Political Censorship in British Hong Kong

Drawing on archival materials, Michael Ng challenges the widely accepted narrative that freedom of expression in Hong Kong is a legacy of British rule of law. Demonstrating that the media and schools were pervasively censored for much of the colonial period and only liberated at a very late stage of British rule, this book complicates our understanding of how Hong Kong came to be a city that championed free speech by the late 1990s. With extensive use of primary sources, the free press, freedom of speech and judicial independence are all revealed to be products of Britain's China strategy. Ng shows that, from the nineteenth to the twentieth century, Hong Kong's legal history was deeply affected by China's relations with world powers. Demonstrating that Hong Kong's freedoms drifted along waves of change in global politics, this book offers a new perspective on the British legal regime in Hong Kong.

Michael Ng is Associate Professor of the Faculty of Law at the University of Hong Kong and has published widely on the legal history of China and Hong Kong in the nineteenth and twentieth centuries. He has been appointed as visiting fellow of the University of Cambridge, visiting scholar of the University of Melbourne and the National University of Singapore, and visiting Associate Professor of National Taiwan University. He was a founding officer and executive committee member of the International Society for Chinese Law and History.

Since 1970, the Law in Context series has been at the forefront of a movement to broaden the study of law. The series is a vehicle for the publication of innovative monographs and texts that treat law and legal phenomena critically in their cultural, social, political, technological, environmental and economic contexts. A contextual approach involves treating legal subjects broadly, using materials from other humanities and social sciences, and from any other discipline that helps to explain the operation in practice of the particular legal field or legal phenomena under investigation. It is intended that this orientation is at once more stimulating and more revealing than the bare exposition of legal rules. The series includes original research monographs, coursebooks and textbooks that foreground contextual approaches and methods. The series includes and welcomes books on the study of law in all its contexts, including domestic legal systems, European and international law, transnational and global legal processes, and comparative law.

Books in the Series

Palmer & Roberts: *Dispute Processes: ADR and the Primary Forms of Decision-Making, 3rd Edition*

Picciotto: *International Business Taxation*

Probert: *The Changing Legal Regulation of Cohabitation, 1600–2010: From Fornicators to Family, 1600–2010*

Radi: *Rules and Practices of International Investment Law and Arbitration*

Reed: *Internet Law: Text and Materials*

Richardson: *Law, Process and Custody*

Roberts & Palmer: *Dispute Processes: ADR and the Primary Forms of Decision-Making, 2nd Edition*

Rowbottom: *Democracy Distorted: Wealth, Influence and Democratic Politics*

Sauter: *Public Services in EU Law*

Scott & Black: *Cranston's Consumers and the Law*

Seneviratne: *Ombudsmen: Public Services and Administrative Justice*

Seppänen: *Ideological Conflict and the Rule of Law in Contemporary China: Useful Paradoxes*

Siems: *Comparative Law, 3rd Edition*

Stapleton: *Product Liability*

Stewart: *Gender, Law and Justice in a Global Market*

Tamanaha: *Law as a Means to an End: Threat to the Rule of Law*

Tuori: *Properties of Law: Modern Law and After*

Turpin & Tomkins: *British Government and the Constitution: Text and Materials, 7th Edition*

Twining: *General Jurisprudence: Understanding Law from a Global Perspective*

Twining: *Globalisation and Legal Theory*

Twining: *Human Rights, Southern Voices: Francis Deng, Abdullahi An-Na'im, Yash Ghai and Upendra Baxi*

Twining: *Jurist in Context: A Memoir*

Twining: *Karl Llewellyn and the Realist Movement, 2nd Edition*

Twining: *Rethinking Evidence: Exploratory Essays, 2nd Edition*

Twining & Miers: *How to Do Things with Rules, 5th Edition*

Wan: *Film and Constitutional Controversy*

Ward: *A Critical Introduction to European Law, 3rd Edition*

Ward: *Law, Text, Terror*

Ward: *Shakespeare and Legal Imagination*

Wells & Quick: *Lacey, Wells and Quick: Reconstructing Criminal Law: Text and Materials, 4th Edition*

Zander: *Cases and Materials on the English Legal System, 10th Edition*

Zander: *The Law-Making Process, 6th Edition*

International Journal of Law in Context: A Global Forum for Interdisciplinary Legal Studies

The *International Journal of Law in Context* is the companion journal to the Law in Context book series and provides a forum for interdisciplinary legal studies and offers intellectual space for ground-breaking critical research. It publishes contextual work about law and its relationship with other disciplines including but not limited to science, literature, humanities, philosophy, sociology, psychology, ethics, history and geography. More information about the journal and how to submit an article can be found at http://journals.cambridge.org/ijc

Political Censorship in British Hong Kong

Freedom of Expression and the Law (1842–1997)

Michael Ng

University of Hong Kong

CAMBRIDGE
UNIVERSITY PRESS

University Printing House, Cambridge CB2 8BS, United Kingdom

One Liberty Plaza, 20th Floor, New York, NY 10006, USA

477 Williamstown Road, Port Melbourne, VIC 3207, Australia

314–321, 3rd Floor, Plot 3, Splendor Forum, Jasola District Centre, New Delhi – 110025, India

103 Penang Road, #05–06/07, Visioncrest Commercial, Singapore 238467

Cambridge University Press is part of the University of Cambridge.

It furthers the University's mission by disseminating knowledge in the pursuit of education, learning, and research at the highest international levels of excellence.

www.cambridge.org
Information on this title: www.cambridge.org/9781108830027
DOI: 10.1017/9781108908580

© Michael Ng 2022

First published 2022

Printed in the United Kingdom by TJ Books Limited, Padstow Cornwall

A catalogue record for this publication is available from the British Library.

ISBN 978-1-108-83002-7 Hardback

Contents

Figures

x

Tables

Acknowledgements

This book was written during challenging times in Hong Kong. It would not have been possible without advice and assistance from many of my friends and colleagues.

My deepest thanks go to the scholars who provided me with comments and suggestions at different stages of the project: Christopher Munn, John Wong, Jed Kroncke, Scott Veitch, Marco Wan, Matthew Erie, Elizabeth Sinn, Fu Hua-ling, Teemu Ruskola, Carol Tan, Billy So, Ghassan Moazzin, Simon Potter, David Clayton, Fu Po-shek, Michael Palmer, Max Wong, Simon Young, Joshua Getzler, Kevin Tan, Humphrey Ko, Mark Chi-kwan, Chu Wai-li and Andrew Harding. I am also very grateful to Florence Mok, Katrina Lam, Leo Shum, Calvin Cheung and Simone Lee for their dedicated research assistance. My gratitude also goes to the staff members of the Hong Kong Public Records Office, the Law Library and the Special Collections of the University of Hong Kong Libraries and the National Archives at Kew, London, for their helpful support, advice and assistance in accessing historical materials. I also thank Joe Ng and Finola O'Sullivan of Cambridge University Press for their continuous support of my work. I am grateful to the anonymous reviewers for their critical comments and encouragement. The book manuscript benefits hugely from the meticulous editing of Erika Hebblethwaite. I am also thankful to the Hong Kong Government's Research Grants Council and the Faculty of Law of the University of Hong Kong for funding this legal history project.[1] I would like to thank Taylor and Francis for consenting to the reproduction of my published article in this book.[2]

I want to express my heartfelt gratitude and respect to Ng Bar-ling, the late senior editor of what was once a major Chinese-language newspaper, *Wah Kiu Yat Po*, whom I never had the honour to meet. His careful preservation of

---

[1] The work described in this book was substantially supported by grants from the Research Grants Council of the Hong Kong Special Administrative Region, China (Project Nos. HKU 17605917 and HKU 17616920).

[2] Chapters 1 and 2 contain materials previously published in 'When Silence Speaks: Press Censorship and Rule of Law in British Hong Kong (1850s–1940s)', *Law and Literature* 29.3 (2017): 425–56.

original documents during his time as a journalist and editor from the 1920s to the 1970s provides valuable evidence to attest to the operation of the little-known political censorship regime in colonial Hong Kong.

Last but not the least, I am deeply indebted to my family for the unconditional love, patience and indulgence they have given me during every adventure I have undertaken.

Abbreviations

BBC	British Broadcasting Corporation
CCP	Chinese Communist Party
CPCO	Control of Publications Consolidation Ordinance
CPG	Chinese Central People's Government
CR	Commercial Radio
CUHK	Chinese University of Hong Kong
ERO	Emergency Regulations Ordinance
FCO	Foreign and Commonwealth Office (UK)
FEER	*Far Eastern Economic Review*
GIS	Government Information Services
HK	Hong Kong
HKFS	Hong Kong Federation of Students
HKFTU	Hong Kong Federation of Trade Unions
HKU	University of Hong Kong
HRC	UN Human Rights Committee
ICCPR	International Covenant on Civil and Political Rights
ISD	Information Services Department
JUSTICE	International Commission of Jurists
KMT	Kuomintang (Chinese Nationalist Party)
LIC	Local Intelligence Committee
MFA	Ministry of Foreign Affairs (China)
NCNA	New China News Agency
OPO	Objectionable Publications Ordinance
PLA	People's Liberation Army
PRC	People's Republic of China
RDF	Rediffusion
RHK	Radio Hong Kong
ROC	Republic of China (Taiwan)
RTHK	Radio Television Hong Kong
SAR	Special Administrative Region
SASI	Secretary for Administrative Services and Information
SCMP	*South China Morning Post*

SCOPG	Standing Committee on Pressure Groups
TVB	Television Broadcasts Limited
UK	United Kingdom
UN	United Nations
UPGC	University and Polytechnic Grants Committee
US	United States of America
WKYP	*Wah Kiu Yat Po*

Introduction

Around noon on 3 June 1919, nine schoolboys aged eight to seventeen walked westwards along Queen's Road in the Central District of Hong Kong clad in their school uniforms and holding open oil-paper umbrellas made in mainland China. The umbrellas featured Chinese characters reading 'Chinese people should buy native goods'. The boys attracted the attention of passers-by, with more than 100 joining them to form an impromptu parade. They also attracted the attention of a police inspector surnamed Brazil, who stopped the crowd and asked one of the students whether he had obtained a permit. The student said no, but that one of their teachers had instructed them to march. Inspector Brazil arrested the nine students on the spot and then went to the teacher's residence to arrest him as well. All of those arrested were charged with participating in a procession without the necessary permit under the Regulation of Chinese Ordinance, and the teacher was also charged with aiding and abetting the organisation of an illegal procession. After a four-day trial, Magistrate Lindsell sentenced Wu, the student who had headed up the procession, to pay HK$10, an amount equivalent to several months' wages for a workman.

In his concluding submission, the prosecutor, a man named Wolfe, who was also the police chief superintendent, made explicit the political motive behind the trial. It was not the prosecution's aim to impose a heavy penalty on the students, he said, but rather for the court to deliver a punishment sufficiently severe to deter further similar activities. Wolfe cited the recent wave of student anti-Japanese protests that had spiralled out of control in many mainland Chinese cities, including Beijing and Tianjin, noting that Hong Kong had to adopt preventive measures to avoid activists using the colony as a launchpad to wreak mayhem on the mainland. Finally, he averred, students should focus on their studies rather than become involved in social movements.[1]

Almost 100 years later, umbrellas were once again unfurled in protest on the streets of Hong Kong. On 28 September 2014, tens of thousands of

---

[1] For an analysis of the case, see Michael Ng, 'Rule of Law in Hong Kong History Demythologised: Student Umbrella Movement of 1919', *Hong Kong Law Journal* 46.3 (2016): 829–47.

demonstrators, many of them secondary school and university students, occupied major roads in the Central District of Hong Kong to protest against the electoral reform package imposed on the city by the Central People's Government in Beijing. The protesters opened their umbrellas to deflect the pepper spray fired on them by the Hong Kong police attempting to disperse them. The Occupy Central Movement, which thus became popularly known internationally as the Umbrella Movement, lasted for seventy-nine days. Large numbers of protestors, including the students who had led and participated in the movement, were subsequently arrested, prosecuted and convicted. Less than five years later, in 2019, millions of citizens took to the streets to protest against an amendment of the extradition law that purported to allow the extradition of fugitives arrested in Hong Kong to mainland China for trial. The subsequent Anti-Extradition Law Amendment Bill Movement led to some of the most violent riots and demonstrations in recent Hong Kong history. More than 10,200 people were arrested, with over 2,500 prosecuted to date, including students, teachers and legislative councillors, amongst others. Some of these cases are still undergoing judicial proceedings as this book goes to press.[2]

Conventionally regarded as one of the most politically stable cities in Asia, Hong Kong has in fact witnessed numerous protests, social movements and even civil unrest over the past hundred years, with its citizens taking to the streets to demand rights, freedoms and better governance from both the colonial and post-colonial governments. The Umbrella Movement and Anti-Extradition Law Amendment Bill Movement not only showcased another fight for freedom and democracy by the Hong Kong people following the reversion of sovereignty to China but also triggered an unexpected – and rather nostalgic – movement in favour of the laws and governance of the colonial era, a movement perhaps unique among former British colonies. The movement's supporters claimed that individual liberties, including freedom of expression, and the rule of law had been better protected under British colonial rule than they were in post-colonial Hong Kong under China's sovereignty. The flag of colonial Hong Kong was a common sight during demonstrations during and after the 2014 Occupy Central Movement and during the Anti-Extradition Law Amendment Bill Movement (Figure 0.1).[3] It is not only nostalgic demonstrators who associate freedom of speech and the rule of law with British rule in Hong Kong, a number

---

[2] *New York Times*, 28 May 2020.

[3] The phenomenon has been widely reported in the press; for example, 'Colonial nostalgia drives the young to reject Beijing', *The Times*, 15 June 2019; 'Hong Kong's frustration with Beijing is no excuse for nostalgia for the British Empire', SCMP, 28 September 2018; 'Chen Zuo-er aims another salvo at Hong Kong, but what's the target?', SCMP, 22 September 2015; 'Chris Patten "flattered" by nostalgic Hongkongers who miss colonial days', SCMP, 22 March 2014. For a recent academic study of colonial nostalgia in post-colonial Hong Kong, see John Lowe and Eileen Yuk-Ha Tsang, 'Securing Hong Kong's Identity in the Colonial Past: Strategic Essentialism and the Umbrella Movement', *Critical Asian Studies* 50.4 (2018): 556–71.

Figure 0.1 A colonial Hong Kong flag being waved by a protester during the
2019 Anti-Extradition Law Amendment Bill Movement.
Source: Courtesy of Keith Tsuji.

of senior legal practitioners, law academics and politicians have also helped to
reinforce such nostalgic fantasies of a former golden age.

Sir Anthony Mason, former chief justice of the High Court of Australia and
later a non-permanent judge of the Hong Kong Court of Final Appeal,
expressed the following views on Hong Kong's history of law in the 2005
Common Law Lecture, a prestigious annual seminar in which distinguished
jurists address lawyers and law teachers in Hong Kong:

The common law also stands for a set of concepts, interests and values which it
has protected during the course of its *long history*. They include the rule of law, the
independence of the judiciary, access to the courts, the separation of the powers of
government, liberty of the individual, *freedom of expression*, freedom of
association. ... These values have both generated and informed legal principles,
including the rules of statutory interpretation. ... The common law stands both as
a symbol and as a *link between Hong Kong's past, its present and its future.*
[Emphasis added.][4]

---

[4] Anthony Mason, 'The Role of the Common Law in Hong Kong', in *The Common Law Lectures
Series 2005*, ed. Jessica Young and Rebecca Lee (Hong Kong: Faculty of Law, Hong Kong
University, 2005), 1–2.

These views were echoed in a recently published, and widely used, law textbook introducing the legal system of Hong Kong, which states that 'Hong Kong's legal system has remained firmly embedded in the common law tradition'; that is:

> The common law, in short, embodies the inherent social order of a free, just and reasonable community that constantly evolves.[5]

Renowned constitutional law scholar Albert Venn Dicey (whose works remain orthodox starting texts for common-law students in the UK and former British colonies) wrote in the late nineteenth century about the notion of freedom of the press as a distinct characteristic of English rule of law:

> For about two centuries the relation between the government and the press has in England been marked by all those characteristics which make up what we have termed the 'rule' or 'supremacy' of law, and . . . just because of this, . . . the press, and especially the newspaper press, has practically enjoyed with us a freedom which till recent years was unknown in continental states . . .. This contrast [with continental law] is not only striking in itself, but also affords the strongest illustration that can be found of English conceptions of the rule of law[6]

Mason is not the only person to have mistaken such doctrinal teaching for the law in practice in Hong Kong history. The website of Hong Kong's current Department of Justice also describes the present legal system by connecting it to the venerable common-law tradition:

> In historical terms . . . the rights relating to freedom of speech, freedom of assembly, and freedom from arbitrary arrest or imprisonment have been spelt out in cases which were decided more than three centuries ago. As we have seen, these have now been underpinned by provisions in the Basic Law.[7]

Such a narrative fits very well into what the twenty-eighth and last British governor of Hong Kong, Chris Patten, said at the Hong Kong handover ceremony:

> As British administration ends, we are, I believe, entitled to say that our nation's contribution here was to provide the scaffolding that enabled the people of Hong Kong to ascend. The rule of law. . . . The values of a free society. . . . This is a Chinese city, a very Chinese city with British characteristics. No dependent territory has been left more prosperous, none with such a rich texture and fabric of civil society.[8]

---

[5] Eric Ip, *Law and Justice in Hong Kong* (Hong Kong: Sweet & Maxwell, 2014), 7–9.

[6] A. V. Dicey, *An Introduction to the Study of the Law of the Constitution*, 10th ed. (London: Macmillan, 1959), 247 and 269.

[7] 'Our Legal System', Department of Justice, as on 23 June 2021, www.doj.gov.hk/en/our_legal_system/the_common_law.html

[8] SCMP, 1 July 1997.

As Sally Merry and Peter Fitzpatrick point out, the law has often been conceptualised as a gift from the colonisers to the colonised.[9] English law remains central to the history of former British colonies and is still widely acknowledged by both Hong Kong citizens and colonial historians today as a core contributing factor to the city's development and economic success. The traditional scholarly narrative is that English rule of law, which offers such safeguards of individual liberty as freedom of expression, freedom of assembly, equality before the law and judicial independence, is the most important legacy of British rule in Hong Kong, a legacy that is very often used to distinguish the legal and societal development of Hong Kong from that of mainland China.[10] These confident claims are made despite the fact that no monographic archival work on Hong Kong's colonial legal history exists.

Drawing on previously unexplored archival materials, this book challenges the widely accepted narrative – or myth – that freedom of expression is a legacy of British rule of law in Hong Kong, arguing that it simply does not stand up to scrutiny of the archival record. The book poses this research question: How has Hong Kong society evolved over its 155-year history from a colony of gelded freedom of expression into a city whose free press and freedom of speech were highly praised globally at the time of Hong Kong's return to China in 1997? By unfolding the history of how the media and schools were consistently and pervasively censored during most of the colonial period and how they were liberated at a very late stage of colonial rule, the book argues that the free press, freedom of speech and even judicial independence that so many people in Hong Kong are eager to preserve today are the result of the larger China strategy that Britain employed in preparing Hong Kong for China. It thus also raises the provocative question of whether the colonial government would ever have granted the freedoms so valued by the people of Hong Kong today if no agreement had been struck to decolonise Hong Kong and return it to China. Any discussion of freedoms and the rule of law in Hong Kong needs to be situated in an informed understanding of this history. This book, however, is not solely concerned with repeating the claims of scholarship showing imperial-era colonial law and legal systems to have been characterised by racism, inequality and oppression of the colonised. Rather, it explains these and other features of colonial rule in Hong Kong in light of the historical context, thereby revealing the

---

[9] Peter Fitzpatrick, 'Custom as Imperialism', in *Law and Identity in Africa*, ed. Jamil Abun-Nasr, Ulrich Spellenbert and Ulrike Wanitzek (Hamburg: Buske, 1990); for how English law is conceptualised in colonial narratives, see Sally E. Merry, 'Law and Colonialism', *Law and Society Review* 25.4 (1991): 889–90.

[10] For acknowledgement of rule of law in Hong Kong as an important colonial legacy, see, for example, Steve Tsang, 'Commitment to the Rule of Law and Judicial Independence', in *Judicial Independence and the Rule of Law in Hong Kong*, ed. Steve Tsang (Hong Kong: Hong Kong University Press, 2001), 1; also Ming Chan, 'The Legacy of the British Administration of Hong Kong: A View from Hong Kong', *China Quarterly* 151 (1997): 567.

complex factors, both local and global, that drove and constrained the 'legal imperial' in running its silencing regime in the British Empire's most important trading post in East Asia.[11] What has defined and confined the Hong Kong people's right to speak has not, unfortunately, been how dearly held the values of common law are or how hard the Hong Kong people have fought to secure that right. What has mattered more, I argue, has been the bigger picture of global and regional politics: the political–economic situation of China, China's relations with the major world powers and those powers' China strategies over time, as we shall see in this book's archival discovery. As the book will show, such China strategies render the colonial legal history of Hong Kong a unique case among former British colonies, as well as an important geopolitical episode in both world and Chinese history of the late nineteenth and twentieth centuries, an episode whose impacts can still be felt in the global geopolitics being played by China, Hong Kong, Britain and the United States today. Hence, well-rehearsed narratives that attribute the freedoms enjoyed in Hong Kong to common-law traditions without situating them in the global history this book tells are seriously inadequate, if not misleading.

More specifically, the book seeks answers to the following questions. What drove the colonial Hong Kong government to enact laws and regulations aimed at censoring the media and schools? How were its political censorship measures carried out, and how did they evolve over time? What kinds of media and schools were targeted for censorship? How was the notion of freedom of expression understood by the colonisers and the colonised? How was that notion negotiated and compromised in practice? How was such compromise and negotiation justified by colonial officers, judges and legislators in Hong Kong, as well as by government officials in London, in light of the domestic governance, national interest and international relations issues faced by the Hong Kong and London governments? How did the political, social and economic situation of China and China's relationship with the major world powers, especially Britain, Japan and the United States, influence the evolution of the law and practice of political censorship in Hong Kong? How and why were such law and practice phased out, and the notions of the rule of law and freedom of speech awakened, as a pressing political agenda in the last decade of colonial rule in the 1980s?

This book constitutes the first in-depth empirical study of the practice and experience of the political censorship of mass media and schools in British Hong Kong in a broader historical context connecting the history of Hong Kong with the histories of China, Britain and global geopolitics in Asia

---

[11] The phrase 'legal imperial' is borrowed from John McLaren, 'Afterword: Looking from the Past into the Future', in *The Grand Experiment: Law and Legal Culture in British Settler Societies*, ed. Hamar Foster, Benjamin L. Berger, and A. R. Buck (Vancouver: University of British Columbia Press, 2008), 276.

in the nineteenth and twentieth centuries. It aims to demythologise the well-rehearsed history of the rule of law in Hong Kong and to unfold the history of freedoms in colonial Hong Kong that was unrelated to the ideal of the rule of law told by Sir Anthony Mason and likeminded jurists or historians. The book adds the legal history of this important former colony in East Asia to the emerging body of scholarship on the global and comparative study of law and colonialism. Its significance also lies in the richness of the unexplored archival data on censorship practice of which it makes ample use. The history of freedom of expression and the law in Hong Kong also informs us that regardless of how the rule of law is idealised as transcending the governing authority, its operation has seldom taken place in isolation from politics, global geopolitics and power structures in the modern era, particularly when the government is not democratically elected.

Colonial Version of English Common Law

The common-law system practised in former British colonies as diverse as India, North America, the West Indies, Africa and Australia has been subjected to a critical review in the past decade in the flourishing scholarship on the practice of English law and its impact on indigenous communities.[12] Martin Chanock, for example, demonstrates how administrative control and the demand for obedience dominated court rulings against the indigenous populations of African colonies in the early to mid-twentieth century,[13] and Julie Evans highlights the large gap between the idealised rule of law and its practice in mid-eighteenth-century Australia.[14] Elizabeth Kolsky argues that racism and violence were central to the practice of British law in nineteenth- to early twentieth-century India.[15] Nick Cheesman's recent study shows that the oppressive law and order practised in colonial Burma's courts contributed to the lack of a rule of law in the country's contemporary legal regime.[16] In his 1,100-page archival study *Human Rights and the End of Empire*, Brian Simpson powerfully argues that the British government was uninterested in,

---

[12] A very useful summary of literatures on the history of British colonies can be found in John McLaren, 'Chasing the Chimera: The Rule of Law in the British Empire and the Comparative Turn in Legal History', *Law in Context* 33.1 (2015): 21–36.

[13] Martin Chanock, *Law, Custom and Social Order: The Colonial Experience in Malawi and Zambia* (Cambridge: Cambridge University Press, 1985).

[14] Julie Evans, 'Colonialism and the Rule of Law: The Case of South Australia', in *Crime and Empire 1840–1940*, ed. Barry Godfrey and Graeme Dunstall (Portland, OR: Willan Publishing, 2005), 57–75.

[15] Elizabeth Kolsky, *Colonial Justice in British India* (New York: Cambridge University Press, 2010).

[16] Nick Cheesman, *Opposing the Rule of Law: How Myanmar's Courts Make Law and Order* (Cambridge: Cambridge University Press, 2015).

and even immune to international pressure for, any guarantee of human rights or freedom of speech or the press in its colonies until as late as the 1960s.[17]

At the same time, efforts have also been made to rebalance this revisionist historiography of colonial justice. David Murray contends that case records provide no evidence of widespread corruption and partiality in the administration of justice in mid-nineteenth-century British Niagara,[18] for example, and Martin Wiener argues that the rule of law practised by the British colonisers improved in India in the late nineteenth to early twentieth century.[19] Other scholars explain the colonial legal system in its historical context, arguing that the colonial version of British common law was bound to differ from the original for good reason. Carol Tan regards the departure from due process in the semi-colony of Weihaiwei of Shandong province in China in the late nineteenth to early twentieth century as a sympathetic integration of Chinese customs,[20] echoing Lauren Benton's view that the culture and religion of indigenous subjects in British colonies were factors in the making, alteration and interpretation of English law as applied on the ground.[21] Hamar Foster, Benjamin Berger and A. R. Buck demonstrate how local life and culture in select colonies influenced, and were influenced by, the ideology of the rule of law that accompanied the British colonial project.[22]

The debates among the celebratory and the accusatory, and those in between, about the nature of colonial justice and the role played by the rule of law in colonial governance are flourishing, judging from the numerous monographs published in the past decade. These scholarly works cover a wide spectrum of former British colonies, encompassing those in North America, the West Indies, Africa, Australia and India. However, Hong Kong, the last major colony returned and still one of the most important global cities in international trade and finance, is missing from these narratives.

With the exception of James William Norton-Kyshe's chronological work published in 1898 on the history of the laws and courts of nineteenth-century Hong Kong, no monographic work on Hong Kong's colonial legal history

---

[17] Brian Simpson, *Human Rights and the End of Empire: Britain and the Genesis of the European Convention* (Oxford: Oxford University Press, 2001).

[18] David Murray, *Colonial Justice: Justice, Morality, and Crime in the Niagara District, 1791–1849* (Toronto: University of Toronto Press, 2002).

[19] Martin Wiener, *An Empire on Trial: Race, Murder, and Justice under British Rule, 1870–1935* (Cambridge: Cambridge University Press, 2009).

[20] Carol Tan, *British Rule in China: Law and Justice in Weihaiwei 1898–1930* (London: Wildy, Simmonds & Hill, 2008).

[21] Lauren Benton, *Law and Colonial Cultures: Legal Regimes in World History, 1400–1900* (Cambridge: Cambridge University Press, 2002).

[22] Hamar Foster, Benjamin L. Berger, and A. R. Buck, eds., *The Grand Experiment: Law and Legal Culture in British Settler Societies* (Vancouver: University of British Columbia Press, 2009).

exists.[23] Norton-Kyshe viewed the export to Hong Kong of the British notion of the rule of law as a civilising gift to China. That view persisted in the histories of Hong Kong written from the viewpoint of the colonisers to memorialise the colony's growth and development under British rule, as notably seen in the works of G. B. Endacott and Frank Welsh.[24] A later generation of historians, including but not limited to Elizabeth Sinn, Tsai Jung-fang and John Carroll, broke away from this colonial narrative and adopted the perspective of the Chinese population but did not treat legal history as a crucial part of the story.[25] It took a century for the colonial narrative of the rule of law to be contested by Christopher Munn in his well-researched book on the early colonial history of Hong Kong (1840s–1870s).[26] His three chapters on crime and justice rewrite the legal history of the colony in this period by highlighting the discriminatory nature of the justice system and the discrepancies between the representation and practice of the rule of law. Criminologist Carol Jones, in her work on crime and the criminal justice system in Hong Kong, also alerts us that geopolitics, rather than crime rates, often drove the practice of the criminal justice system in colonial Hong Kong.[27] Poshek Fu's and Kenny Ng's works on post-war film censorship and Lu Yan's book on the government's repressive measures against labour activism are important recent studies that begin to examine how freedoms in Hong Kong were affected by geopolitics.[28] These works serve as important references in constructing the historical context of the present book.

---

[23] James William Norton-Kyshe. *The History of the Laws and Courts of Hong Kong from the Earliest Period to 1898* (Hong Kong: Vetch and Lee, c. 1971; originally published by London: T. Fisher Unwin, 1898).

[24] G. B. Endacott, *A History of Hong Kong* (London: Oxford University Press, 1958); Frank Welsh, *A History of Hong Kong* (London: HarperCollins, 1993).

[25] Elizabeth Sinn, *Power and Charity: The Early History of the Tung Wah Hospital, Hong Kong* (Hong Kong: Oxford University Press, 1989); Tsai Jung-fang, 香港人之香港史 *1841–1945* [Hong Kong people's history of Hong Kong 1841–1945] (Hong Kong: Oxford University Press, 2001); John M. Carroll, *Edge of Empires: Chinese Elites and British Colonials in Hong Kong* (Hong Kong: Hong Kong University Press, 2007).

[26] Christopher Munn, *Anglo-China: Chinese People and British Rule in Hong Kong 1841–1880* (Hong Kong: Hong Kong University Press, 2009). For discriminatory legislation, see Peter Wesley-Smith, 'Anti-Chinese Legislation in Hong Kong', in *Precarious Balance: Hong Kong between China and Britain, 1842–1992*, ed. Ming K. Chan and John D. Young (Hong Kong: Hong Kong University Press, 1994), 91–106.

[27] Carol Jones, *Criminal Justice in Hong Kong* (London: Routledge-Cavendish, 2007).

[28] Poshek Fu, 'More Than Just Entertaining: Cinematic Containment and Asia's Cold War in Hong Kong, 1949–1959', *Modern Chinese Literature and Culture* 30.2 (2018): 1–55; Kenny K. K. Ng, 'Inhibition vs. Exhibition: Political Censorship of Chinese and Foreign Cinemas in Postwar Hong Kong', *Journal of Chinese Cinemas* 2.1 (2008): 23–35; Yan Lu, *Crossed Paths: Labor Activism and Colonial Governance in Hong Kong, 1938–1958* (New York: Cornell University Press, 2019).

Organisation of the Book

The book opens with Chapter 1, 'Punitive Censorship and Libel Lawsuits against the Press', which examines the imperial silencing regime in Hong Kong from the early colonial years to the turn of the nineteenth century, a regime I call 'punitive censorship'. The chapter details how for the first fifty years of British rule in Hong Kong, following its inception in 1841, criminal prosecutions under libel law were wielded by the colonial government as the major tool against newspaper editors who criticised government officials and/ or policies. Libel prosecutions aimed not only to suppress criticism of the colonial government but also to manage Britain's geopolitical interests in East Asia, particularly its relationship with China. In addition to suppressing the Hong Kong press through judicial proceedings, the colony's censorship regime also featured legislative measures that, for example, forbade the import of anti-imperial China and anti-colonial materials into Hong Kong

Chapter 2, '"Reading Every Line": Era of the Daily Vetting of Newspaper Proofs', uncovers how the political censorship regime in Hong Kong evolved from punitive censorship to what I call 'pre-emptive censorship', a measure that imposed the mandatory daily vetting of newspaper proofs by government censors. During the China-backed large-scale strikes that occurred in 1922–6, the colonial government faced the most serious challenge to its legitimacy to date. In response to the resulting anxiety over its continued rule in Hong Kong, particularly in the face of the united front presented by the Nationalists, also known as the Kuomintang (KMT), and the Chinese Communist Party (CCP) during the anti-imperialist movement of 1924, the colonial government further stretched its control of the press by enacting newspaper regulations. Press control was expanded from punishing editors for what they had already published to day-to-day political vetting of the content of Chinese newspaper proofs before they were printed for sale to the public. The operations of the censors' office produced newspapers with weird dots and crosses concealing censored material. News manuscripts banned from publication featured a big chop from the government's Press Censorship Office, as shown on the cover of this book. The daily operation of this mysterious office, hitherto unknown to scholarship, will be described in detail in this chapter.

Chapter 3, '"Communist China Now Contiguous to Hong Kong": Censorship Imposed by the "Free World"', shows how the civil war in China after the Second World War and then the takeover of China by the CCP contributed to the further expansion and strategic modification of Hong Kong's political censorship regime. The loss of China to communism, mass influx of Chinese refugees into Hong Kong, outbreak of the Korean War, global Cold War geopolitics, and ongoing ideological warfare between KMT and CCP in Hong Kong through their respective newspapers and schools hugely increased the complexity of operating effective media censorship while maintaining a free flow of information for trading and business purposes. The colonial government could no longer rely solely on pre-emptive daily vetting to contain undesirable content and comments. During the second half of the twentieth century, political censorship of the media and education sector was facilitated and supplemented by large-scale surveillance operations carried out through a collaborative network of local departments informed by global intelligence collected through London and British embassies around the world. Intelligence collected by this network allowed the colonial government to nip trouble in the bud and resulted in a number of 'troublemakers' (including journalists, editors, publishers, teachers, students and principals) being arrested, detained and even deported without trial without any due regard to whether such actions were lawful. Chapter 3 provides a comprehensive account of such surveillance and censorship operations targeting the media and education sector from the late 1940s to the late 1950s against the backdrop of rising Cold War tensions and the new Communist China's relations with the world.

Chapter 4, '"Patriotism to You Can Be Revolutionary Heresy to Us": Hardened Control of Media, Schools and Entertainment', details the encroachment of the government's silencing machine on Hong Kong citizens' daily lives at the height of the Cold War. The period from the 1950s to the 1960s saw CCP cultural infiltration into various sectors of Hong Kong in an attempt to propagate anti-colonial patriotic ideas and communist ideologies. The CCP not only published, directly or indirectly, newspapers, books and magazines in Hong Kong but also sponsored schools and film studios and staged theatrical performances. Together with the co-existence of KMT supporters and intelligence agents of other world powers in the colony, Hong Kong became an important ideological battleground of the Cold War in Asia. The colonial government responded by hardening its monitoring of newspapers and schools, suppressing them when necessary. It also monopolised the preparation of news bulletins for radio broadcasting and imposed political censorship on radio entertainment programmes, films and theatrical performances. Radical movements of the KMT and CCP also led to the two most violent riots in colonial Hong Kong history, in 1956 and 1967, respectively, in which a large number of political dissidents were deported, detained without trial and imprisoned for speech offences.

Chapter 5, 'Preparing to Negotiate with China: Overt Loosening and Covert Control', reveals how Hong Kong's freedom of expression was defined and confined by changes in the China strategies of Britain and other world powers. The diplomat Murray MacLehose assumed Hong Kong's governorship in 1971 with an express mandate from London to build civic pride and raise living standards in Hong Kong to maximise the British bargaining position in negotiations over Hong Kong's future with a post-Mao regime. In addition to the well-known expansion of social services and efforts to combat crime and corruption, MacLehose's governorship also featured a hitherto understudied loosening of media control. Yet behind the overt building of a free city were the covert surveillance of political activists and unchanged draconian laws of political censorship that were used to crack down on anti-government dissent whenever it overstepped the government's political red lines.

Chapter 6, 'Liberating Hong Kong for China: De-silencing the City', traces the trajectory of a renewed consciousness of the rule of law and various freedoms in the final decade of colonial rule and unpacks the geopolitical concerns and motivations of the British government in de-silencing Hong Kong before the handover in 1997. The conclusion in 1984 of negotiations between Britain and China on the reversion of Hong Kong's sovereignty marked the opening of an era of liberalistic rule of law and individual freedoms in Hong Kong. Former Chief Justice Denys Roberts, a barrister who had never been a judge but had been both a colonial secretary and attorney general of Hong Kong before being appointed chief justice in 1979, was succeeded in 1988 by Yang Ti-liang, a professional Chinese judge who had served only the judiciary throughout his career, to showcase the colony's judicial independence under a British legal system prior to its return to China. Laws and regulations that had been used to suppress free speech, control publication and prosecute political protesters were loosened or repealed one after another in the late 1980s and early 1990s. Hong Kong's first statute expressly recognising freedom of speech, assembly and association was passed only in 1991, just six years before the colonial era came to an end. Not only were laws and senior judicial appointments liberalised in the last decade of British rule, but the 1980s and 1990s also witnessed unprecedented levels of public discussion of, and official and media narratives on, the importance of free speech and the rule of law to Hong Kong.

Colonial Hong Kong not only brokered trade and culture between China, Britain and the world, it also played an important risk arbitrage function for Britain and its allies in global politics at the Eastern frontier by leveraging the changing economic–political situation of China. Hence, Hong Kong's 155-year legal history offers not only a history of local statutes and court judgments but a very useful lens for visualising global politics and international relations. Hong Kong's legal history was deeply affected by China's relations with world powers, particularly Britain and the United States, and those powers' China strategies from the nineteenth to the twentieth century. Hong Kong's freedoms drifted along on these waves of change in global politics without much of a push from much-vaunted common-law values, as this book is about to show.

1 Punitive Censorship and Libel Lawsuits against the Press

It is to be remembered that, in so small a community as that of Hong Kong, concentrated, moreover, within so narrow a space, the Press is sure to be at once more personal and less influential than in larger and more scattered communities. Here it is, of course, impossible to preserve that mystery which elsewhere enhances the power of the Press. Hong Kong Governor Bowen[1]

Libel Prosecutions against the Press

For the first fifty years of British rule in Hong Kong following its inception in 1841, criminal prosecutions under libel law were amongst the major tools used by the colonial government against newspaper editors for criticisms of government policies.[2] For example, William Tarrant, the editor of *Friend of China*, one of the earliest English-language newspapers in Hong Kong, was fined and imprisoned in 1857 and 1858, respectively, for publishing corruption allegations against then Colonial Secretary William Thomas Bridges and Acting Governor William Caine. Soon after Tarrant's release from jail, the paper closed its Hong Kong operations and moved across the border to Canton (now Guangzhou).[3]

Yorick Jones Murrow, the editor of another major English-language newspaper, the *Hong Kong Daily Press* (established in 1857), was prosecuted for libel and sentenced to six months' imprisonment and a fine of £100 in 1858 for publishing an article on the alleged favouritism shown by Governor John Bowring towards a large trading firm in which the governor's son was a partner.[4]

---

[1] Letter from Hong Kong governor to Earl of Derby, 20 July 1883, CO 129/210.

[2] Newspapers in Britain were also threatened by government's libel lawsuits during the nineteenth century. For details, see Martin Hewitt, 'The Press and the Law', in *Journalism and the Periodical Press in Nineteenth Century Britain*, ed. Joanne Shattock (Cambridge: Cambridge University Press, 2017), 147–64; also Mark Hampton, *Visions of the Press in Britain, 1850–1950* (Champaign: University of Illinois Press, 2004), 30–9.

[3] See Munn, *Anglo-China*, chapter 7, in particular pp. 317–19 for details of and events leading to the prosecution against Tarrant.

[4] *China Mail*, 22 April 1858, CO 129/67.

The *Hong Kong Telegraph*, an English-language newspaper established in 1881, became the target of prosecution soon after its launch owing to its numerous outspoken reports on the alleged corrupt behaviour of government officials.

For example, in 1881, harbour master Captain H. G. Thomsett was alleged by the paper to have erroneously issued a licence allowing a vessel carrying 835 Chinese passengers to leave Hong Kong for Australia. Under Hong Kong law, such a licence could be issued only if the harbour master personally determined that the passengers in question were travelling of their own volition and able to pay their passage, and hence were not contracted labourers being illegally transported to Australia. According to the verbatim *Hong Kong Telegraph* report, however, Captain Thomsett for reasons known only to him failed to carry out the required due diligence but let the vessel depart anyway:

It [the examination] is very rarely conducted honestly towards the emigrants .... Although certain powerful companies in Australia would like to see for their own special benefit a great deal of cheap Chinese labour in the country, the great mass of the people are strongly averse to their towns being inundated with an alien race .... The emigrants themselves are doubtless willing enough to try their luck in other lands, but they are of a class who cannot afford to pay for their own passages, hence the contract system, which under some circumstances is a sort of debased slavery ... no doubt associations... arranging the contracts, getting the coolies from [China] and seeing them safely housed and shipped ... make vast sums out of the traffic.[5]

As there can be little doubt that emigration from this port to the colonies and other places has been tainted with many evils, it is incumbent on the Government to see that all examinations are conducted with a strictness to defy imposition in any shape or form.[6]

The colonial government prosecuted the editor of the *Hong Kong Telegraph* for these allegations.

Another report in the paper about the allegedly corrupt tendering process for public works directed by Surveyor-General John Price was met with criminal prosecution. The newspaper queried the way in which public works tenders were granted in reports on 25 June and 3 September 1883:

We frequently observe in the Government Gazette notices inviting tenders for government contract, which would seem to indicate that everything is carried out independently and impartially .... This, however, may be altogether deceptive. ...

It is generally believed that this [tender] system is strictly adhered to in placing all contracts for Government works in Hongkong; but that can hardly be, excepting in theory, otherwise the hints and suggestions which are constantly current as to certain officials 'arranging' contracts with their friends for a consideration would scarcely be so generally accepted in well informed circles as matters of fact. ...[7]

---

[5] *Hong Kong Telegraph*, 12 July 1881, CO 129/193.
[6] *Hong Kong Telegraph*, 25 July 1881, CO 129/193.
[7] *Hong Kong Telegraph*, 25 June 1883, CO 129/210.

In Saturday's Gazette appear several Government notifications inviting tenderers for certain local works of some magnitude. The reclamation of Causeway Bay and the construction of a sea wall, swing bridge, basin . . . . Why, then, does the custom prevail in the Colonial Secretary's office of confining the advertisements inviting the public tenders for these works to the semi-privacy of the columns of the Government Gazette, a publication which is seldom seen outside the government's offices?[8]

It is worthy of note that such prosecutions were not simply actions taken by the attorney general's office in Hong Kong but constituted high-stakes political decisions endorsed by government departments concerned in Hong Kong and by the British government in London. Archived correspondence shows that decisions to bring libel prosecutions against the press were not made independently by the attorney general but rather were collective political decisions initiated by the government department against whom the allegation was directed, advised by the Hong Kong attorney general, approved by the colonial secretary and governor, and reported to London through the governor to the secretary of state for the colonies. Governor Pope Hennessy and Henry March wrote to London in 1881 and 1883, respectively, to seek an endorsement from London to prosecute the editors of the *Hong Kong Telegraph* for the aforementioned newspaper reports.[9]

Libel prosecutions against the press aimed not only at suppressing criticism of the colonial government but also at managing Britain's geopolitical interests in East Asia, especially its relationship with China.

An increase in the Chinese population of Hong Kong in the late nineteenth century raised demand for Chinese-language newspapers, a considerable number of which were launched between the 1870s and 1890s. Early Chinese newspapers focused more on news from mainland China than on local affairs, particularly during an era of rising internal disturbances and ongoing warfare with foreign powers on the mainland. The political stance of these papers, some of which were believed to have been founded by revolutionaries, was closely monitored by the Hong Kong government. Legal actions were instituted against them if the reports they carried were found to undermine the legitimacy of the colonial government or jeopardise the interests of the British Empire and its allies in East Asia and mainland China. For example, in 1884, criminal actions were directed against four Chinese newspapers, two of which were the major papers in Hong Kong (*Wa Tsz Yat Po* and *Tsun Wan Yat Po*), for their publication of an imperial edict issued by the governors of Guangdong and Guangxi provinces calling for collective action against French military aggression on the mainland after the outbreak of the Sino-French War. A report from

---

[8] *Hong Kong Telegraph*, 3 September 1883, CO 129/211.
[9] Letter from Acting Governor Henry Marsh to Earl of Derby, 25 September 1883, CO 129/211; Letter from Governor Pope Hennessy to Earl of Kimberley, 27 July 1881, CO 129/193.

the Hong Kong government to London indicated that the prosecution of such major Chinese papers constituted an important political decision requiring London's endorsement:

My Lord, I have the honour to report that, on the recommendation of the Attorney General, and with the full concurrence of the Executive Council, I have directed criminal proceedings to be taken against the Editors of four local Chinese Newspapers namely: 1. Wa Tsz Yat Po . . ., 2. Tsun Wan Yat Po, 3. Chung Ngoi San Po, 4. Wai San Yat Po for publishing what purported to be an Edict issued by the Viceroy of the Two Kwang and the Governor of Kwang Tung . . . In [the edict], Chinese subjects residing in Hongkong are exhorted to 'secretly kill some French Commander, or destroy by fire their munitions of war, or cooperate with the Chinese Officers and soldiers in attacking them from within and without, with a view to their being entirely swept away'.[10]

In addition to suppressing the press within Hong Kong through judicial proceedings, the colony's censorship regime also featured legislative measures that, for example, forbade the import of revolutionary materials into Hong Kong. In 1900, the Post Office Ordinance was amended, giving the governor power to prohibit dispatching and delivering of any letter, newspaper, book or pamphlet into Hong Kong. Anyone importing a publication into Hong Kong without going through the Hong Kong Post was liable to be charged with an offence. However, having the postmaster serve as the gatekeeper in preventing revolutionary materials from entering Hong Kong soon proved inadequate to alleviate the growing anxiety of the colonial administration arising from worsening instability across the border.[11]

Legislating Press Control

After the failure of the Hundred Days' Reform in 1898, key figures of the Chinese revolution, if not arrested or executed by the Qing government, were driven underground or overseas, where they continued their revolutionary activities. A rising number of revolutionary publications were launched overseas at the turn of the century and then distributed in mainland China. Many of the exiles used Hong Kong as a relatively safe haven to organise and promote revolutionary activities, and a number of new Chinese-language newspapers were started around the turn of the century, some of which were believed to be founded or backed by revolutionaries and their financiers.[12]

The rising number of anti-Qing publications and activists in Hong Kong was a headache for the Hong Kong government. Given the then British stance of

[10] Letter from Acting Governor Henry Marsh to Earl of Derby, 25 September 1884, CO 129/217.

[11] Post Office Ordinance 1900.

[12] Lee Siu-nam, '香港的中西報業' [Chinese and English press in Hong Kong], in 香港史新編/ *Hong Kong History: New Perspectives*, ed. Wang Gung-wu (Hong Kong: Joint Publishing, 2017), 2:563–604.

supporting the Qing government, the laws and courts of Hong Kong were repeatedly used to combat the anti-Qing press and revolutionary activities. In 1907, for example, legislation targeting the suppression of anti-Qing publications was passed. The new law – 'owing to the proximity of the Colony of Hongkong to the mainland of China and to the tendency to create internal dissension in that country' – punished any person who published or distributed materials calculated to excite disorder in China, regardless of whether they were printed on the mainland or in Hong Kong. Those convicted of these charges would be liable to imprisonment for any term not exceeding two years and to a fine not exceeding HK$500.[13]

During the Legislative Council meeting considering the legislation, then Colonial Secretary Francis Henry May and Attorney General Rees Davies made the objective of stricter press control clear. The law aimed 'to prevent Hongkong becoming a place where seditious pamphlets may be printed and circulated with a view to distribution in China' and 'to prevent this Colony being made a centre for seditious publications'.[14]

The colonial secretary justified the passing of the law by saying that the stance of 'the native press in this Colony towards the reigning dynasty in China has been a serious source of embarrassment'. While addressing the Legislative Council, he held up a publication sold in Hong Kong 'in which were represented some of China's leading statesmen sitting with their heads in their hands' (as shown in Figure 1.1). 'That is', the colonial secretary said, 'nothing more or less than inciting persons to deliberate rebellion against the great and friendly empire which lies so close to our border'.[15]

Confidential correspondence addressed to the governor of the Straits Settlements Sir John Anderson revealed that the Chinese government had a role to play in enacting this ordinance in the empire's colonies in East Asia:

Sir, I have the honour to transmit to you for your information a copy of Hongkong Ordinance no. 15 of 1907 [Chinese Publications (Prevention) Ordinance] together with copies of correspondence with the Foreign Office with regard to the request of the China Government that similar enactments should be passed in the Straits Settlements and other British territories in the Far East in order to prevent the publication there of books or newspapers containing matter calculated to excite dissension in China.[16]

Not long after passage of the Chinese Publications (Prevention) Ordinance, the British Empire itself also faced anti-imperialist movements and nationalist attacks in its colonies, India in particular. A further measure was thus taken to curb the

---

[13] Chinese Publications (Prevention) Ordinance 1907.
[14] *Hong Kong Hansard*, 3 October 1907.
[15] *Ibid.*
[16] Confidential note from Hong Kong government to Governor John Anderson, 19 June 1908, CO 129/351.

Figure 1.1 China's leading statesman losing his head, as depicted in *Min Bao* (1907).

spread of anti-British sentiments to Hong Kong. In 1914, the Seditious Publications Ordinance was passed with the aim of prohibiting anti-government publications against colonial rule. Much stronger and more detailed than the earlier ordinance, the new legislation empowered the government not only to punish the publisher of anti-government materials but also to search for, seize and confiscate such materials. During the Legislative Council meeting held to consider the new ordinance, the colonial secretary spoke of the empire's growing unease over its colonies. He noted that 'newspapers and documents of a highly objectionable character' had been recently imported into Hong Kong. Although Section 12 of the Post Office Ordinance 1900 empowered the postmaster to stop such import, many publications 'of a highly seditious and disloyal character' entered Hong Kong by means other than through the Post Office. Hence, the government needed legal powers to 'detain any articles suspected of containing seditious publications and to declare them "to be forfeited"'. Further, it needed the power 'to issue search warrants for such publications and for seizure'. What worried colonial officials even more was that anti-imperialistic feelings amongst the Indian population of Hong Kong might be incited by some of the publications emanating from Indian sources. Their publication and appearance in India had already been prohibited.[17]

17 *Hong Kong Hansard*, 23 April 1914.

The Seditious Publications Ordinance of 1914 and its revisions of 1915 were passed, providing that any person who published or knowingly had in his or her possession any newspaper, book or other document containing any seditious material (which was broadly defined to include, amongst other material, any words likely to incite violence or excite hatred or disaffection towards the British government) would be liable to a fine not exceeding HK$500 and imprisonment of no more than two years. Extensive powers of search and seizure were also afforded the governor in council and the police with respect to seditious materials. Furthermore, defendants charged with possessing such materials bore the burden of proving their absence of knowledge that the materials were seditious.[18]

Juridifying Press Control

Contrary to previous scholarship's description of the press control legislation of British Hong Kong as something that for most of the time was 'stand-by legislation' that was 'sparingly used',[19] the laws for controlling unwanted opinion were in fact by no means an empty threat. They were resolutely applied, sometimes with heavy penalties, over many years, primarily against Chinese-language newspapers, during the early twentieth century to actively suppress materials containing criticisms of the mainland Chinese government, materials antagonistic to British rule in Hong Kong and materials that might affect Britain's diplomatic relations with other powers, as the following court cases show. Although during the Legislative Council meetings in which the aforementioned legislation was passed, the government explicitly stated that the legislation applied to articles in both the English- and Chinese-language press that might excite tumult, its actual application shows that Chinese and European papers were not in fact treated equally before the common law

---

[18] Ss. 2, 3, 3A, 3B and 4, Seditious Publications Ordinance 1914 (as amended by No. 6 of 1915).

[19] Previous scholarship on the history of media laws in British Hong Kong wrongly assumes that the extensive powers granted under those laws were used sparingly and that the press was thus generally free. For example, commenting on the censorship power afforded the governor in the 1910s, Norman Miners writes: 'The Hong Kong Government made use of these sweeping powers only on one occasion', see Norman Miners, 'The Use and Abuse of Emergency Power', *Hong Kong Law Journal* 26, no. 1 (1996): 51. In *Censorship: A World Encyclopedia*, Kees Kuiken's entry on early colonial Hong Kong notes: 'In spite of their draconian powers [to suppress freedom of expression], most British governors left the Hong Kong press quite free'; see Kees Kuiken, 'Hong Kong and Macau', in *Censorship: A World Encyclopaedia*, ed. Derek Jones (New York: Routledge, 2001), 2:1096–102, at 1096. Also see similar image portrayed in Lee Siu-nam, '香港的中西報業', 597; Francis Lee, *Talk Radio, the Mainstream Press, and Public Opinion in Hong Kong* (Hong Kong: Hong Kong University Press, 2014), 32; Anne Cheung, *Self-Censorship and the Struggle for Press Freedom in Hong Kong* (The Hague: Kluwer, 2003), 66. This book provides a corrective to these conventional narratives.

system practised in Hong Kong, as the prosecution against the Chinese news-paper *Chung Kwok Yat Po* (*China Daily*) shows.[20]

In May 1911, Li Hon-chi, the editor of *Chung Kwok Yat Po*, a newspaper founded by the revolutionary Chen Shao-bai in 1900, was charged with pub-lishing an article calculated to excite tumult, disorder or crime in mainland China in breach of the Chinese Publications (Prevention) Ordinance. The offending article contained such remarks about the oppressive behaviour of Qing government officials as 'If there were no Tsing [Qing] officials there would be no famine-stricken people ... the officials were contemplating selling the country'.[21] The article also called for actions against such officials. In defending Li, barrister Eldon Potter highlighted the unequal treatment in law of English and Chinese newspapers in his cross-examination of A. W. Brewin, the registrar general of the Hong Kong government, who was responsible for Chinese affairs in Hong Kong, including the monitoring of Chinese news-papers. Brewin was giving evidence that the article was calculated to excite tumult in China.

Potter read to Brewin a quote from an article in an English-language newspaper: 'They [the Qing government] stand out to day in the eyes of all the world, as the most incapable, corrupt, decadent and hopeless race, into whose hands have fallen, the destinies of any conquered people.' He then asked Brewin: 'Does that not mean the Manchu conquered China and are the worst rulers that the people have even seen? Is it not as strong as anything in here [the *Chung Kwok Yat Po* article]?' Brewin replied: 'Yes I suppose it is.'

Potter then submitted that

it was a vindictive prosecution. It was an unfair thing to bring a prosecution after eight months had gone. The Government had translations in their possession in 1910 and yet they did not take any steps until the present time. They should not have one law for the Chinese and another for Europeans. They boasted that the law was the same for an Englishman as for a foreigner. But, unfortunately, in the administration of that particular ordinance, the Chinese were picked out and were prosecuted while others, who were publishing literature much stronger were passed by. ... It was not fair that Europeans should be passed by and that Chinese should be singled out for punishment.[22]

He continued, noting that the case was of the utmost importance to both European and Chinese papers, which may contain articles criticising very freely the state of affairs in China. The judge hearing the case, Chief Justice

---

[20] The Attorney General explained to the Legislative Councillors that the Chinese Publications (Prevention) Ordinance applied also to materials printed in the English language if such materials were found by the court to have excited tumult or disorder in China; see *Hong Kong Hansard*, 3 October 1907.

[21] SCMP, 23 May 1911.   [22] *Ibid.*

Sir Francis Piggott (CJ Piggott hereafter), in directing the jury, did not consider the foregoing point relevant to the trial:

A great deal had been said of the other papers in the colony. They [the jurors] had to remember, however, that two wrongs did not make a right, and that question, so far as they were concerned, was totally irrelevant.[23]

CJ Piggott's remarks also reveal the deeper political anxiety of the empire, which in his view should be afforded a higher priority than free speech and equality before the law:

They all know that China subjected herself to criticism, but the basis of the law was that the King's Government had undertaken certain obligations, of friendship and of commerce with the Emperor of China, and it was bound to recognise the existence of the Government as much as the French or German Governments .... It was no new principle.[24]

After the collapse of the Qing dynasty, such obligations of friendship seem to have been inherited by the Beiyang warlord government under Yuan Shi-kai in Beijing. Possibly under the principle mentioned by CJ Piggott, Chinese newspapers continued to be prosecuted during Yuan's reign for criticisms of his government. From 1913 to 1916, the editors of a number of Chinese newspapers and periodicals in Hong Kong, including but not limited to *Shat Po*, *Chi Po* and *Yin Cheong*, were prosecuted for publishing articles critical of Yuan and his plan to restore monarchy in China.[25]

Taking editors to court and exposing in newspaper reports the rather political debates between colonial judges and defending counsels sometimes caused the government embarrassment rather than conferring any benefit. To avoid the theatrics of trial hearings and get rid of 'naughty' editors in a more efficient yet less visible way, the colonial government very often made use of the wide deportation power vested in the governor by the Peace Preservation Ordinance and Banishment and Conditional Pardons Ordinance to banish newspaper editors from Hong Kong.[26] Not only was the colonial government sensitive to articles critical of the British Empire, the colonial government or the Chinese government, but its censorship net extended to lyrics and cartoons that might arouse anti-European sentiments or embarrass British allies. In 1904, two editors and a manager of *Wai San Yat Po* were banished for publishing the Chinese lyrics of a song called 'Curry Rice'. The colonial government translated the lyrics into English (as shown in Figure 1.2) and discussed them in an Executive Council meeting. A lyric encouraging yellow curry sauce (which

---

[23] *Ibid.*   [24] *Ibid.*

[25] The prosecution of Shat Po was reported in SCMP, 26 September 1913, that of Chi Po in SCMP, 23 November 1915, and that of Yin Cheong in SCMP, 21 April 1916.

[26] Peace Preservation Ordinance 1886; and Banishment and Conditional Pardons Ordinance 1882.

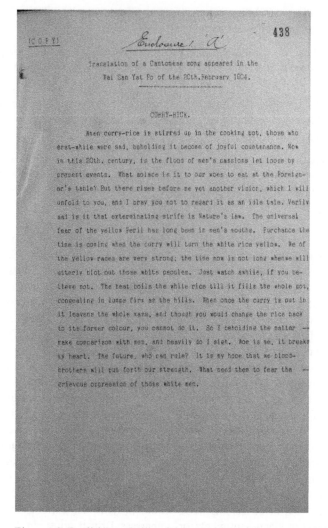

Figure 1.2 English translation of the song 'Curry Rice' prepared by the Hong Kong government for Executive Council discussion. Source: Francis Henry May, Officer Administering the Government of Hong Kong to Alfred Lyttelton, Secretary of State for the Colonies, 24 March 1904, CO 129/322, 434–42. Source: Courtesy of The National Archives of the UK.

could be analogised to 'yellow' Chinese) to penetrate and conquer white rice (analogised to white Europeans) was thought by the governor in council to be intended to stir up 'hatred and distrust of the foreigner'. Hence, an order of banishment was issued against the paper's editors and managers.[27] In 1905, three editors of *Kung Yik Po* were deported for publishing an offensive cartoon of Alice Roosevelt, the daughter of the then US president, shortly before her visit to Hong Kong.[28]

In the Name of War: On the Path to Pre-emptive Censorship

During the First World War, anti-government censorship regulations were further tightened in the name of defence and military security. Censorship regulations were passed between 1914 and 1916 on the Orders of the British King in Council, which empowered the Hong Kong government not only to prosecute newspapers found to have published articles that were seditious, caused hatred of or disaffection with the British Empire or reported sensitive war information but also to request that the press submit pre-publication newspaper scripts for censorship.[29] A Press Censor's office headed by a lieutenant was established in Hong Kong for the purpose. Two letters from the Hong Kong government requesting that all press in Hong Kong submit materials for pre-emptive censorship are shown in Figures 1.3 and 1.4.

21 August 1914

Sir,

I am directed by His Excellency the Governor to request you to submit to the Censor, General Staff, Headquarter Officers, before publication, all reports, notices or other information which you propose to insert in your newspaper.

(Signed) Claud Severn

Colonial Secretary

Figure 1.3 Letter asking the press to submit all reports for pre-censorship. Source: Letter from Hong Kong Governor to Andrew Bonar Law, MP, 24 October 1916, CO 129/435.

---

[27] Francis Henry May, Officer Administering the Government of Hong Kong to Alfred Lyttelton, Secretary of State for the Colonies, 24 March 1904, CO 129/322, 434–42.

[28] For the wide power of deportation possessed and used by the colonial Hong Kong government, see Christopher Munn, 'Our Best Trump Card: A Brief History of Deportation in Hong Kong, 1857–1955', in *Civil Unrest and Governance in Hong Kong: Law and Order from Historical and Cultural Perspectives*, ed. Michael H. K. Ng and John D. Wong (London: Routledge, 2017), 26–45. For the report of the offensive cartoon of Alice Roosevelt, see p. 32 of the same book.

[29] Censorship Regulations, 1916 attached to Letter from Hong Kong governor to Andrew Bonar Law, MP, 24 October 1916, CO 129/435.

4 September 1916

I am directed to inform you that it is the Governor's desire that all items of news referring in any way to the following subjects should be sent to the Press Censor prior to publication:-

(1) The 'Chou-an-hui' or 'Peace Preservation Society'.

(2) Revival of the Monarchy in China.

(3) Any matters arising in China or Japan which have been referred to the British Legations.

(4) The situation between China and Japan.

(5) News or information regarding India and Indians wherever situate[d] ...

The above is simply a general statement of the subjects which should invariably be sent up for censorship. There are possibly however others which must be left to our discretion but His Excellency wishes me to impress on you the desirability of submitting such for censorship whenever there might be any doubt as to the desirability of publication.

(Signed) Claud Severn

Colonial Secretary

Figure 1.4 Letter requesting that the press submit specific reports for pre-censorship. Source: Letter from Hong Kong Governor to Andrew Bonar Law, MP, 24 October 1916, CO 129/435.

Sometimes the Hong Kong government would make individual enquiries concerning a particular item of news reported in a newspaper, as shown in the following letter from the colonial secretary of Hong Kong to the SCMP dated 14 April 1916.

14 April 1916

Sir,

I am directed to request you to explain how the heading to a [R]euters' telegram on page 7 of today's issue of your newspaper 'The Laurentic's Captures' came to be inserted. There is no mention of the 'Laurentic' in the telegram and the mention of the name of the vessel is a serious breach of the instructions issued to the public press in this Colony.

(Signed) Claud Severn

Colonial Secretary

Figure 1.5 Letter asking the SCMP for an explanation of a newspaper report. Source: Letter from Hong Kong Governor to Andrew Bonar Law, MP, 24 October 1916, CO 129/435.

During the 1914–19 period, a number of papers, both European and Chinese, were sent enquiries, warned or prosecuted for breaching the censorship regulations. Several of these actions are summarised in Table 1.1.

Table 1.1 *Hong Kong government's actions against the press, 1915–18*

Date of newspaper report	Name of newspaper	Content of complaint	Action against paper
23 September 1915	SCMP	Publishing news referring to the supply of munitions to Russia	Referred to colonial secretary, who sent a letter of warning[30]
12 October 1915	SCMP	Publishing an article referring to Rosyth Dockyard	Colonial secretary interviewed the editor, who promised to submit everything in future[31]
5 November 1915	SCMP	Publishing two telegrams referring to Japanese military information	Editor warned by press censor on 6 November 1915[32]
27 July 1916	SCMP	Publishing an article relating to Russia's navy	Editor was warned[33]
17, 18 August 1917	*Chung Ngoi Sun Po*	Publishing an article against the president of China	Prosecuted for making statements and spreading reports likely to cause disaffection with the British Crown and promote Chinese enmity amongst British subjects in contravention of the censorship regulations[34]
15 May 1917	*Hong Kong Daily Press*	Publishing an article about the arrival of two steamers in Hong Kong	Prosecuted for breaching the censorship regulations[35]
11 May 1918	*Hong Kong Telegraph*	Publishing an article relating the movement of British ships	Prosecuted for breaching the censorship regulations[36]

[30] Summary of actions against the press attached to Letter from Hong Kong governor to Andrew Bonar Law, MP, 24 October 1916, CO 129/435.
[31] *Ibid.* [32] *Ibid.* [33] *Ibid.* [34] SCMP, 3 September 1917. [35] SCMP, 18 May 1917.
[36] SCMP, 7 June 1918.

Pre-emptive censorship did not end with the Great War. A number of large-scale strikes during the early 1920s added to fears over rising anti-Japanese and anti-colonial sentiment in Hong Kong, giving the colonial government an opportunity to establish a permanent censorship mechanism governing only the Chinese-language press in Hong Kong. That mechanism was kept in place for at least another three decades into the 1950s. The next chapter uncovers how the political censorship regime in Hong Kong evolved from punitive censorship to regular pre-emptive censorship, a measure that imposed the mandatory daily vetting of newspaper proofs by government censors. Press control was expanded from punishing editors for what they had already published to day-to-day political vetting of the content of Chinese newspaper proofs before they were printed for sale to the public. The operations of the censors' office produced newspapers with weird dots and crosses concealing censored material, as shown in the next chapter.

'Reading Every Line': Era of the Daily Vetting of Newspaper Proofs

Daily Pre-emptive Censorship (1920s–1940s)

The colonial government faced the most serious challenge to its legitimacy to date during the large-scale strikes that occurred between 1922 and 1926.[1] In response to the resulting anxiety over its continued rule in Hong Kong, particularly in the face of the united front of the Nationalists and the Communist Party in the anti-imperialist movement of 1924, the government further stretched its reach in controlling the press. Press control was expanded from punishing editors for what had been published contrary to the law to day-to-day censorship of the content of Chinese newspaper proofs. The legislative and judicial branches again became important components of this routine press censorship machine. During a seamen's strike in 1922, the Emergency Regulations Ordinance (ERO), which was said to have been rushed through in just three minutes without debate, was passed,[2] giving power to the governor to make regulations on, amongst other matters, censorship and the control and suppression of publications. Any person contravening any regulation under the ordinance was liable to a fine not exceeding HK$1,000 and to imprisonment for a term not exceeding one year. During the Canton–Hong Kong Strike and Boycott of 1925, the governor established more detailed newspaper censorship regulations (Newspapers Regulations) under the power vested in him by the ERO. Under these regulations, the extensive power of censorship of newspapers and other types of publication was vested in the secretary for Chinese affairs, and the governor was even afforded the power to suspend a newspaper from publication.

1. No person shall print, publish, or distribute any newspaper, placard or pamphlet containing any matter *in the Chinese language* (other than

---

[1] For an account of these strikes, see Tsai Jung-Fang, 香港人之香港史 *1841–1945/The Hong Kong People's History of Hong Kong 1841–1945* (Hong Kong: Oxford University Press, 2001), 109–67; Ming K. Chan, 'Hong Kong in Sino-British Conflict: Mass Mobilization and the Crisis of Legitimacy', in *Precarious*, ed. Ming K. Chan and John D. Young (New York: Routledge, 1994), 27.

[2] As noted by Lo Man Kam in the Legislative Council Meeting on 26 August 1936. See *Hong Kong Hansard* of the same date.

a bona fide trade advertisement) which has not been ***previously submitted to and passed by*** the Secretary for Chinese Affairs. [Emphasis added]

2. No person shall import, print, publish, reproduce, have in his possession or under his control, post up or distribute any newspaper, placard, pamphlet, writing or pictorial representation calculated or tending to persuade or induce any person or persons, whether individually or as members of the general public, (1) to refrain from dealing with, trading with, working for or hiring any person or persons in the course of trade, business, occupation, or employment; (2) to do any act calculated or tending to cause a breach of the peace; (3) to interfere with the administration of the law or with the maintenance of law and order.

3. No person shall, without the permission of the Secretary for Chinese Affairs, import any newspaper, placard or pamphlet containing any matter in the Chinese language other than a bona fide trade advertisement. No person shall have in his possession any newspaper, placard or pamphlet imported without permission.

4. The Governor in Council shall have power to suppress for such period as he may think fit or until further order the printing and publication of any newspaper.[3]

These regulations ushered in an era of the active and pre-emptive press censorship of Chinese newspapers in Hong Kong, in addition to such punitive censorship measures as bringing criminal libel lawsuits against unfriendly editors and newspapers. The ERO was enacted in the context of maintaining law and order (from the colonial government's viewpoint) in the midst of the largest-scale strikes in Hong Kong history, but the pre-censorship measures within it nevertheless continued to operate after the eighteen-month strike ended in the autumn of 1926. In 1931, the censorship regulations were tightened to empower policemen to seize and detain the printing machinery and writing materials of suppressed newspapers.[4] Not surprisingly, English-language newspapers were not subject to the mandatory daily pre-censorship requirement.

'Reading Every Line': How the Censors Worked

Although it is not easy for a researcher to find in the archival records government documents detailing how the censorship of newspaper proofs was carried out on a daily basis, the testimonies of government censors and press editors reported in newspaper coverage of censorship prosecution cases reveal how pervasive daily censorship operations were in early twentieth-century

---

[3] G.N. No. 369 of 1925, Hong Kong Government Gazette, 25 June 1925.
[4] G.N. No. 621 of 1931, Hong Kong Government Gazette, 2 October 1931.

Hong Kong and how closely censors and editors worked together in the evening prior to sending newspaper proofs to printers. The diary and personal collection of Ng Bar-ling, a long-time editor of one of the major Chinese-language newspapers in colonial Hong Kong, *Wah Kiu Yat Po* (WKYP), also contain valuable information and documents on how the hitherto little known Press Censorship Office operated.

During the Canton–Hong Kong Strike and Boycott, the pre-censorship of newspaper proofs was carried out on a part-time basis by three Chinese justices of the peace, one Chinese staff member of the Secretariat for Chinese Affairs and two Chinese staff members of the Education Department. After the strike, this pre-censorship work was institutionalised under the newly established Press Censorship Office under the leadership of an ethnically Chinese deputy secretary for Chinese affairs by the name of Liu Zhi-ping. Liu was a highly educated man who had served as the county governor of China at Bao An county in Guangdong province, which neighbours Hong Kong.[5] The Press Censorship Office began operating on 17 May 1928.[6] Liu supervised two full-time censors who were charged with 'the task of reading every line' that appeared in the proofs of all Chinese newspapers every day. One of the censors was on duty from 4:00 to 6:00 in the afternoon and the other from 6:00 to 8:00 in the evening. Censorship hours were later extended to 11:00 p.m., and subsequently to as late as 1:30 a.m., to cater for late news coming in from mainland China.[7] Figure 2.1 shows a notice kept by the Chinese press about the opening hours of the Press Censorship Office during the 1930s. The censors sometimes had to ring up the papers at 12:45 a.m. to tell them that if they had any articles to be censored, they were to send them along as quickly as they could. Any later telegrams arriving from China after 1:00 a.m. had to be sent to the residence of a designated censor for approval.[8] The method of censorship entailed the censors 'delet[ing] any objectionable matter by striking it through with a red or blue pencil or an ink cross or line, which indicated that the matter was not passed for publication, or to place his initials in the corner of any objectionable paragraph, which indicated that the particular paragraph was passed for publication'.[9]

If the censors struck out objectionable words or sentences from the newspaper proofs, editors had to delete those words or sentences from the proofs. In an age without computer software, editors were left with insufficient time to manually rearrange newspaper layouts to accommodate such deletions.

[5] Description of Liu and newspaper report of 7 April 1970 on Liu's death and his background, Ng Bar Ling Collection (1904–1976), Special Collections of the University of Hong Kong Libraries.

[6] Ng Bar-ling, Manuscript of 'Materials of Hong Kong Press History' and diary entries of Ng Bar-ling, Ng Bar Ling Collection (1904–1976), Special Collections of the University of Hong Kong Libraries.

[7] SCMP, 21 June 1928; SCMP, 15 June 1928. Two additional censors were subsequently added to the operation, see *Hong Kong Hansard*, 26 August 1936.

[8] SCMP, 5 February 1931.   [9] SCMP, 21 June 1928.

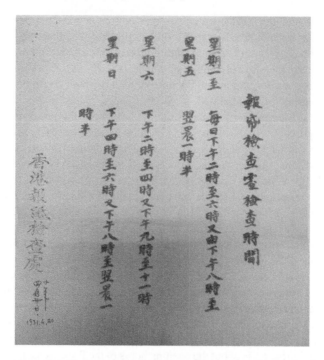

Figure 2.1 Notice kept by the Chinese press about the opening hours of the Press Censorship Office in 1931. It informs the press that the office operates from 2:00 to 6:00 p.m. and 8:00 p.m. to 1:30 a.m. from Monday to Friday; from 2:00 to 4:00 p.m. and 9:00 to 11:00 p.m. on Saturday; and from 4:00 to 6:00 p.m. and 8:00 p.m. to 1:30 a.m. on Sunday. Source: Ng Bar Ling Collection (1904–1976), Special Collections of the University of Hong Kong Libraries.

Instead, they had to either replace the deleted words or sentences with a blank space marked 'censored' in Chinese (Figure 2.2) or replace them with dots, crosses and/or squares (Figures 2.3 to 2.8) before sending the revised proofs to the printers in a hurry. Veteran journalists later recalled that the government had not liked the idea of revealing to readers that a news story had been censored but could do nothing about it.[10] It was therefore not uncommon to see newspapers filled with dots, crosses and squares for sale in the streets. In addition to striking out individual words and sentences in a newspaper proof, the press censors could also prohibit an entire news story from being published. As

---

[10] A Chinese newspaper report (newspaper title missing), 22 August 1974, Ng Bar Ling Collection (1904–1976), Special Collections of the University of Hong Kong Libraries.

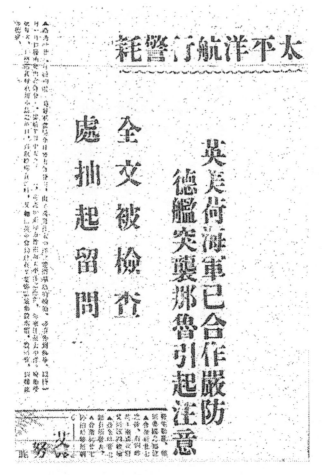

Figure 2.2 Censored newspaper report. The blank space with words 全文被
檢查處抽起留問 reads 'Entire story was kept by Censorship Office for
investigation'. Source: *Wa Tsz Yat Po*, 29 December 1940.

shown in Figures 2.9 and 2.10, a censor would sometimes cross out an entire
news report and stamp it with an official chop to signify his disapproval. The
characters on the outer circle of the chop shown in Figures 2.9 and 2.10 reads
'Hong Kong Press Censorship Office', and the inner one reads 'This script is
not allowed to be published'.[11]

[11] Ng Bar-ling, Manuscript of 'Materials of Hong Kong Press History', Ng Bar Ling Collection
(1904–1976), Special Collections of the University of Hong Kong Libraries.

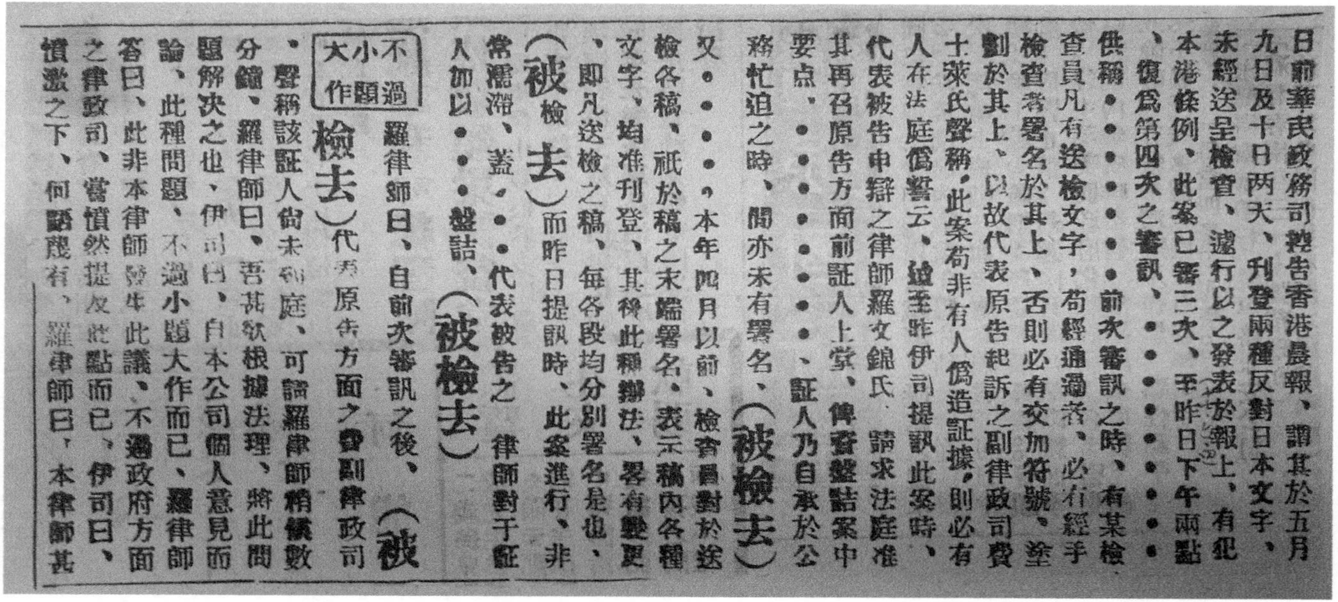

日前華民政務司控告香港晨報、謂其於五月
九日及十日兩天、刊登兩種反對日本文字、
未經送呈檢查、遽行以之發表於報上、有犯
本港條例、此案已審三次、至昨日下午兩點
、復爲第四次之審訊、●●●●●●●
供稱●●●●●●前次審訊之時、有某檢
查員凡有送檢文字，苟經通過者、必有經手
檢查者署名於其上、否則必有交加符號、塗
劃於其上、以故代表原告起訴之副律政司費
士萊氏聲稱、此案苟非有人僞造証據、則必有
人在法庭僞誓云、繼至昨伊司提訊此案時、
代表被告申辯之律師羅文錦氏、請求法庭准
其再召原告方面前証人上堂、俾審盤詰案中
要点、●●●●●●●、証人乃自承於公
務忙迫之時、間亦未有署名、（被檢去）
又●●●●●，本年四月以前、檢查員對於送
檢各稿、祇於稿之末端署名、表示稿內各種
文字、均准刊登、其後此種辦法、略有變更
、即凡送檢之稿、每各段均分別署名是也、
（被檢去）而昨日提訊時、此案進行、非
常濡滯、蓋●●●代表被告之 律師對于証
人加以●●●盤詰、（被檢去）

不過小題大作

羅律師曰、自前次審訊之後、（被
檢去）代表原告方面之費副律政司
、聲稱該証人尚未到庭、可請羅律師稍候數
分鐘、羅律師曰、吾甚欲根據法理、將此問
題解決之也、伊司曰、自本公司個人意見而
論、此種問題、不過小題大作而已、羅律師
答曰、此非本律師發生此議、不過政府方面
之律政司、嘗憤然提及此點而已、伊司曰、
憤激之下、何語罷有、羅律師曰、本律師甚

Figure 2.3 Newspaper report with dots replacing the censored sentences. Words in brackets (被檢去) read ‘censored’. Source: Newspaper clippings of June 1928 (date and title of newspaper missing), Ng Bar Ling Collection (1904–1976), Special Collections of the University of Hong Kong Libraries.

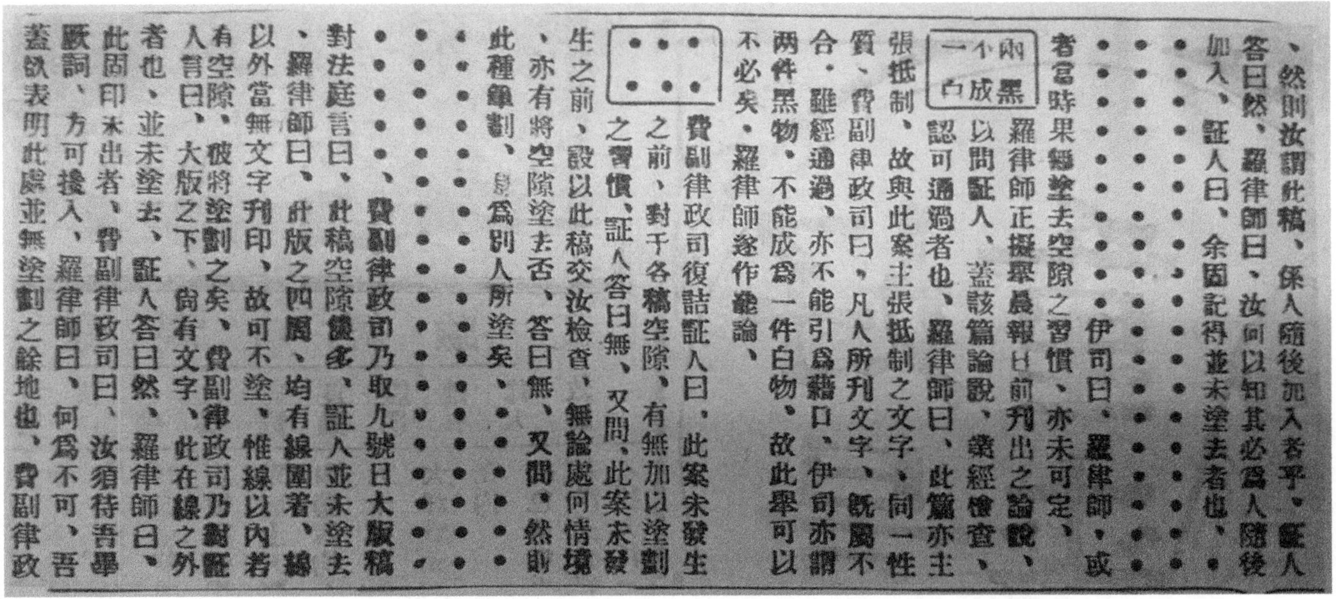

、然則汝謂此稿、係人隨後加入者乎。証人答曰然、羅律師曰、汝何以知其必爲人隨後加入、証人曰、余固記得並未塗去者也、●●●●●●●●●●●●●●●●●●●●●●●●●●●●●●●●●●●伊司曰、羅律師、或者當時果曾塗去空隙之習慣、亦未可定、

一个兩
白成黑

羅律師正擬舉晨報日前刊出之論說、以問証人、蓋該篇論說、業經檢查、認可通過者也、羅律師曰、此篇亦主張抵制、故與此案主張抵制之文字、同一性質、費副律政司曰、凡人所刊文字、既屬不合、雖經通過、亦不能引爲藉口、伊司亦謂兩件黑物、不能成爲一件白物、故此舉可以不必矣、羅律師遂作罷論、

●●●
●●●

費副律政司復詰証人曰、此案未發生之前、對于各稿空隙、有無加以塗劃之習慣、証人答曰無、又問、此案未發生之前、設以此稿交汝檢查、無論處何情境、亦有將空隙塗去否、答曰無、又問、然則此種鏟劃、是爲別人所塗矣、●●●、費副律政司乃取九號日大版稿對法庭言曰、此稿空隙儘多、証人並未塗去、羅律師曰、此版之四圍、均有線圍着、線以外當無文字刊印、故可不塗、惟線以內若有空隙、彼將塗劃之矣、費副律政司乃對証人言曰、大版之下、尚有文字、此在線之外者也、並未塗去、証人答曰然、羅律師曰、此固印未出者、費副律政司曰、汝須待吾畢厥詞、方可插入、羅律師曰、何爲不可、吾蓋欲表明此處並無塗劃之餘地也、費副律政

Figure 2.4 Newspaper report with dots replacing the censored sentences. Source: Newspaper clippings of June 1928 (date and title of newspaper missing), Ng Bar Ling Collection (1904–1976), Special Collections of the University of Hong Kong Libraries.

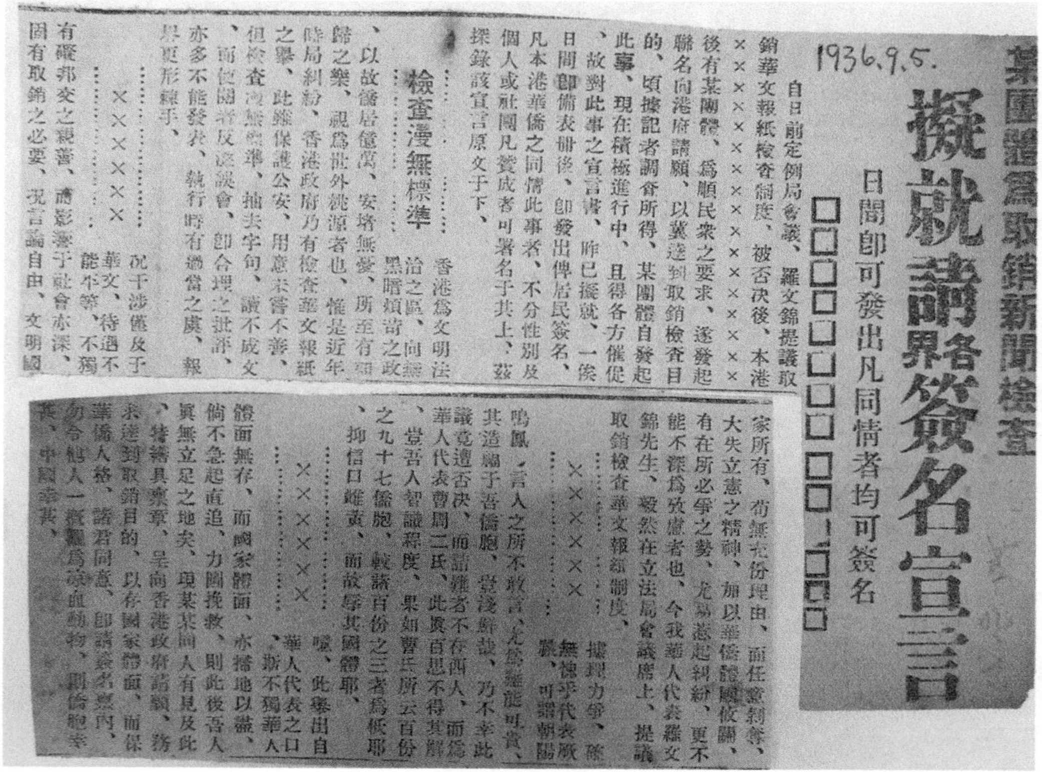

1936.9.5.

華團體為取銷新聞檢查

擬就請各界簽名宣言

日間即可發出凡同情者均可簽名

□□□□□□□□□□□□□

自日前定例局會議、羅文錦提議取銷華文報紙檢查制度、被否決後、本港××××××××××××××××後有某團體、為順民衆之要求、遂發起聯名向港府請願、以冀達到取銷檢查目的、頃據記者調查所得、某團體自發起此事、現在積極進行中、且得各方催促、故對此事之宣言書、昨已擬就、一俟日間即備表冊後、即發出俾居民簽名、凡本港華僑之同情此事者、不分性別及個人或社團凡贊成者可署名于其上、茲探錄該宣言原文于下、

……檢查漫無標準……

香港為文明法治之區、向無黑暗煩苛之政、以故僑居億萬、安堵無憂、所至有如歸之樂、視為世外桃源者也、惟是近年時局糾紛、香港政府乃有檢查華文報紙之舉、此雖保護公安、用意未嘗不善、但檢查漫無標準、抽去字句、讀不成文、而使閱者反滋誤會、即合理之批評、亦多不能發表、執行時有過當之處、報界更形棘手、

……××××××……

況干涉僅及于華文、待遇不能平等、不獨有礙邦交之親善、尤影響于社會亦深、固有取銷之必要、況言論自由、文明國家所有、苟無充份理由、而任意剝奪、大失立憲之精神、加以華僑體顧攸關、有在所必爭之勢、尤易惹起糾紛、更不能不深為致慮者也、今我華人代表羅文錦先生、毅然在立法局會議席上、提議取銷檢查華文報紙制度、

……××××××……

據理力爭、旗無愧乎代表厥職、可謂朝陽鳴鳳、言人之所不敢言、尤為難能可貴、其造福于吾僑胞、豈淺鮮哉、乃不幸此議竟遭否決、而諸難者不在西人、而為華人代表曹周二氏、此實百思不得其解、豈吾人智識程度、果如曹氏所云百份之九十七僑胞、較諸百份之三者為低耶、抑信口雌黃、而故辱其國體耶、

……××××××……

噫、此舉出自華人代表之口、斯不獨華人體面無存、而國家體面、亦掃地以盡、倘不急起直追、力圖挽救、則此後吾人眞無立足之地矣、現某某同人有見及此、特籌具衆章、呈向香港政府請願、務求達到取銷目的、以存國家體面、而保華僑人格、諸君同意、即請簽名其內、勿令他人一瞥屬為殘血動物、則僑胞幸甚、中國幸甚、

Figure 2.5 Newspaper report with crosses and squares replacing the censored sentences. Source: Newspaper clippings of 5 September 1936 (title of newspaper missing), Ng Bar Ling Collection (1904–1976), Special Collections of the University of Hong Kong Libraries.

Figure 2.6 Newspaper report with crosses replacing the censored sentences. Source: *Ta Kung Pao*, 6 May 1939, courtesy of *Ta Kung Pao*.

Figure 2.7 Newspaper report with squares and crosses replacing the censored sentences. Source: *Kung Sheung Daily News*, 21 September 1936, courtesy of The Robert H. N. Ho Family Foundation.

Furthermore, censors sometimes had face-to-face meetings with editors in which they would tell them what not to report. When one editor was cross-examined in court about what he had been told by a censor, he said, 'What he [the censor] told us was not to publish anything violent against Japan'.[12] The secretary for Chinese affairs also sent notices to the press via the Newspapers

[12] SCMP, 15 June 1928.

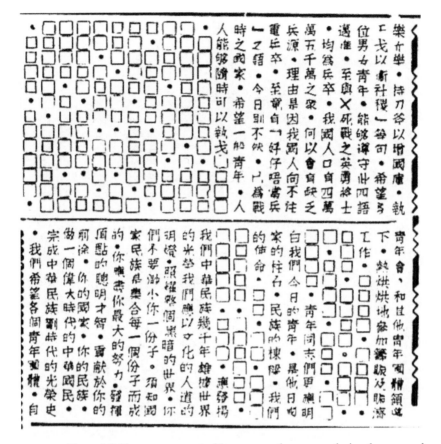

Figure 2.8 Newspaper report with squares and crosses replacing the censored sentences. Source: WKYP, 8 May 1939, courtesy of SCMP.

Association setting out topics that the press should not report on. For example, a notice kept by Ng Bar-ling shows that the government asked the press not to write stories that would 'jeopardize loyalty to the British Empire', 'affect British relations with China' or 'promote communism'.[13] Newspapers could be prosecuted under the Newspapers Regulations if they published any articles that had not been approved.[14]

[13] A translated letter (undated but it is likely that it was written in 1936 as it refers to the Legislative Council debate in 1936) from Secretary for Chinese affairs to representatives of the Newspaper Association, Ng Bar Ling Collection (1904–1976), Special Collections of the University of Hong Kong Libraries.

[14] For example, four Chinese newspapers were prosecuted for evasion of the censorship, SCMP, 5 February 1931.

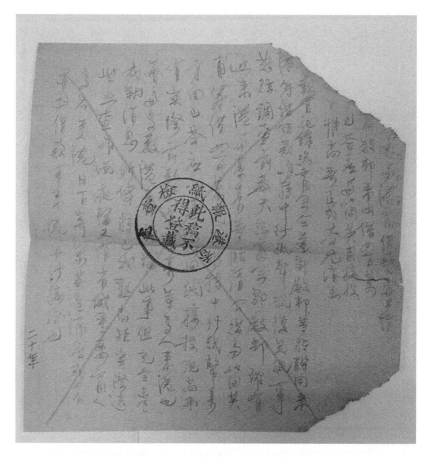

Figure 2.9 Original manuscript of a news story written in 1931 that was banned by the Press Censorship Office. The story reported that merchants from China had come to Hong Kong to seek a loan to help stabilise currency issuance in China. Source: Ng Bar Ling Collection (1904–1976), Special Collections of the University of Hong Kong Libraries.

What kinds of news stories were banned from publication? What kinds of words warranted deletion by the censors? As we will see in the following sections, the colonial government was particularly sensitive to reports that criticised its governance of the colony, jeopardised the British Empire's geo-political interests in East Asia, upset the power equation in the region or instigated political activism in the Chinese populace. Censorship measures thus became an additional political tool allowing the colonial government to suppress any news that might be deemed troublesome for the British Empire,

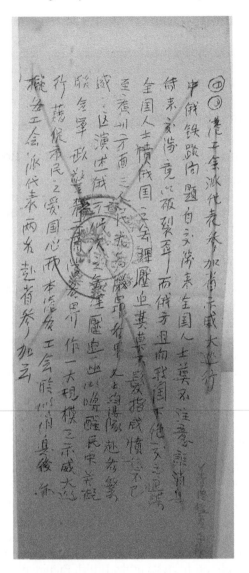

Figure 2.10 Original manuscript of a news story that was banned by the Press Censorship Office. The story reported that representatives of trade unions in Hong Kong had joined the demonstration held in Guangzhou to protest against the USSR and in support of China during a railway dispute in 1929. Source: Ng Bar Ling Collection (1904–1976), Special Collections of the University of Hong Kong Libraries.

which was experiencing challenges to its legitimacy in the region in the midst of rising nationalist and communist movements. A left-wing newspaper known as *Siu Yat Po* was suppressed under the aforementioned regulation not long after it commenced publication.[15] The empire's anxieties and priorities are clearly reflected in two important censorship prosecutions under the Newspapers Regulations that took place in 1928 and 1931 and involved five major Chinese newspapers in Hong Kong.

'Prevention Is Better Than Cure': The Shun Po Case, 1928

Military conflicts between the Kuomintang and Japanese armies that took place in Jinan in Shandong province in May 1928, resulting in the death of over 6,000 Chinese, stirred up another wave of anti-Japanese protests and boycotts in China. Censorship measures and prosecutions against Chinese-language newspapers were again used by the colonial government to suppress the spread in Hong Kong of anti-Japanese sentiments that might jeopardise the British relationship with Japan.

Shun Po, a Chinese newspaper in Hong Kong, reported on the aforementioned incidents and published a number of patriotic editorials. The paper's printers and publisher were subsequently arrested for breaching regulation 1 of the Newspapers Regulations because certain sentences and paragraphs contained in a published news report had not been approved by the Censor's Office. Those sentences were also said to be inducing support for a boycott in contravention of regulation 2. The offending sentences were as follows:

Warning to our Chinese . . . all of us who wish to maintain our nationality must refrain from using Japanese goods. If your enthusiasm is going to last for only five minutes, you might as well prepare to become slaves in a lost country . . ..

All our countrymen arise in a body and be active. The Japanese have challenged us and cruelly murdered our Chinese Officials and people. Be unanimous in severing economic relations with Japan.[16]

The four-day trial of *Shun Po*'s printers and publisher received detailed press coverage in Hong Kong, with news reports recording conversations amongst the prosecution, magistrate and defence counsel. The following snapshot of those conversations reveals how the judicial process and the law together helped to protect the geopolitical interests of the British Empire in East Asia in favour of Japan, with which Britain was on friendly terms until the outbreak of the Second World War, at the expense of a weakening China. It also clearly shows the awareness of Chinese elites of the importance of a free press, which,

---

[15] For the pro-communist background of *Siu Yat Po*, see Yang Guo-xiong, 香港戰前報業 [Hong Kong pre-war newspaper industry] (Hong Kong: Joint Publishing, 2013), 210–25.
[16] SCMP, 21 June 1928.

to their disappointment, was not afforded them under the English legal system practised in Hong Kong.

The defendants were represented by Lo Man-kam, a prominent Chinese lawyer who later became a legislative councillor. Lo argued that the use of the Newspapers Regulations in this case went beyond the legal purpose for which they had originally been established and drew the court's attention to the preamble of the ERO, which stated that 'on any occasion which the Governor in Council may consider to be an occasion of emergency or public danger he may make any regulations whatsoever which he may consider desirable in the public interest'. Lo pointed out that this preamble constituted a 'blank cheque' to the governor and must be construed strictly in the context of the circumstances in which the ordinance had been enacted (i.e. the disorder caused by the strikes of the 1920s). Lo further stated that there was and must be some limit to 'judicial ignorance', remarking that the court did and should know that a state of emergency did not exist to justify the regulations. He submitted that in every civilised country one could find laws against seditious, obscene, scandalous or libellous publications and asked the magistrate whether it was feasible to imagine that no protest would be voiced if the government tried to 'censor the Press, to muzzle the Press and to prevent it from having any freedom'. Lo added: 'The Tsinan [Jinan] incident was a matter of great and personal interest to the Chinese and there was no reason why the Chinese papers in Hongkong, catering for the Chinese public ... should not give a dispassionate account of what had happened.'[17]

The magistrate, Lieutenant Colonel Eaves, ignoring the accusation of judicial ignorance, refused to accept Lo's argument:

I cannot accept this view. Considering the possible danger to the public of one single publication of (say) seditious matter, for the purpose of preventing publication an occasion of 'public danger' may be said to exist continuously from day to day and prevention is obviously better than cure.[18]

The magistrate did not comment on Lo's point about freedom of the press, but clearly spelled out what in his view was a more important consideration in colonial legality:

If the defendants had had the slightest idea of civic responsibility, they must have realised that in the then state of Chinese feeling, the publication of such matter might excite further feeling between the Chinese and Japanese in this Colony.[19]

As a result, Eaves handed down a heavy sentence against the defendants. All partners of the printing company were fined HK$250 and the publisher was fined HK$500. All of them were also sentenced to imprisonment for one month.

---

[17] SCMP, 15 June 1928.   [18] SCMP, 21 June 1928.   [19] Ibid.

An additional unusual and humiliating punishment was also imposed on the defendants to address the magistrate's concern over the feelings of the Japanese community in Hong Kong:

When a person wrongs others through the medium of the press, the least he can do to right the wrong is publicly to apologise through the same medium. I therefore add that if, at the expiration of seven days, the defendants have printed and published in the Hongkong Morning Post [*Shun Po*] for two consecutive daily issues an expression of regret and apology to the Japanese community in Hong Kong in the following terms, I shall be prepared to recommend to the proper authority, remission of the remainder of the defendants' sentences of imprisonment.

The terms of the apology are: 'We ... trading as the Chung Fat Company, Printers, and Leung Chan, Publisher, all of Hongkong, the Printers and Publisher respectively of the *Hongkong Morning Post*, having on the 9th and 10th May last unlawfully printed and published in the Chinese language in the said newspaper certain matter advocating a boycott of Japanese goods, calculated in its result to injure the Japanese community in Hongkong, and, having been sentenced therefor to fines and imprisonment, hereby express our regret and apologise to the Japanese Community in Hongkong and further counsel and advise the Chinese inhabitants of Hongkong loyally to live in peace and amity and to continue to trade as heretofore with all persons irrespective of their nationality.'[20]

The sentences in this case, although in line with Britain's stance of remaining neutral in China's conflicts with Japan and suppressing anti-Japanese sentiments in Hong Kong, aroused not only discontent in the Chinese community but also the resentment of the English press. The SCMP, although not itself subject to the government's pre-censorship measures, reacted strongly, arguing in an editorial that the judgment against *Shun Po* 'open[ed]the door to a complete denial of the elementary British right of free speech'. It further complained that 'censorship such as has been operated in Hongkong [is] intolerable'.[21]

Faced with such a large fine and an inability to pay it, *Shun Po* was forced to cease publication from 21 June 1928.[22]

'Who But the Governor Is the Judge?': The Four Chinese Newspapers Case, 1931

The daily pre-emptive censorship exercise of the colonial government aimed not only at managing Britain's relationship with other powers and safeguarding its geopolitical interests in East Asia but also at silencing domestic voices of discontent in Hong Kong.

In February 1931, four vernacular newspapers (*Wah Kiu, Nam Keung, Nam Chung* and *Chung Hwa*) were together prosecuted for breaching the

[20] *Ibid.*   [21] *Ibid.*   [22] SCMP, 22 June 1928.

Newspapers Regulations under the ERO by publishing a series of news reports on protests and strikes amongst prisoners in Victoria Gaol without the prior consent of government censors. On the four consecutive days from 17 to 20 December 1930, the four newspapers reported that over 300 prisoners had refused to work in protest at not being given enough food. Armed police were sent into the prison to suppress the protests and place the strikers into separate custody. According to the news reports, for four days and nights the prisoners continued to shout through the windows of the prison that they were nearly dying of starvation, attracting a large number of people to gather in the vicinity.[23]

The prosecution alleged that these news reports had not been censored in accordance with the Newspapers Regulations. The trial hearing, which attracted considerable public discussion, was held at the Central Magistracy and widely reported in both the Chinese and English press.

In the trial hearing on 4 February 1931, the defendants' counsel, F. H. Loseby, before calling witnesses (including the government censor responsible for censoring the newspaper articles in question) for cross-examination, questioned the applicability of the Newspapers Regulations in peacetime Hong Kong. In the event that they were inapplicable, he averred, the charges should be dropped. He also submitted that the use of emergency regulations once times of danger and emergency has passed was a gross abuse of power. The prosecution, in contrast, insisted on the statutory interpretation that the regulations remained in force until repealed by the governor:

MAGISTRATE LINDSELL: Who is to say that the danger has passed?
MR LOSEBY: The evidence of that is 'what have we got left.'
MAGISTRATE LINDSELL: The greater part of the danger may have passed but some of it may have remained.[24]

The magistrate ruled against the defendants on this legal point, holding that:

The answer to this contention [of the defendants' counsel] seems to be: who but the Governor in Executive Council is the judge as to whether the emergency is past? The worst of it may be over, and yet some danger still remains. Again there seems to me to arise the presumption that inasmuch as these particular regulations have not been repealed ... the state of emergency in which they must have been made has not wholly passed away. On all points therefore the defence fails and the case must go on.[25]

Magistrate Lindsell then adjourned the hearing for a week until 12 February, when cross-examination of the government censor would take place. Surprisingly, when the day of the adjourned hearing arrived, the prosecution

---

[23] SCMP, 5 February 1931. For original newspaper reports containing articles complained of, see WKYP and *Nam Keung Yat Po*, 18–20 December 1930.
[24] SCMP, 29 January 1931.   [25] SCMP, 5 February 1931.

applied to drop all charges because the censor in question, a Mr Leung, was unable to appear. The SCMP reported the remarkable way in which the case concluded and its suspicions that the government had made Mr Leung leave the colony 'to avoid embarrassing disclosures and [the] provocation of further friction'.[26]

In the same column, the SCMP editor criticised the continued censorship of the Chinese press, as such a mechanism also affected European-run newspapers such as the SCMP that were not subject to the pre-censorship regime because readers would 'wrongly think, or affect to think, that the Government exercises control of the news we [Europeans] publish'. He urged the government to set Chinese newspapers free during normal times and to return British freedom of speech to Hong Kong.[27]

Censorship of Anxiety and Anxiety about Censorship: The 1936 Debate

Protests against the censorship of Chinese newspapers continued until the outbreak of the Second World War, and the arguments between the Chinese community and the colonial government were not confined to courtroom debates. In 1928, the leading Chinese newspapers in Hong Kong filed a joint petition with the secretary for Chinese affairs for the lifting of the censorship system, albeit without success.[28] In July 1936, fifty editors of Chinese news-papers in Hong Kong submitted a jointly signed letter to Lo Man-kam, now a Chinese legislative councillor, requesting that the matter of censorship be raised in the Legislative Council, which Lo duly did in its session on 26 August 1936:

LO: I rise, Sir, to propose the motion standing in my name: 'That in the opinion of this Council, the present censorship of the Chinese Press should be abrogated.'[29]

I have set out the Regulations imposing the censorship and the [Emergency Regulations] Ordinance under which they were made. Now, what were the circum-stances under which the Ordinance was passed by this Council? The Colony was then going through one of the most critical crises of its existence. The outlook was grave; disorder threatened. On the 28th February 1922, an emergency meeting of this Council was convened. At this meeting ... [Governor] Sir Reginald Stubbs, in addressing the Council on the measure, spoke inter alia as follows: –

'It is essential for the safety of the Colony that steps should be taken as early as possible, to confer upon the Executive the most drastic powers for dealing with a situation which may at any moment result in disorder owing to the misguided efforts of persons who are under the influence of Bolshevist doctrine.'

---

[26] SCMP, 13 February 1931.   [27] Ibid.   [28] SCMP, 17 April 1928.
[29] Hong Kong Hansard, 26 August 1936, 179.

It will be seen that under the cloak of an authority which the Governor-in-council is to exercise only on an occasion of emergency or public danger the Government has, in effect, imposed a permanent system of censorship upon the Chinese Press.[30]

Lo then further attacked the unequal treatment of the Chinese and English press:

Hon. Members of this Council may recall that on the 19th [of] March [1936] I introduced a motion in this Council, and Hon. Members might have read some of the comments on the debate which appeared in the English press. One Chinese newspaper translated one of the leading articles from the English press for insertion on Saturday, the 21st. This mere translation of a leader in an English paper was held up [by the censors] for consideration, and publication was not permitted until Monday, the 23rd. Another Chinese paper wished to publish, on Sunday the 22nd March, a leader on the debate, which also dealt with the present Constitution of the Colony, but the whole of this article was suppressed [by the censors] ....[31]

Just before luncheon today I received various complaints from the Chinese Press. It has been represented to me that an article on the debate which is to be held this afternoon was absolutely suppressed and there are other matters dealing with censorship which have been suppressed in most cases .... I have here a letter written by the Chinese Press Association which represents the whole of the Chinese Press of this Colony and is dated July 27. It asks me, because of the injustice they feel about this censorship, to take up this matter. The communication contains the signatures of about 50 editors and reporters and is chopped by all the leading newspapers of Hong Kong.[32]

In fact, Lo was correct in stating that the debate in question had been censored in the vernacular papers. As shown in Figure 2.11, a news report on the joint letter by the newspaper editors and the proposed motion were severely censored. The squares and dots in the figure represent the sections that were struck out by the censor. The paragraph preceding the first group of dots appearing in the image states that the censorship system was begun to cope with the emergency situation, a situation that had ended eleven years previously. The sentence that follows the dots states that 'therefore the [press] industry operators jointly requested that Chinese representative Lo Man-kam petition the Government to abolish the censorship system over the Chinese press'. It is likely that the sentences replaced with dots laid out the reasons for such abolition, criticised the censorship system or supported calls for its abolition by the Chinese press. Such material no doubt struck a nerve with the colonial government, and hence was struck out by the censors.

Lo then cited a number of English legal authorities in support of his argument that Hong Kong was deprived of what had long been enjoyed in Britain and in some other colonies:

Freedom of the press is now an accepted fact in England, and as far as I know, in all colonies under her rule. As is succinctly stated in a work of reference which I consulted: In 1693 the Government of England formally abandoned the preventive censorship of printing, and began the punitive... Blackstone states that – 'the liberty

---

[30] *Ibid.*, 181–2.   [31] *Ibid.*, 183.   [32] *Ibid.*, 183, 190.

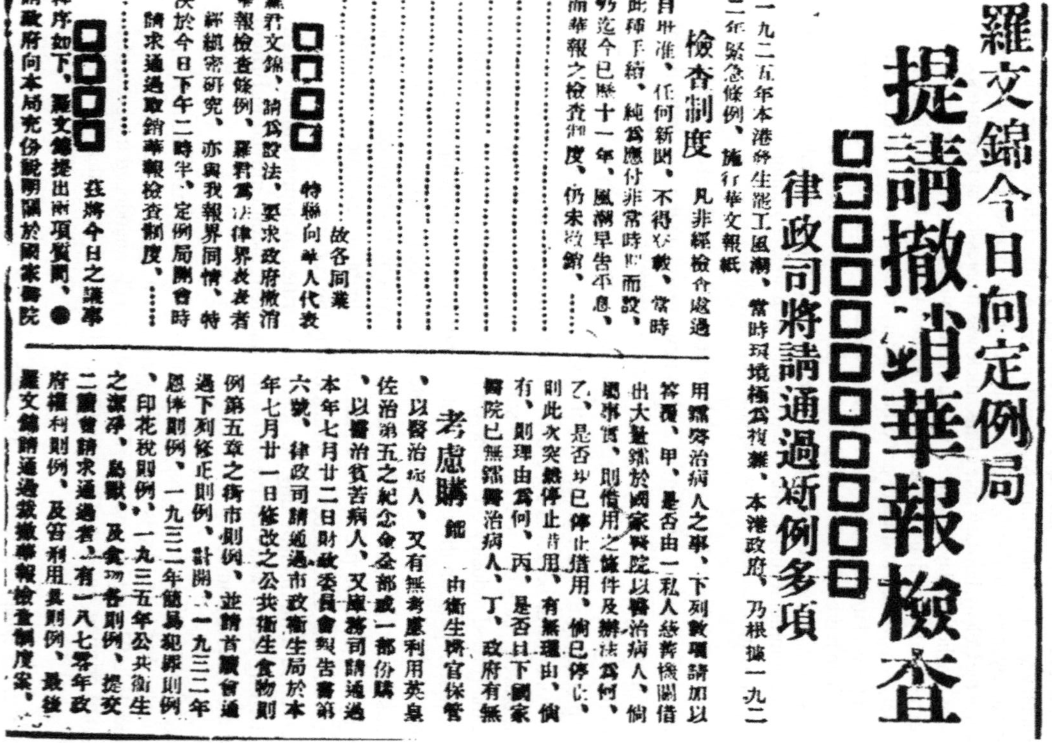

羅文錦今日向定例局

提請撤消華報檢查

□□□□□□□□□□□□

律政司將請通過新例多項

一九二五年本港發生罷工風潮、當時環境極爲複雜、本港政府、乃根據一九二二年緊急條例、施行華文報紙檢査制度、凡非經檢查處通過目卅准、任何新聞、不得登載、當時此種手續、純爲應付非常時期而設、乃迄今已歷十一年、風潮早告平息、而華報之檢査制度、仍未取銷、……

故各同業特聯向華人代表羅君文錦、請爲設法、要求政府撤消華報檢查條例、羅君爲法律界表表者、經縝密研究、亦與我報界同情、特決於今日下午二時半、定例局開會時、請求通過取銷華報檢査制度、……

□□□□

茲將今日之議事程序如下、羅文錦提出兩項質問、●請政府向本局充份說明關於國家醫院……

Figure 2.11 Censored Chinese newspaper reporting legislative councillor Lo Man Kam’s motion for the abolition of the press censorship system. Source: *Wa Tsz Yat Po*, 26 August 1936.

of the Press ... consists in laying no previous restraints upon publication and not in freedom from censure for criminal matter when published'.

Halsbury's Laws of England, Vol. 6. (Second Edition), on page 590, dealing with constitutional law, states as follows: 'The Crown cannot, apart from the rules of law relating to the licensing of stage plays, or to blasphemous or seditious libels, or the publication of reports of judicial proceedings, exercise any control over the public press'. ... The same authority's reference, on page 712, to the British Colonies makes rather pathetic reading in view of the circumstances prevailing in Hong Kong: 'In the British colonies the press is as free as it is in England.'[33]

In support of Lo's motion, another councillor, J. P. Braga, said:

[Lo] has made it clear that the Chinese Press has been in a sense muzzled for the past 11 years, and muzzled in a manner that the Emergency Regulations confer powers for the closing down of any offending Chinese newspaper .... The author of the motion has demonstrated that such emergency has not existed now for some time. It does not exist today.[34]

Braga seems to have been the only supporter of the motion, with most councillors sharing the government's position. Opposing the motion, Councillor J. J. Paterson said:

I remained unconvinced. The power of the Press is very great and it is because of that power, Your Excellency and because of the delicate nature of the situation the whole world finds itself in today, that I think it would be better to keep the censorship for the time being at any rate.[35]

The colonial secretary, representing the Hong Kong government, responded, making it clear that the administration's anxiety justified the continuation of stringent censorship of the Chinese press. In a rebuttal of Lo's arguments, he spoke of the public danger outlined in the ERO:

That danger exists still, and will continue to exist until a definitely stable government exists in China .... The welfare of Hong Kong depends on good relations with her customers in trade and ... nothing will sooner prejudice those relations than an impression that the Colony can with impunity be made a base from which to foment disorder .... None will defend interference with the reasonable freedom of the press .... [However,] so long as unrestrained publication can do very serious injury to our relations with China, and with other friendly Powers and so to the Colony itself, just so long is prevention better than cure. Apart from the possibility that an article might cause serious harm, ... the Government feels that fear of possible consequences will not with any certainty prevent the publication of matter open to objection, and that once the harm is done, it cannot be completely undone even if the publisher is convicted in a Court of Law. For these reasons the Government is unable to accept the motion.[36]

[33] *Ibid.*, 182–3.   [34] *Ibid.*, 184–5.   [35] *Ibid.*, 186.   [36] *Ibid.*, 188.

Lo rose again to rebut the colonial secretary's notion that prevention is better than cure:

If the Chinese Press is to have only a measure of the freedom of the Press while that definition of public danger exists, then I feel that I for one will not live to see the day it is free .... If you are going to give freedom to the Chinese Press only at a time when there is an idealist state, blissful inertia and benevolent governments without armaments, then I say to you, Sir, don't give it, because there will be nobody in this world to enjoy it![37]

Not all Chinese councillors shared Lo's view that the censorship of Chinese newspapers should be lifted. One such councillor, S. W. Tso, was against it based not only on the perceived danger to Hong Kong but also on his view that the intelligence level of certain sections of the Chinese populace rendered them undeserving of press freedom. Tso said:

Hong Kong is situated on the outskirts of China with a population of no less than 97 per cent Chinese. While there is, at the present moment, so much unrest and uncertainty in the political atmosphere in the Far East, it is very easy and quite natural for the Chinese papers to over-step their bounds by giving expressions to their feelings .... Such expressions, if undesirable and unchecked, might create misunderstandings outside and stir up trouble inside the Colony. I consider prevention is better than cure. For, if bad feeling or bad blood is stirred among the mass[es], especially among the less intelligent section of the Chinese community, it is most difficult to restrain or pacify .... The intelligence of the 9[7] per cent Chinese are not all equal.[38]

Lo's motion, unsurprisingly, was defeated, and censorship measures remained in place in Hong Kong. Not only were the newspaper censorship regulations and practices maintained, but they were further tightened – and extended to the English-language press – after the outbreak of the Sino-Japanese War to give more power to the governor. In 1939, the government was empowered to require English newspapers to submit for pre-censorship particular news stories or reports whenever the government deemed necessary.[39] Hence, in that period the SCMP occasionally published news reports with the word 'censored' in brackets to indicate that certain words had been deleted by the government. An example of a censored English newspaper report whose description of the Chinese who worked for the Japanese was deleted is shown in Figure 2.12. Chinese newspapers in Hong Kong were still closely pre-censored on a daily basis during the late 1930s. In line with the Hong Kong government's desire to maintain neutrality in the Sino-Japanese War prior to the Japanese invasion of Hong Kong, numerous words relating to Japan or the Japanese were struck out of news reports, resulting in many 'x's' in censored

---

[37] *Ibid.*, 189.   [38] *Ibid.*, 187, 190.
[39] G.N. No. 622 of 1939, Hong Kong Government Gazette, 4 August 1939.

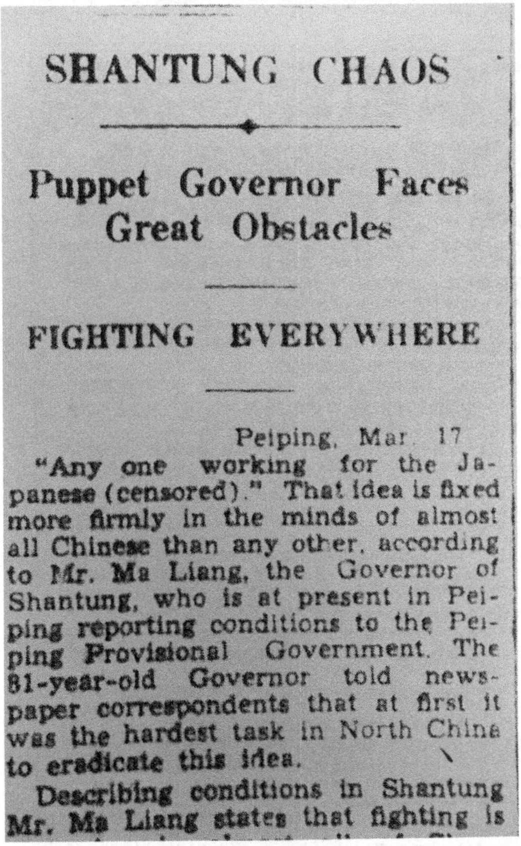

SHANTUNG CHAOS

---◆---

Puppet Governor Faces Great Obstacles

FIGHTING EVERYWHERE

Peiping, Mar. 17

"Any one working for the Japanese (censored)." That idea is fixed more firmly in the minds of almost all Chinese than any other, according to Mr. Ma Liang, the Governor of Shantung, who is at present in Peiping reporting conditions to the Peiping Provisional Government. The 81-year-old Governor told newspaper correspondents that at first it was the hardest task in North China to eradicate this idea.

Describing conditions in Shantung Mr. Ma Liang states that fighting is

Figure 2.12 Censored news report appearing in the SCMP on 19 March 1938. Source: Courtesy of SCMP.

newspapers, as shown in Figures 2.13 and 2.14, which depict censored news reports from 1939.[40]

When Silence Speaks: Empire's Anxiety in East Asia and Political Censorship

This chapter reveals the secretive operation of pre-emptive press censorship in British Hong Kong. It also offers a corrective to previous scholarship that

---

[40] For Britain's accommodative policies towards Japan's aggression in China, see Yoichi Kibata, 'British Imperialism in Asia and Anglo-Japanese Relations, 1930s–1950s', in *The International Order of Asia in the 1930s and 1950s*, ed. Shigeru Akita and Nicholas J. White (Farnham, England: Ashgate, 2010), 49–60.

Figure 2.13 Censored Chinese newspaper *Wa Tsz Yat Po*, dated 12 June 1939, reporting the military attack of various cities in mainland China by the Japanese air force.

Figure 2.14 Censored Chinese newspaper WKYP, dated 4 May 1939, reporting the military attack of Chongqing city in mainland China by the Japanese air force. Source: Courtesy of SCMP.

wrongly assumes that the extensive powers granted under the colony's press regulations and censorship laws were used only sparingly by the colonial government and that the press remained generally free. A number of explanations for the colonial government's insistence on controlling the Chinese press through the legal system despite widespread awareness amongst colonisers and colonised alike of the importance of a free press and the existence thereof in Britain itself can be gleaned from the foregoing archival study. Although not everyone in the colonial government of the day may have agreed with Tso's view that depriving Hong Kong of a free press was justified by the limited intelligence of its Chinese population, the colonial administrators clearly did believe, even before the geopolitical disturbances in East Asia from the 1900s to the 1920s, that press control was well justified in Hong Kong. In a letter dated 20 July 1883 from Governor Bowen to the Earl of Derby, the then secretary of state for the colonies, regarding the government's intended prosecution of the *Hong Kong Telegraph*, Bowen wrote of the reason for that prosecution:[41]

It is to be remembered that, in so small a community as that of Hong Kong, concentrated, moreover, within so narrow a space, the Press is sure to be at once more personal and less influential than in larger and more scattered communities. Here it is, of course, impossible to preserve that mystery which elsewhere enhances the power of the Press.

Freedom of expression seems never to have been an intended part of the legal system for the crown colony of Hong Kong. Fears arising from the revolutions in China in the 1900s, the struggles between the Nationalists and Beiyang warlords in the 1910s, the growing anti-Japanese movement, the power dynamics between the Nationalists and the Communist Party and the 1920s labour movement in Hong Kong all served to solidify the existing government policy of press control, which continued to tighten. Censorship measures were also in place in other British colonies in Asia.[42]

This chapter also shows the embarrassing and difficult situation in which the colonial government found itself in the broader historical context of Hong Kong, China and British interests in Asia in the early twentieth century. The British colonisers began to encounter legitimacy issues in their colonies and concessions in this period, triggered in part by nationalist and communist movements in mainland China and elsewhere in Asia. It was well known that the Western powers, Britain included, backed Japan's claim to Qingdao under the terms of the Treaty of Versailles of 1919. Japan was also exerting increased pressure on the Western powers to acquiesce to its territorial ambitions. Neither Britain's early alliance with Japan nor its subsequent neutrality in the Sino-Japanese conflict did justice to its ruling role in Hong Kong, where there was mass resentment against Japanese aggression in China. In the absence of a strong government in China, suppressing anti-Japanese and anti-colonial sentiments through press censorship may have seemed the best way of easing the empire's anxiety over its questionable legitimacy in Hong Kong and the troubling geopolitics of East Asia.

Once granted censorship power, the colonial government continued to make use of it far beyond the context of the actual crisis or fears from which it arose. An imagined state of danger even during periods of relative peace conveniently allowed the colonial administrators in Hong Kong to continue through

---

[41] Letter from Hong Kong Governor to Earl of Derby, 20 July 1883, CO 129/210.
[42] See SCMP, 28 March 1928, reporting the arrest of four people on 4 March 1928 on New Bridge Road, Singapore, for posting and possessing political posters.

censorship to suppress the circulation of domestic grievances or criticisms of government measures, as the aforementioned cases brought against newspapers for reporting on the prisoners' strike and the censorship debate show. The discourse surrounding the notion that 'prevention is better than cure', which was repeatedly used by senior government officials, judges and legislative councillors to justify the censorship regime, underscores the usefulness of such an imagined state of danger in supporting continued censorship in Hong Kong. As we have seen, press censorship was not restricted to emergency situations or wartime, but continued to operate in peacetime through the colonial government's asserted perpetual state of danger. Sharing the empire's anxiety over the region's troubling geopolitics, such colonial judges as C. J. Piggott, Magistrate Lindsell and Magistrate Eaves also collaborated with the executive in controlling and censoring the press. The efforts of the judiciary, like those of the legislature and executive, did not serve the rule of law, at least not in its ideal form described by A. V. Dicey, but rather a colonial legal order that served the empire's objective of maintaining and exerting strong control over its colonies in East Asia and managing the power equation in the region.

The British colonial pre-censorship regime continued to operate until Hong Kong was occupied by Japan in December 1941.[43] The post-war era also saw the further expansion and strategic modification of Hong Kong's political censorship regime. The loss of China to communism, mass influx of Chinese refugees into Hong Kong, outbreak of the Korean War, global Cold War geopolitics, and ongoing ideological warfare between the Nationalist and Communist parties in Hong Kong through their respective newspapers and magazines, as well as the rise of new mass media forms such as live radio broadcasts, hugely increased the complexity of operating effective media censorship while maintaining a free flow of information for trading and business purposes. The colonial government could no longer rely on pre-emptive daily vetting to contain undesirable content and comments. In addition, the expansion of schools run by supporters of the CCP and KMT extended the colonial control of information and ideas from public media to private instruction in schools.

As we shall see, during the second half of the twentieth century, political censorship of the media and education sector was facilitated and supplemented by large-scale surveillance operations carried out through a collaborative network of local departments informed by global intelligence collected through London and British embassies around the world. The intelligence collected by the network allowed the colonial government to nip trouble in the bud and

---

[43] Notes of recollection by Ng Bar-ling, Ng Bar Ling Collection (1904–1976), Special Collections of the University of Hong Kong Libraries.

resulted in a number of 'troublemakers' (including journalists, editors, publishers, teachers, students and school principals) being arrested, detained and even deported without trial without any due regard to whether such actions were lawful. Chapters 3 and 4 provide a comprehensive account of such forceful surveillance and censorship operations against the media and education sector from the late 1940s to the late 1960s against the backdrop of rising Cold War tensions and China's relations with the world.

3 'Communist China Now Contiguous to Hong Kong': Censorship Imposed by the 'Free World'

After the Second World War, Hong Kong's return to the British Empire following Japanese occupation was not without geopolitical controversy. The Nationalist Chinese government, in particular, made its opposition known.[1] The colonial Hong Kong government was sensitive to newspaper reports that might stir up patriotic feelings amongst the Chinese citizens of Hong Kong and potentially challenge British reoccupation of the colony. The increasing numbers of newspapers with either KMT or CCP backing that were moving their publication base to Hong Kong to avoid China's Civil War also caused fears that that war might spill over into Hong Kong.[2] Although the colonial government decided not to spare any of its already tight resources to continue with the daily pre-censorship of Hong Kong's growing number of newspapers, it warned the publishers and editors of Chinese-language newspapers not to report any sensitive stories including stories that might jeopardise Britain's relations with China. Government officials also reminded editors that the press could be suppressed if that warning was ignored.[3] During the very short post-war governorship of Mark Young, the pre-war Newspapers Regulations were used to suppress the KMT-supported *Kwok Man Yat Po* in June 1946 for publishing an editorial advocating for the extradition to China of the publisher of the major Chinese newspaper *Wah Kiu Yat Po*, whom the Hong Kong government had befriended (the gazetted suppression notice was reported in the

---

[1] For the Nationalist government's diplomatic efforts to reclaim Hong Kong's sovereignty, which failed because of US President Truman's support for Britain's repossession of the colony after the Second World War, see Tsai, 香港人之香港史, 270, and Sun Yang, 國民政府對香港問題的處置 [Nationalist government's policies towards the Hong Kong question] (Hong Kong: Joint Publishing, 2017), 82–105.

[2] For the relocation of the CCP's and KMT's newspapers to Hong Kong after the Second World War, see Lee Siu-nam, '香港的中西報業' [Chinese and English press in Hong Kong], in 香港史新編/*Hong Kong History: New Perspectives*, ed. Wang Gung-wu (Hong Kong: Joint Publishing, 2017), 2:563–604.

[3] Notes of meeting held with government official on 27 February 1946 contained in Ng Bar Ling Collection (1904–1976), Special Collection of The University of Hong Kong Libraries.

Figure 3.1 Notice of suppression of *Kwok Man Yat Po* reported in *Kung Sheung Daily News*, 9 June 1946. The report mentions that *Kwok Man Yat Po* was suppressed for encouraging the disrespect of law and order by advocating for the extradition of *Wah Kiu Yat Po*'s publisher. Source: courtesy of The Robert H.N. Ho Family Foundation.

newspaper, as shown in Figure 3.1).[4] Not long after the suppression of this KMT-backed newspaper, the Hong Kong government began to realise that it was the CCP, not the KMT, that posed the real threat.

[4] For detailed political reasons of the suppression, see Sun, 國民政府對香港問題的處置, 142–8; for the suppression notice and reaction from the press, see *Kung Sheung Daily News*, 9 and 21 June 1946.

'Labour, Education and the Press Thoroughly Infiltrated by Communists'

Alexander Grantham succeeded Mark Young's governorship of Hong Kong at another critical juncture in the global geopolitics of the twentieth century: regime change in China. Just a few months after his arrival in Hong Kong in July 1947, Grantham was tasked with assessing the impact on Hong Kong and other British Asian territories if the KMT was to 'lose' China to the Communists. Assisted by the Special Branch of the Hong Kong Police ('Special Branch' hereafter), Grantham and the British Embassy in Nanjing collaborated in collecting, collating and assessing intelligence on the progress of the Chinese Civil War and communist activities in Hong Kong for circulation not only to the Colonial Office in London but also to the colonial governments of Singapore, Malaya and Sarawak in North Borneo, where communists were considered a serious security concern.[5] As early as April 1948, increasing activities by members of the CCP and other anti-KMT groups such as the China Democratic League and Kuomintang Revolutionary Committee in Hong Kong suggested that 'the end of the Nanking Government [was] not far off'.[6] The Hong Kong government was advised that should China fall into the hands of the CCP, 'communists in Hong Kong would begin to be troublesome' and 'just as irredentist as the KMT'.[7] Although 'the sweeping Communist military and political successes in China ha[d] stimulated [the] activities and morale [of the communists] in the Colony',[8] various sources of information indicated that the CCP did not envisage the immediate recovery of Hong Kong even if it won the civil war and regained China from the KMT.[9] Despite the slim likelihood of a direct attack on Hong Kong, London agreed to reinforce garrisons in Hong Kong as the People's Liberation Army (PLA) advanced towards the south,[10] and Grantham organised comprehensive surveillance and formulated

---

[5] Letter from Grantham to Arthur Creech Jones, Secretary of State for the Colonies, 2 August 1949, FCO 141/14419. The Special Branch was a specialised unit responsible for anti-communist operations, see Hua-ling Fu and Richard Cullen, 'Political Policing in Hong Kong', *Hong Kong Law Journal*, 33.1 (2003): 199–230. For similar units in other former British colonies see Kah-choon Ban, *Absent History : The Untold Story of Special Branch Operations in Singapore, 1915–1942* (Singapore: Raffles, 2001), and Leon Comber, *Malaya's Secret Police 1945–60 : The Role of the Special Branch in the Malayan Emergency* (Singapore: Institute of Southeast Asian Studies, 2008).

[6] A note on 'political situation in China as it affects Hong Kong' prepared by Wallace for Colonial Office in April 1948 (date missing), CO 537/3726.

[7] *Ibid.*

[8] Report on Communist Activities in Hong Kong for the six months ending 31 December 1948, enclosed in memo from Colonial Office to Colonial Secretary of Singapore, Chief Secretary of Malaya and Australian Commissioner in Malaya, 9 March 1949, FCO 141/14419.

[9] Chi-kwan Mark, *Hong Kong and the Cold War: Anglo-American Relations 1949–1957* (Oxford: Oxford University Press, 2004), 26–30, and John M. Carroll, *A Concise History of Hong Kong* (Lanham, MD: Rowman and Littlefield, 2007), 135–6.

[10] Carroll, *A Concise History*, 136.

targeted measures to 'guard against the contingency of trouble at short notice' in Hong Kong.[11]

To achieve this objective, Grantham needed detailed information on communist organisations and their activities in Hong Kong. On 11 December 1948 and 21 April 1949, Special Branch raided the residence of a communist leader at Tin Hua Temple Road in Causeway Bay, as well as an alleged undercover CCP office on Wing Kut Street in Central.[12] During these raids, 'valuable documents were seized revealing Communist intentions over a wide sphere of activities'.[13] From these documents, Special Branch in June 1949 compiled an eighteen-page secret report entitled 'The Chinese Communist Party in Hong Kong', which provided 'a basic summary' of the CCP's penetration of Hong Kong, as well as an organisational chart and list of the key personnel of the CCP's Hong Kong Municipal Committee (which Special Branch believed to be under the command of the CCP's South China Bureau). The report also offered details of 'practically every known communist organisation of importance in Hong Kong'.[14] Particularly alarming was the report's revelation that 'labour, education and the press [were] thoroughly infiltrated by Communists' under the committee's leadership.[15] The Labour Section of the Hong Kong Municipal Committee was said to exercise influence over thirty-eight workers' unions affiliated with the Hong Kong Federation of Trade Unions (HKFTU). These unions represented the workers of a wide range of industries, from the employees of Hong Kong's major utilities, including the Tramway, Hong Kong Electric, China Gas, Kowloon Docks, Hong Kong Telephone and the Dairy Farm, to seamen, carpenters, rickshaw pullers, rattan workers and tea packers.[16] Further, the Propaganda Section was said to comprise five newspapers (including three daily newspapers, *Wen Wei Po*, *Ta Kung Pao* and *Hwa Shiang Pao*), nine magazines, eight printers and seventeen bookshops in Hong Kong. The Hong Kong Branch of the New China News Agency (NCNA) had been established under the Propaganda Section in 1947 at the former office of the East River Column, a CCP-backed anti-Japanese guerrilla force, at Nathan Road in Kowloon. The NCNA was being used as 'a distribution centre of communist propaganda', including news materials to newspapers, the report stated.[17] There was also evidence suggesting that the CCP was using 'Hong Kong as a control and propaganda centre for South China and

---

[11] Report on Communist Activities in Hong Kong for the six months ending 31 December 1948.
[12] Record of such raids and searches prepared by the Special Branch (date illegible) and letter from Security Intelligence Far East at Singapore to Commissioner-General of Singapore, 11 May 1949, CO 537/4815.
[13] Letter from Grantham to Arthur Creech Jones, 2 August 1949.
[14] 'The Chinese Communist Party in Hong Kong', compiled by the Hong Kong Police Special Branch, 30 June 1949, 'Foreword' and organisation chart in Appendix X, FCO141/14419.
[15] Letter from Grantham to Arthur Creech Jones, 2 August 1949.
[16] 'The Chinese Communist Party in Hong Kong', 5–8 and Appendix I.   [17] *Ibid.*, 9–10.

South East Asia'.[18] Further, the Youth Section, 'responsible for the political education of all young workers, farmers, soldiers, employees, youth and young intelligentsia',[19] had, as of April 1949, recruited through its Youth Corps approximately 3,700 members between the ages of fourteen and twenty-five. Special Branch believed that the Youth Corps was 'firmly entrenched' in the colony and that it was a dangerous and effective agency for the 'infiltration of schools and labour unions'.[20] The Youth Section was also said to exercise control or significant influence through a number of teachers' associations over a large number of schools in Hong Kong. Of the long list of schools allegedly influenced by communists, ninety were classified as either 'Communist dominated' or 'infiltrated' with CCP sympathisers, aggregating in about 11 per cent of the roughly 800 schools in Hong Kong.[21] According to the report, an Education Committee comprising representatives of fourteen communist-controlled schools 'organised political indoctrination in schools controlled or infiltrated by their agents',[22] who were 'disguised' as teachers or students.[23] The student agents were instructed to organise student bodies such as reading clubs or singing groups to spread communism, and sometimes also took their schoolmates out for long picnics in the countryside, where '"*Yangko*" [folk] dancing [was] indulged and indoctrination ... carried out'.[24] Communist newspapers and publishing houses reinforced such political indoctrination by supplying schools with leftist newspapers and periodicals for students' consumption. Special Branch worried that not only vernacular schools but also missionary schools were affected.[25] Although the number of CCP members in Hong Kong was not thought to be large (approximately 2,000 CCP members and 4,000 CCP Youth Corps members based on Special Branch's estimation), they were 'strategically placed in all spheres of daily life' and were able to 'create a great deal of trouble when and if they [chose] to do so' through their 'influence in labour, in the press and other fields of propaganda'.[26] Given such 'an unenviable and dangerous situation', Governor Grantham believed that 'measures ... had to be taken to counter the growing scale of malignant Communist influence in education and other fields'.[27] Such measures, Grantham warned, would restrict 'democratic rights' but were necessary to

---

[18] Telegram from the Secretary of State for the Colonies to the Governor of Hong Kong, 17 March 1949, CO 537/4815.

[19] 'The Chinese Communist Party in Hong Kong', 11.   [20] *Ibid.*, 12, FCO 141/1441.

[21] Savingram from the Governor to the Secretary of State for the Colonies, 17 November 1952, CO 968/259.

[22] 'The Chinese Communist Party in Hong Kong', 13–14.   [23] *Ibid.*, 14.

[24] Letter from J. F. Nicoll, Officer Administering the Government of Hong Kong, to James Griffiths, Secretary of State for the Colonies, 21 July 1950, FCO 141/14419.

[25] 'The Chinese Communist Party in Hong Kong', 14.   [26] *Ibid.*, 18.

[27] Letter from Grantham to Arthur Creech Jones, 2 August 1949.

protect the structure of Hong Kong society, whose 'rights and freedoms the Communists utilise and abuse in order to destroy it'.[28]

Drawing Red Lines

Faced with the dual threats of growing communist propaganda and the likelihood of a CCP victory in China, however, Grantham did not consider a 'drastic suppression of all communist activities' in Hong Kong to be a wise policy change. Rather, the 'traditional policy of non-interference and neutrality in the political affairs of China'[29] while 'vigilantly keeping an eye on communist activities and curbing them when they overstep the mark' would, in his opinion, continue to work well for Hong Kong for pragmatic reasons.[30] Taking drastic measures to suppress communist activities, he advised London, would not only 'hamper in advance the possibilities of trade between Hong Kong and Communist China' but also 'drive communism under cover', leading to the possibility of general strikes and even terrorism. He was not willing to take the risks that a policy of all-out suppression would entail as long as he could 'be assured that adequate military reinforcement [was] available within [a] reasonably short time'.[31] Accordingly, the principles that guided Grantham's policy towards Communist China and its penetration into Hong Kong for the rest of his governorship were to perform 'a balancing act' at all times, to neither provoke nor appease the communists, and to act swiftly to curb any communist activities that overstepped the legal mark.[32]

Two weeks after Mao Zedong declared the establishment of the People's Republic of China (PRC) at Tiananmen Square in Beijing on 1 October 1949, Grantham saw communist forces appear at the Hong Kong border. Although intelligence indicated that 'the Reds' denied any claim to Hong Kong and that an immediate military assault on the colony was unlikely, Grantham did not underestimate the potential threat to Hong Kong's security caused by infiltration of CCP into the society of Hong Kong after witnessing the widespread flying of the new five-star national flag of the PRC throughout the colony in October 1949.[33] Nonetheless, these pressures did not shake Grantham's policy

---

[28] *Ibid.*

[29] Colonial Office's report on recent changes in policy towards Chinese Communists in Hong Kong, 12 August 1949, CO 537/4815.

[30] Letter from Grantham to the Secretary of State for the Colonies, 27 March 1949, CO 537/4815.

[31] *Ibid.*

[32] Alexander Grantham, *Via Ports: From Hong Kong to Hong Kong* (Hong Kong: Hong Kong University Press, 1965), 139 and 169.

[33] For the report on China's official denial of claims for Hong Kong, see *New York Herald Tribune* (Paris edn.), 14 February 1950, CO537/6054. For the Hong Kong government's assessment of the chance of direct attack and China's immediate recovery of Hong Kong, see Report on Communist Activities in Hong Kong for the six months ending 31 December 1949 enclosed in a letter from Grantham to James Griffiths, Secretary of State for the Colonies, 6 March 1950,

of 'combating the spread of Communist influence in Hong Kong', as he advised London in March 1950:

The policy in combatting the spread of Communist influence in Hong Kong has not been one of stern suppression ... which would, it is consider[ed], merely exacerbate the situation and drive the movement underground completely, but one of striking at it when it oversteps the limits of the law. If all Communist manifestations were suppressed merely on the grounds that they were Communist, it would delight the Communists by giving them grounds to criticise Government as being 'undemocratic'. Also once the movement is driven underground it will become much more difficult to identify and it may well adopt terrorism as a weapon.[34]

Grantham's government followed a 'policy of arresting and deporting the individuals who clearly overstep the mark and render themselves legally liable to penalty'. Communists who breached the tightened laws would be liable to be 'sent back to enjoy [the] "new democracy" inside China'. He believed the fact that living conditions in Hong Kong remained better than those inside China and that fundamental rights such as those of freedom of speech and the press and liberty of movement were still 'basically preserved' would deter communists and their supporters from stirring up large-scale unrest in the colony because 'most Communists in the Colony do not wish to be sent back to China, however much they may preach the blessings of the New China'.[35] Despite official recognition of the PRC by the British government in January 1950, the British Cabinet had actually considered adopting more drastic measures to suppress communist activities in Hong Kong.[36] After deliberation amongst ministers, however, London deferred to Grantham's appraisal of the local situation, explicitly leaving him to devise strategies and legal measures that in his opinion fit Hong Kong's geopolitical context to curb 'Chinese Communist abuse of Hong Kong's hospitality'.[37] Since the autumn of 1948, Grantham had been preparing for regime change in China by tightening the law to significantly restrict the rights of assembly, association, expression and the press to contain the increasing 'infiltration of Chinese Communists into the Colony and to deal with difficulties and dangers which might arise from

---

FCO 141/14419; and letter from J. F. Nicoll to James Griffiths, 21 July 1950; also Carroll, *A Concise History*, 135. For military preparation, see Mark, *Hong Kong and the Cold War*, 40–9.

[34] Report on Communist Activities in Hong Kong for the six months ending 31 December 1949.

[35] *Ibid.*

[36] For the problem Britain faced in its decision to recognise the PRC, that is to protect British interests in the mainland while maintaining solidarity with the United States, see Mark, *Hong Kong and the Cold War*, 84–93; and Chi-kwan Mark, *The Everyday Cold War: Britain and China, 1950–1972* (London: Bloomsbury, 2017), 14–19. For a list of works on the accounts of such a decision and the United States' attitude towards recognition of the PRC, see James T. H. Tang, 'From Empire Defence to Imperial Retreat: Britain's Postwar China Policy and the Decolonization of Hong Kong', *Modern Asian Studies* 28. 2 (1994): 326–7, footnotes 32 and 33.

[37] Telegram from the Secretary of State for the Colonies to the Governor of Hong Kong, 17 March 1949, and letter from N. D. Watson to Sidebotham, 23 March 1949, CO 537/4815.

their activities'.[38] His first move was to see the Societies Ordinance amended in May 1949. Following the amendment, organisations affiliated with foreign political parties were unable to register as lawful societies in Hong Kong, and thus became illegal organisations.[39] The law was intended to prevent the CCP from establishing 'an overt organisation in the Colony', although CCP membership was not itself made unlawful. Another intention was to control cultural and media groups such as 'singing groups and dramatic societies which are known to be vehicles for Communist propaganda and penetration'.[40]

The Hong Kong government saw ample evidence showing the CCP existed covertly in Hong Kong for 'the usual function of penetrating and spreading Communist ideas among all sections of the Chinese community, with the object of gaining a dominant position and influence in the Colony'.[41] To counter the dissemination of communist, anti-imperialist and nationalist ideas, especially in the areas of education, labour and the press, where accumulating communist influence was noticed,[42] new legal powers were put in place to set the limits within which freedom of expression was to be defined and confined in Hong Kong for several decades to come. The colonial government was very vigilant in 'keeping [an] eye on communist activities and curbing them when they overstep[ped] the mark',[43] as will become clear in the following sections.

Counter-Communist Bureau of Education Department

Education was regarded as a critical battlefield against communist infiltration to attempt to win the hearts and minds of the younger population of Hong Kong. Under Grantham's governorship, new powers were granted under the law to enable the government to engage in the political screening of teachers and school mangers, censor teaching materials, and shut down any schools that were believed to have overtly indoctrinated their students with communist, anti-imperialist and nationalist ideas. The Education Ordinance was amended in December 1948 to widen the power of the governor in council to close a school, remove its manager and de-register a teacher if it appeared to him or her that the school/manager/teacher was 'prejudicial to the interests of the Colony or of the Commonwealth or of the public or of the pupils in any school'.[44] The Education Regulations were also rewritten in April 1949 to

---

[38] Colonial Office's report on recent changes in policy towards Chinese Communists in Hong Kong.
[39] Societies Ordinance (Cap. 151), s. 5.
[40] Colonial Office's report on recent changes in policy towards Chinese Communists in Hong Kong.
[41] Letter from J. F. Nicoll to James Griffiths, 21 July 1950.
[42] Minutes to Sir T. Lloyd, 24 August 1949, CO537/4816 (author's name illegible).
[43] Letter from Grantham to the Secretary of State for the Colonies, 27 March 1949.
[44] Education Amendment (No. 2) Ordinance 1948, s. 10.

explicitly prohibit political propaganda in schools.[45] The revised Education Ordinance also required teachers to apply to the director of education for permission to teach.[46] Although permission was granted primarily on the basis of 'educational considerations', all applications were to be referred to Special Branch for 'a more exhaustive examination'[47] to guard against 'the evils which [would] result from the introduction of political indoctrination into education'.[48] The revised ordinance also required that all textbooks, pamphlets and the like used in school classrooms be approved by the director of education.[49]

Hitherto unknown in scholarship on the anti-communist efforts of the colonial Hong Kong government, a specialised counter-communist unit was established within the Education Department in July 1949. Known as 'the Special Bureau' and headed by 'a senior European education officer',[50] the unit was tasked with two major responsibilities: one 'repressive' and the other 'creative'.[51] The bureau's repressive responsibility was to investigate and contain the spread of communist, anti-imperialist and nationalist ideas in schools and to suppress communist activities in schools when necessary.[52] Its creative responsibility was to advance in schools 'the ideals of liberal and democratic education' to counter communist propaganda.[53]

On the repressive side, the Special Bureau worked closely with Special Branch to monitor and make inquiries into the activities of school managers and teachers, to identify pro-communist sympathisers in schools and make recommendations about teaching staff dismissals, and even to take control of schools when necessary. The Special Bureau was expected to have a 'constant inter-change of information on all matters affecting education' with Special Branch, which was also directly involved in the monitoring of school activities and teaching staff. The governor and the director of education were provided with secret monthly reports on the communist tendencies of schools and their staff members in which the names of staff members suspected of being pro-communist sympathisers and/or involved in communist activities were mentioned. Staff movements across schools were monitored to detect possible 'systematic infiltration' by communist teachers moving from one school to

---

[45] Education Regulations 1949, reg. 34.

[46] Education Amendment (No. 2) Ordinance 1948, s. 5.

[47] Report tabled by T. R. Rowell, Director of Education of Hong Kong for the Second Conference of Directors and Deputy Directors of Education, held in the Department of Education, Fullerton Building, Singapore, on 4 and 5 September 1950, Appendix VIII, CO 968/259.

[48] Explanation of the objectives of Education Amendment (No. 2) Ordinance 1948 given by the Attorney General of Hong Kong during Legislative Council meeting, 22 December 1948, Hong Kong Legislative Council Official Report of Proceedings.

[49] Report tabled by T. R. Rowell; Education Regulations 1949, reg. 30(3).

[50] A proposal paper entitled 'Counter-Communist Education' appended to the report tabled by T. R. Rowell, CO 968/259.

[51] *Ibid.*   [52] *Ibid.*   [53] *Ibid.*

another, with Special Branch launching inquiries into and conducting interviews with those suspected.[54] It was not only the classroom activities of
teaching staff working in schools categorised by Special Branch as CCP-
dominated or -infiltrated that were monitored, teachers working at public
schools and Christian schools were also a target of Special Branch surveillance.
For example, two Chinese teachers with the surnames Lam and Lo employed
by the Chinese Methodist Church School were reported to be propagating
communism in their classes and encouraging their pupils to read communist
literature. Similarly, the headmaster of Ching I Public School was reported to
have held weekly meetings at his house during which speeches were made and
'Communist dances performed'.[55] Upon receipt of information indicating that
the teachers of a particular school were disseminating communist propaganda,
its teachers' quarters were searched, leading to Special Branch's discovery of 'a
library of CCP literature' and 'essays by pupils showing left-wing
inclinations'.[56]

The most repressive measure resulting from the collaboration of the Special
Bureau of the Education Department and Special Branch was the closure of
'leftist' schools found to have continuously and overtly engaged in communist
propaganda. One of the earliest such schools to be shut down was the Tat Tak
Institute located on Castle Peak in the New Territories. Established in
September 1946, Tat Tak was a private post-secondary institution whose
faculty 'comprised a number of capable and well-informed professors'.[57]
Most of its 600 students 'were not Hong Kong residents but came from distant
provinces of China and from countries in South East Asia'.[58] When an application for the registration of Tat Tak was submitted for Hong Kong government
approval, it was suspected that the school was affiliated with the CCP and/or an
anti-KMT organisation. Accordingly, approval was withheld for some time
because the 'Director of Education considered that the head-master or manager
of the school had an undesirable political background' and that the school was
merely a 'cloak' for political activities.[59] However, an on-site inspection of the
school by education inspectors found few signs of political activity, 'with the
possible exception of a slight bias in the lectures on political science'. It was
also reported that Tat Tak 'had a better qualified staff than most other institutes

[54] Various extracts of reports by Hong Kong Police Special Branch, November 1952 –
February 1953, CO 968/259.
[55] Extracts of reports by Hong Kong Police Special Branch, November, December 1952 and
February 1953, CO 968/259.
[56] Extracts of reports by Hong Kong Police Special Branch, November 1952, CO 968/259.
[57] Letter from Grantham to Arthur Creech Jones, Secretary of State for the Colonies, 2 April 1949,
CO 537/4815.
[58] Secret savingram No. 51 from the Governor to the Secretary of State, 16 March 1949, CO 537/
4815; letter from Grantham to Arthur Creech Jones, 2 April 1949.
[59] Letter from Grantham to Arthur Creech Jones, 2 April 1949.

in the Colony'.[60] Upon receiving the report, the director of education decided to allow Tat Tak's registration, but he 'personally interviewed' Tat Tak's manager and warned him that 'any political activity likely to cause embarrassment to this Government would result in the closing of the school'.[61] Less than a year after Tat Tak's registration, however, a Special Branch investigation revealed that Tat Tak had not heeded the director's warning. On 7 September 1948, 'a Chinese courier was arrested in Hong Kong, and was found to be in possession of a number of documents' that linked the Tat Tak Institute with a communist organisation. The police also found 'evidence connecting teachers of ... Tat Tak with communist activities in the Colony' and believed that 'the institute had taken an important and active part in the supply of recruits from its student body to the communist forces in China'. Tak Tat was also found to have started a magazine called *Tat Tak Youth* that 'illustrated the political inclinations' of its faculty and students.[62] Acting on the belief that Tat Tak 'was not a genuine place of education but a centre for political indoctrination' and 'had become a hot bed of communist intrigue', Grantham struck off its registration and closed the school on the grounds that allowing it to continue would be 'prejudicial to the interest of the Colony' under the new power granted by section 19A of the Education Ordinance, which had come into effect less than a month previously.[63]

Unlike Tat Tak, whose students were primarily non-Hong Kong resident Chinese, there were also communist-controlled schools run by local communist supporters for a primarily local student body. 'Workers' Children's Schools' were cited as an example of 'how easily institutions can fall into the wrong hands'.[64] These schools had been 'expanded at the instigation of the Bishop of Hong Kong who was eager to provide education for the children of workers'. Colonial government believed that these schools were managed by 'a Committee dominated by extremists of the Labour Union and staffed by unqualified teachers who were encouraged to mix in politics in very generous measure'.[65] There were twelve Workers' Children's Schools in Hong Kong in 1949. If all of them were closed to stop the dissemination of communist, anti-imperialist and nationalist ideas, there would be a need to find replacement schools for the rocketing student population from the late 1940s to the early 1950s that coupled with the influx of refugees from the mainland.[66]

---

[60] *Ibid.* [61] *Ibid.* [62] *Ibid.*

[63] Secret savingram No. 51 from the Governor to the Secretary of State, 16 March 1949; letter from Grantham to Arthur Creech Jones, 2 April 1949; letter from the Colonial Secretariat to the Manager of Tat Tak Institute, 20 January 1949, CO 537/4815; Education Amendment (No. 2) Ordinance 1948.

[64] Report tabled by T. R. Rowell. [65] *Ibid.*

[66] Between 1946 and 1954, the student population increased from 6,000 to 250,000 in Hong Kong, see Kin-Lop Tse, 'The Denationalization and Depoliticization of Education in Hong Kong, 1945–92' (PhD diss., University of Wisconsin, Madison, 1998), 136.

Accordingly, the colonial government used the powers afforded by the Education Ordinance to close seven of them and transfer the children to two new public primary schools 'built specially for the purpose'.[67] The Education Department also replaced the headmasters of the five remaining schools, which would subsequently be 'closely supervised'.[68] Addressing his fellow directors of education from other British colonies in Asia, Hong Kong Director of Education T. R. Rowell summarised Hong Kong's policy for the control of communist schools and communist elements as 'watch[ing] their activities as closely as possible' and 'tak[ing] repressive action against individual teachers when the time seems appropriate'.[69]

The British government's recognition of the CCP government as the government of mainland China in January 1950 did not reduce the Hong Kong government's hostility and vigilance towards China; rather, it prompted the view that 'it was advisable to send official notices to the heads of all registered schools warning them that any misuse of education for political ends would lead to the dismissal of the teachers concerned'.[70] After the issuance of such notices, there were instances 'in which school managers ... dismissed teachers alleged to be communists'.[71] Quick repressive action against individual headmasters and teachers was made possible not only through the powers of dismissal granted under the Education Ordinance but also through the Deportation Ordinance that afforded the governor of Hong Kong very wide discretion to deport anyone in the interest of peace and order in the colony.[72] On the night before the British government announced its recognition of the CCP's Beijing government on 6 January 1950, Lo Tung, headmaster of Heung To School, a 'communist controlled or dominated school', and a 'top Communist in Education matters in the Colony' who also headed 'the Education Section of the Federation of Trade Unions', was deported.[73] British recognition of the Beijing government, which, in Grantham's words, was 'a recognition of fact rather than an act of approbation', perhaps gave the Hong Kong government more apprehension than comfort in combatting the spread of communist propaganda amongst youngsters in Hong Kong[74]: 'With Communist China

[67] Report tabled by T. R. Rowell.

[68] *Ibid.*; Zhou Yi, 香港左派鬥爭史 [History of struggles of leftists in Hong Kong] (Hong Kong: Li Wen, 2002), 19–20.

[69] Report tabled by T. R. Rowell.   [70] *Ibid.*   [71] *Ibid.*

[72] For wide powers of deportation possessed and used by colonial government, see Christopher Munn, 'Our Best Trump Card: A Brief History of Deportation in Hong Kong, 1857–1955', in *Civil Unrest and Governance in Hong Kong: Law and Order from Historical and Cultural Perspectives*, ed. Michael Ng and John Wong (London: Routledge, 2017), 26–45.

[73] Letter from J. F. Nicoll to James Griffiths, 21 July 1950; *Ta Kung Pao*, 8 January 1950; Zhou, 香港左派鬥爭史, 96.

[74] Report on Communist Activities in Hong Kong for the six months ending 31 December 1949 enclosed in a letter from Grantham to James Griffiths, 6 March 1950.

now contiguous to Hong Kong', schools in Hong Kong could be made a centre to 'lure large numbers of students into China for indoctrination courses'. When those students returned to Hong Kong, they would help to spread communism 'as propaganda agents themselves'. A special school for such indoctrination courses was believed to have been established in Huizhou in Guangdong province, a town less than 100 kilometres from the Hong Kong border.[75]

Censoring Textbooks as Part of the 'Ideological Battle'

As noted in the previous section, in addition to repressive measures, the Special Bureau was also responsible for 'creative measures' to combat the dissemination of communist, anti-imperialist and nationalist ideas in schools. One such creative measure was to provide schools with teaching and propaganda materials that exemplified the 'virtues of democracy and the values of the Commonwealth concept of cooperation' to counter communist indoctrination in schools. Believing that 'Communism as a creed must be dealt with as well as Communism as a force', the colonial government tasked the Special Bureau with devising 'well-planned counter-Communist propaganda and counter-Communist educational activities'.[76] To prepare for the design of such materials and activities for schools in Hong Kong, the Special Bureau was asked to make 'a full study of the educational and propaganda methods used by the Communists in the past' to determine the appeal of ideas and ideals not only in Hong Kong but also in North China and Malaya, so that the 'counter plans would utilise similar methods to those employed and proved effective by the Communists, e.g. newspaper articles, special news-sheets, special school-texts, broadcasting and [the] formation of Dramatic and Singing Groups, etc.'[77] At the same time, the bureau was advised not to 'introduce direct political propaganda into education' but to try to 'present a fair and balanced picture of good government'.[78]

Against the backdrop of escalating Cold War tension due to the outbreak of the Korean War in June 1950, a series of secret annual conferences amongst the directors of education in the British colonies of Hong Kong, Singapore, Malaya, Sarawak, Borneo and Brunei and officers from the Colonial Office in London were held in Asia in the early 1950s. One of the major objectives of these conferences was to share amongst British territories in Southeast Asia experiences in 'creative measures' designed to 'safeguard education from Communist indoctrination', inculcate 'a common nationality in the various peoples of each territory' and produce 'text-books

---

[75] *Ibid.* [76] 'Counter-Communist Education'. [77] *Ibid.* [78] *Ibid.*

suitable for use'.[79] The 1950 conference resolved to adopt the opinion that 'if the ideological battle is lost among children and young persons it is generally lost'. In his opening address to the conference, Malcolm MacDonald, commissioner-general for Southeast Asia, pleaded for the establishment of 'one language [i.e. English] as the medium of instruction in any one ... territory' so as to 'bring into being a national loyalty to the country of domicile'. He reminded the colonial education directors in attendance that 'the progress of the human race depended on the preservation of freedom of thoughts, particularly among children'. Of course, communist thoughts were to be precluded from such freedom in his opinion because 'Communist Governments with their tyrannical control over men's thoughts and opinions' aimed to produce 'slave-minds'. Hence, MacDonald stressed that providing suitable textbooks was a matter of 'urgency' for the colonies.[80] In a report addressing his fellow directors of education at the same conference, T. R. Rowell, the director of education of Hong Kong, introduced the 'creative works' that the Special Bureau had so far accomplished: putting into press six textbooks for primary schools, preparing a further series of textbooks for secondary schools in both Chinese and English, issuing materials and syllabuses for civics courses to schools, establishing syllabus committees for vernacular schools, sponsoring a radio storyteller, cooperating with the British Council and US Information Service on a travelling display of educational pictures, and posting materials to teachers' private addresses to disseminate 'covert propaganda'.[81] He said that the Special Bureau had also produced short 16mm films and been asked to 'keep a library of films specially selected as exemplifying good government and well-ordered living'.[82] The education directors attending the conference agreed that 'the most dangerous vehicles for undesirable propaganda were text-books in General Knowledge, Civics, History and Geography'. Rowell reported in response that a history textbook for Chinese schools was being prepared by the Education Department in Hong Kong, which was acknowledged as being 'in an advanced position when compared with other territories in the provision of Chinese text-books'.[83] It appears, however, that the Hong Kong government did not view preparing and supplying textbooks to all vernacular Chinese schools in Hong Kong as a sustainable solution, as most such schools were private schools that did not receive government subsidies. Instead, a Syllabus and Textbook Committee was formed after the

[79] Report of the Second Conference of Directors and Deputy Directors of Education, held in the Department of Education, Fullerton Building, Singapore, on 4 and 5 September 1950, 2, CO 968/259.

[80] Report of the Second Conference of Directors and Deputy Directors of Education, 1.

[81] Report tabled by T. R. Rowell.   [82] Ibid.; and 'Counter-Communist Education'.

[83] Report of the Second Conference of Directors and Deputy Directors of Education, 9.

conference in 1952 to design syllabuses and advise the director of education on the adoption of textbooks published by commercial presses, thereby censoring undesirable teaching materials. Textbooks that satisfied the government's syllabus and curriculum requirements were classified as 'recommended' or 'approved', with a list of approved textbooks issued to schools prior to the commencement of each academic year.[84]

The Education Ordinance and Regulations were also extensively rewritten in 1952 to tighten the government's control of educational content and activities. The new law expressly prohibited in schools 'instruction, education, entertainment, recreation and propaganda or activity of any kind which shall be in any way of a political or partly political nature'.[85] Syllabuses, timetables and all instructional materials were also now subject to the director of education's approval,[86] and school inspections were to be 'carried out without previous notice being given' to check whether there were any activities and materials of a communist nature.[87] The colonial directors of education participating in the 1952 conference agreed that it was the duty of colonial education authorities to provide training to teachers to enable them to 'inculcate in their pupils a lively awareness of the advantages of democracy and of the dangers to such a way of life which are inherent in any totalitarian ideology'.[88] The issue of 'emergency training' for teachers had also been discussed in detail at the 1950 conference. Against this backdrop, the first full-time Teacher Training College was established in Singapore in 1950, and, a year later, a similar training college named after Governor Grantham was established in Hong Kong, both for the training of primary school teachers.[89]

Despite the combination of the aforementioned repressive and creative measures, Rowell admitted the inadequacy of official efforts to contain the spread of communist ideas amongst students. For instance, censoring the textbooks used in the classroom did not preclude indoctrination amongst students that was 'carried out in so-called "self-study" groups, or in extra-curricular activities, walks, or excursions'.[90] Further, despite the background screening jointly conducted by Special Branch and the Special Bureau of the Education Department, 'many teachers without previous records had been able to pass the security check and had later turned out to

---

[84] Paul Morris and Anthony Sweeting, 'Education and Politics: The Case of Hong Kong from an Historical Perspective', *Oxford Review of Education* 17. 3 (1991): 249–67.

[85] Education Regulations 1952, reg. 88.   [86] *Ibid.*, reg. 87.   [87] Report tabled by T. R. Rowell.

[88] Extract from a report of the Fourth Annual Conference of Directors of Education and Senior Education Officers held in the Office of the Commissioner-General for South East Asia on 9 September 1952, CO 968/259.

[89] Report of the Second Conference of Directors and Deputy Directors of Education, 12.

[90] Report tabled by T. R. Rowell.

be pro-Communist'.[91] Another problem was communist literature sold outside schools, which constituted 'a grave handicap to [the Education Department's] efforts at keeping schools free from dangerous propaganda material'. Yet another was the display of propaganda films and cartoons to young persons, especially when such films and cartoons were shown in private places, thereby rendering the censorship requirement for all films screened in public under the Places of Public Entertainment Ordinance inapplicable.[92]. After five years of governorship, Grantham reported to the secretary of state for the colonies on what he had achieved in constraining communist 'influence in proportion to the expansion of the school system'. The proportion of schools in Hong Kong considered to be dominated or infiltrated by communists or to have CCP sympathies, he wrote, had declined from 11 per cent (90 schools) in 1949 to 8 per cent (83 schools) in 1952. The percentage of students 'possibly subject to indoctrination' had declined from 12.5 per cent (16,196 students) to 8.5 percent (16,732 students) during the same period.[93] However, as we will see in the next chapter, communist influence in Hong Kong's education sector continued to be a major headache for Grantham's successors.

Actions against the Press: Amethyst Incident

Outside the classroom, Grantham's government fought communist and anti-imperialist propaganda disseminated through the leftist press and news agencies, in particular *Wen Wei Po*, *Ta Kung Pao*, *Hwa Shiang Pao* and the NCNA, which were believed to be voicing 'only directives of [the] Chinese Communist propaganda machine'.[94] News reports that embarrassed the British government were also considered to be 'overstepping the limits' and thus to warrant sanctions.[95] In April 1949, for example, a British warship, HMS *Amethyst*, was shelled by the CCP's batteries in the lower Yangtze River. The *Amethyst*'s captain was killed and a large number of its crew members injured. The damaged ship was held captive by the PLA for ten weeks before escaping to Hong Kong in late July. Leftist Chinese newspapers in Hong Kong published news reports and editorials distributed by the NCNA that portrayed the incident

---

[91] Report of the Second Conference of Directors and Deputy Directors of Education, 11.

[92] Report tabled by T. R. Rowell; extract from a report of the Fourth Annual Conference of Directors and Senior Education Officers.

[93] Savingram from the Governor to the Secretary of State for the Colonies, 17 November 1952.

[94] Telegram from R. Stevenson of the British Embassy in Nanking to the Foreign Office, 13 June 1949, CO 537/5116.

[95] 'Overstepping the limits' was a test that was frequently used by the governor and the secretary of state for the colonies in discussing whether suppressive actions should be taken; see examples of such discussions in the telegram from the Secretary of State for the Colonies to the Governor, 18 August 1949, CO 537/5116.

as a military victory for the PLA in defending Chinese territory against British imperialist aggression, as the *Amethyst* had been attempting to prevent the PLA from crossing the Yangtze River for Nanjing.[96] These reports and editorials depicted the British Empire as only a 'paper tiger'.[97] Prior to the Amethyst incident, there had already been 'a series of outspoken attacks on British and American policy (particularly in regard to the Atlantic Pact)' by leftist newspapers that Grantham found 'increasingly difficult to tolerate'. The incident presented him with 'the right opportunity for action' against these papers. Grantham at once proposed to the Colonial Office that the NCNA and 'communist controlled newspapers' be closed under the Emergency Regulations Ordinance or the Societies Ordinance.[98] His proposal was, however, held back on the advice of R. Stevenson, the British Ambassador in Nanjing, who wished to 'avoid any action likely to diminish the chance of arranging a safe passage out' for the *Amethyst* and her crew who were 'at present at the mercy of the Communists'.[99] The ambassador also worried that such actions would be 'open to charges of interference with [the] freedom of the press' and risked prejudicing the position of Reuters and *North China Daily*, which were operating in CCP-controlled Shanghai.[100] He advised that any repressive action against the communist-controlled press and news agency 'should not be based upon its affiliation with [the] Chinese Communist party (even were this relatively easy to establish) but rather upon a specific subversive article for which prosecution would be presumably practicable' under the existing legislation of Hong Kong.[101] Stevenson also thought that given the impracticability of excluding communist news altogether from Hong Kong, 'there may be benefit in permitting it[s] centralised distribution through a known agency which can be punished each time it oversteps certain established limits'.[102] Grantham ultimately agreed to this cautious diplomatic strategy and promised that the NCNA would not be dealt with under the Societies Ordinance, which prohibited societies from being politically affiliated with a foreign political party but rather under legislation against the press or press articles that 'overstep limits'.[103]

The NCNA's reaction to the successful escape of the *Amethyst* on 30 July 1949 caused Grantham to consider that the limits had been overstepped and that action should be taken against the agency. On 3 August, the day the

---

[96] *Ta Kung Pao*, 21, 24 and 26 April 1949.
[97] Savingram from Grantham to the Secretary of State for the Colonies, 11 May 1949, CO 537/5116.
[98] Telegram from Grantham to the Secretary of State for the Colonies, 23 April 1949, CO 537/5116.
[99] Telegram from R. Stevenson to the Foreign Office, 25 April 1949, CO 537/5116.
[100] Telegram from R. Stevenson to the Foreign Office, 13 June 1949, CO 537/5116.   [101] *Ibid.*
[102] *Ibid.*
[103] Telegram from Grantham to the Secretary of State for the Colonies, 22 June 1949, CO 537/5116.

Amethyst arrived in Hong Kong waters, the NCNA, through leftist newspapers in Hong Kong, published what Grantham called a 'vindictive, offensive and distorted' version of the incident.[104] The NCNA accused the *Amethyst* of sinking a Chinese steamer during its escape, drowning many of its passengers.[105] The NCNA's commentary further described the British ship's escape as adding 'another serious crime to its serious crimes of invading into the Yangtze River and the defence line of the People's Liberation Army' on 20 April. The incident, it continued, served to 'teac[h] the Chinese people [of] the viciousness, hypocrisy and shamelessness of imperialists'. The agency's commentary also repeated a PLA general's appeal to the Chinese to 'mourn for their compatriots who were sacrificed on 20 April and 30 July and seek retribution for their death'.[106] Regarding such news reports as an outrageous abuse of freedom of the press and 'a smear on the name of the Royal Navy', Grantham considered three courses of action: to prosecute the NCNA under the Defamation and Libel Ordinance and the Sedition Ordinance for the articles it had published; to close down the NCNA completely; or to issue 'a strong warning to [the NCNA] that in any further case[s] firm action would be taken' and that such action 'might mean immediate closure'. Voices from London and Nanjing warned against closing down the NCNA because of British interests in mainland China. Prosecuting the agency would 'necessitate witnesses, possibly including Admiral Brind, appearing in court', which was 'clearly undesirable'.[107] In the circumstances, the colonial secretary of the Hong Kong government opted for the most moderate of these courses of action. He issued a letter to the director of the NCNA on 4 August 1949 warning him that the NCNA's articles 'overstep[ped] the limits' and 'disseminate[d] libellous and seditious matter' and that any further breach of the law would result in legal action against the agency and its director. Less than a week later, Chau Kong-ming, an official of the Hong Kong Literary and Arts Association who was believed by the Hong Kong government to be leading the youth section of CCP organisations in Hong Kong, was deported from Hong Kong, although there is no evidence showing that the deportation was directly linked to the Amethyst incident.[108] Grantham justified the government's

---

[104] Extract from telegram to the Secretary of State for the Colonies from the Governor, 6 August 1949, CO537/5116. For newspaper reports of Amethyst's escape to Hong Kong, see *Wah Kiu Yat Po*, 1 and 3 August 1949.

[105] *Ta Kung Pao*, 3 August 1949.

[106] Translation of NCNA commentary enclosed in telegram from Grantham to the Secretary of State for the Colonies, 5 August 1949, CO537/5116. For original NCNA commentary, see *Ta Kung Pao*, 3 August 1949.

[107] Telegram from Grantham to the Secretary of State for the Colonies, 9 August 1949, CO 537/5116.

[108] Telegram from Grantham to the Secretary of State for the Colonies, 8 August 1949; telegram from the Secretary of State for the Colonies to Grantham, 19 August 1949, CO 537/5116. Reuters, 9 August 1949, CO 537/5116. For leadership role of Chau, see 'The Chinese Communist Party in Hong Kong', 12.

hesitation to close down the NCNA and communist newspapers in his memoirs, relying on the rhetoric of freedom of expression and the press: 'Was our hesitancy a sign of weakness? Were we afraid? No, we were not: but one of the most important things for which the free world stands is freedom of expression of opinion and liberty of the press.'[109] Following the free-world rhetoric that highlights the contrast between 'the Communist Governments with their tyrannical control of men's thoughts and opinions, and the democratic governments which still believed in liberalism and freedom',[110] Grantham emphasised that his preference had been 'to rely on the judicial process rather than to suppress [the press] by executive act', as his predecessors had done through their wide administrative powers.[111] Such free-world rhetoric was thus made subject to the widening legal web within which judicial process could be deployed to suppress the press and penalise editors and publishers who found themselves caught in that web.

Korean War and the New Press Law

In December 1949, Grantham's government consolidated the Emergency Regulations decreed before the Japanese occupation and further expanded them into the Emergency (Principal) Regulations, which comprised 137 regulations enabling the government to censor publications, prohibit the publication of matters that in the government's view were prejudicial to the public interest, and to search the premises of any press organisation that published such matters.[112] These powers would come into effect upon the governor's declaration that he considered there to exist an occasion of emergency or public danger.[113] Two months later, Secretary of State for the Colonies Arthur Creech Jones sent a seven-page secret circular despatch to all colonial governors asking them to evaluate their legal powers to 'deal with subversive activities and propaganda in circumstances which, while not sufficiently serious to warrant the declaration of a state of emergency, may, unless dealt with in the very early stages, lead to a situation in which such a declaration has to be made'.[114] He further asked the governors to 'bring to the attention of all members of the administration the

---

[109] Grantham, *Via Ports*, 148–9.
[110] Opening address of Malcolm MacDonald, the Commissioner-General for South East Asia, in the Second Conference of Directors and Deputy Directors of Education, held in the Department of Education, Fullerton Building, Singapore, on 4 and 5 September 1950, 1, CO 968/259.
[111] Grantham, *Via Ports*, 148–9.
[112] Emergency (Principal) Regulations 1949. Many of these publications remained in the statute books of Hong Kong until their repeal in 1995, see Michael Ng, Shengyue Zhang and Max Wong, 'Who But the Governor in Executive Council Is the Judge?': Historical Use of the Emergency Regulations Ordinance', *Hong Kong Law Journal* 50.2 (2020): 425–61.
[113] For difference from state of emergency, see Ng, Zhang and Wong, 'Who But the Governor in Executive Council Is the Judge?'
[114] 'Powers for Dealing with Subversive Activities', telegram from A. Creech Jones to the Officer Administering the Government of Colonies, 18 February 1950, CO 537/5389.

dangers of the present Communist threat' and to advise the means by which 'the activities of subversive persons and associations, particularly Communists, can be hampered and thwarted'.[115] At the same time, however, as a prudent measure to guard against retaliation, the secretary reminded the governors that 'in legislation of this character no specific mention should of course be made of the fact that it is directed against "Communism" and "Communists"'.[116] In response, the Hong Kong government further tightened existing laws relating to the control of publications, newspapers and news agencies to 'give greater powers to control the entry or the publication within the Colony of literature subversive or prejudicial to the safety of the state'.[117] A new law, known as the Control of Publications Consolidation Ordinance (CPCO), took effect on 17 May 1951 and remained effective in Hong Kong until its repeal in 1987. This legislation consolidated and widened the colony's state powers relating to the printing, publication, sale, distribution, importation, control, registration and licensing of the print media.[118]

One of the most important powers afforded by the new ordinance was the court's power to order the suppression of a newspaper or prohibit the publication of objectionable content. That power had existed under the Emergency Regulations, which could take effect only upon an occasion of emergency or public danger.[119] The CPCO, however, made the power a part of ordinary substantive law exercisable by the state even at times of no emergency or public danger. All that was needed to trigger the suppression or suspension of a newspaper was an application to a magistrate by the attorney general pending a determination of government prosecution against the printer, publisher or editor of the newspaper for one of the listed offences, such as publishing seditious content or inducing individuals to support any foreign political party or group that was considered by the governor in council to be prejudicial to the security of the colony.[120] Once a newspaper was ordered to be suppressed, policer officers were authorised to forcibly enter its premises to seize and detain all equipment and materials used to publish the suppressed newspaper and to remove any personal or material obstructions.[121] Another major change in the law allowed the penalisation of newspapers that maliciously published false news likely to alarm public opinion or disturb public order.[122]

---

[115] *Ibid.*   [116] *Ibid.*

[117] Telegram in reply from the Officer Administering the Government to the Secretary of State, 20 September 1950, CO 537/5389.

[118] The new law consolidated and amended provisions in Printers and Publishers Ordinance 1927 (No. 25 of 1927), the Prohibited Publications Ordinance 1938 (No. 14 of 1938) and the Chinese Publications (Prevention) Ordinance 1907 (No. 15 of 1907).

[119] Emergency Regulations Ordinance, s. 2, and Emergency Regulations 1938, regs. 21–25.

[120] For the offence of seditious publication, see Sedition Ordinance 1938, s. 4; for the offence of inducing to support a foreign political party and conditions for triggering suppression of newspapers, see Control of Publications Consolidation Ordinance 1951, ss. 3 and 4.

[121] Control of Publications Consolidation Ordinance 1951, s. 4(4).   [122] *Ibid.*, s. 6,

This new offence in Hong Kong was sourced from the Press Ordinance of Malta enacted in 1933.[123] In justifying it at a Legislative Council session, Hong Kong Attorney General John Bowes Griffin acknowledged that the suppression of a newspaper could 'result in an interference with the liberty of the press and the liberty of expression which [are] jealously guarded, and rightly so, in the free world'. However, he continued, abuse of such a tolerant attitude could produce 'indulgence in licence rather than liberty'. The new law, which, in his opinion, 'no newspaper which discharges its onerous duties with a sense of responsibility need fear', thus provided 'a guide as to the limits within which the true exercise of the liberty of the press and of expression can proceed'.[124] Whilst the press law enacted in pre–Second World War Hong Kong targeted the control of newspapers and periodicals, the CPCO widened the web of press control to include news agencies, which were now required to register with the government and furnish the personal particulars of their proprietor, printer, publisher, manager and editor or else cease operation. The government was also empowered to cancel such registration if any of these key personnel of a news agency were connected to a suppressed newspaper.[125] The new press law, which was passed in the same month (i.e. May 1951) that the UN General Assembly adopted a resolution to impose an embargo on China owing to its involvement in the Korean War, quickly became a weapon wielded against the leftist press and the NCNA as the Cold War tension in Asia escalated in the early 1950s.

Another Test of Strength with the NCNA

Britain's military involvement in the Korean War in support of the United States and its support of the UN embargo on China made it an official enemy of the PRC. At the beginning of the 1950s, Hong Kong thus became a 'reluctant Cold Warrior' forced to strike a balance between the need to follow London in demonstrating Britain's solidarity with the United States as a close ally in combatting communism and the need to safeguard itself against aggression from neighbouring communist China.[126] While the chiefs of staff and Cabinet Defence Committee in London were deciding to deploy only minimal force to defend Hong Kong in the event of an attack from China, the Hong Kong government was tightening its control of the leftist press, which was openly

---

[123] Press Ordinance 1933 of Malta, s. 13.
[124] *Records of Legislative Council Meeting on 2 May 1951*, Hong Kong Legislative Council.
[125] Control of Publications Consolidation Ordinance 1951, s. 16, and News Agencies Registration Regulations 1951, reg. 15.
[126] For Hong Kong factors in the Anglo-American relationship during the Korean War and the description of Hong Kong as a 'reluctant Cold Warrior', see Mark, *Hong Kong and the Cold War*, 6, 101–10.

subversive in its propaganda.[127] Soon after passing the CPCO, the Hong Kong government requested the NCNA, a major news agency that supplied news stories and propaganda to leftist newspapers in Hong Kong, to register as a news agency, furnish the particulars of its key personnel and make a deposit of HK$10,000 in accordance with the newly enacted ordinance. Beijing, while stalling in its negotiations with London over the establishment of official diplomatic relations at a time when China and Britain were on opposing sides in the Korean War, claimed diplomatic immunity for the NCNA. The Chinese government broadcast through Beijing Radio that the NCNA was a state-owned agency of the PRC, and hence not bound by the local laws of Hong Kong according to international practice and in line with the USSR's immunity claims for TASS, that country's official news agency.[128] Governor Grantham, facing another test of strength with the NCNA not long after the Amethyst incident, advised London to adopt a heavy-handed approach by amending the newly passed CPCO to authorise the police to forcibly break into any unregistered news agency, close it down and confiscate its property.[129] The Colonial Office and Foreign Office, in consultation with the chargé d'affaires in Beijing, rejected such an approach and asked the Hong Kong government 'to take no further action to amend the Ordinance'.[130] Instead, it was instructed to inform the director of the NCNA that the agency must comply with local laws to register or cease publication. The director would also need to be informed that in the event of non-registration, action would be taken against them and other persons concerned under the Deportation of Aliens Ordinance. In explaining its preference for this softer approach, the Colonial Office stressed its concerns about the risk of 'retaliation against the British official staff in China' were Grantham's solutions to be adopted.[131] On 4 April 1952, the director of the NCNA was accordingly asked to register with the Hong Kong Government Registrar within one month. On 5 May, when the one month deadline expired, the NCNA wrote to the Hong Kong government restating its state agency role, and hence that it was not subject to local laws, albeit expressing 'its

---

[127] Both the chiefs of staff suggested 'a policy of bluff' to deter Chinese attack in order not to undermine British efforts in the Cold War elsewhere while the Cabinet Defence Committee were of the view that Britain would not reinforce the colony with forces other than two battalions that had been sent from Hong Kong to Korea, see Mark, *Hong Kong and the Cold War*, 50.

[128] SCMP, 22 August 1951.

[129] Draft amendment to Control of Publications Consolidation Ordinance attached to savingram from Grantham to the Secretary of State (copying Chargé d'Affaires in Beijing), 8 December 1951, FO371/99362.

[130] Savingram from Secretary of the State for the Colonies to the Officer Administering the Government of Hong Kong, 28 February 1952, FO 371/99362.

[131] *Ibid.*

willingness to register as a state news agency'.[132] In the government's reply, the NCNA was for the first time acknowledged as a state news agency, but it was also emphasised that it would be required to register under Hong Kong law despite such status before the extended deadline of 23 May, failing which further action would be taken.[133] On 20 May, Percy Chen, a Chinese lawyer, met with the attorney general of Hong Kong with apparent authority from the NCNA, warning that closing the agency would result in retaliation against British consular officers in China. Furthermore, Chen advised, deportation of the NCNA director would be impractical because he claimed British nationality. He also indicated that the NCNA was prepared to fight any prosecution of NCNA personnel 'to the Privy Council if necessary'.[134] Not only did the NCNA fail to register by the deadline prescribed by the governor, but it published 'seditious articles' that condemned the prosecution and criminal trial of a major leftist newspaper, *Ta Kung Pao*, for publishing articles on the police suppression of a riot that had occurred in March, details of which will be discussed in the next section of this chapter. Following the government's 'weak' response 'in view of the threat of retaliation by the Chinese', the British Foreign Office's China and Korea Department took over the driver's seat 'to give the Chinese one more chance'.[135] Leo Lamb, the British chargé d'affaires in Beijing, was instructed to write to the PRC Ministry of Foreign Affairs (MFA) demanding registration of the NCNA. Lamb's letter, sent on 6 June and addressed to the vice minister of Foreign Affairs of the PRC, stressed that 'continued permission for the [NCNA] to function in Hong Kong' was 'dependent upon the Agency conducting itself in conformity with international propriety and upon compliance with local legal requirements including registration'. Lamb also mentioned in his letter that the state news agencies of other governments had already complied with the

---

[132] Telegram from Grantham to the Secretary of State for the Colonies, 11 May 1952, FO 371/99362.

[133] In the absence of a formal diplomatic relationship between Britain and the PRC, NCNA's state news agency status was 'claimed and virtually admitted', as described by Leo Lamb, Chargé d'Affaires in Beijing, in his telegram to the Foreign Office, 21 May 1952, FO 371/99362.

[134] Percy Chen, according to the governor, 'professed to be speaking without specific authority' in the meeting. Yet he was regarded by London and the Hong Kong government as 'the Chinese Solicitor for the New China News Agency' and the Chinese government's 'adviser in this matter'; see a note on 'New China News Agency in Hong Kong' by C. H. Johnston of the Foreign Office, 27 May 1952, FO 371/99362; and telegram from Grantham to the Secretary of State for the Colonies, 25 May 1952, FO 371/99362. For Percy Chen's relationship with the CCP, see Percy Chen, *China Called Me: My Life Inside the Chinese Revolution* (Boston: Little Brown, 1979).

[135] Response described as 'weak' by the Head of the China and Korea Department of the Foreign Office R. H. Scott in his written comment to the note on 'New China News Agency in Hong Kong' by C. H. Johnston; telegram from the Foreign Office to the Chargé d'Affaires in Beijing, 29 May 1952, FO 371/99362.

registration requirements.[136] The letter was copied to Washington and to British high commissioners around the world to alert them to possible retaliation against consular officers by the Chinese government.[137] On the same day, Grantham wrote to the director of the NCNA informing him that if the agency failed to register by the extended deadline of 21 June, or if it published seditious materials again, it would be closed down without further notice.[138] The director replied two days before the deadline and agreed to register according to the CPCO because the NCNA's 'Hong Kong Branch was recognised as a state agency'. The agency's registration with the Hong Kong Registrar of Newspapers on the same day afforded officials in London and Hong Kong temporary relief from the ongoing struggle amongst four competing forces that would persist for the next two decades of the Cold War period: allying with the US-led battles with communist regimes around the world; protecting British interests in China; safeguarding the security of British colonial rule in Hong Kong; and upholding the rhetoric of a free world standing for freedom of expression and the press. In reviewing the NCNA registration saga, the British Foreign Office regarded it as a 'small but definite success for a policy of cautious firmness with the Chinese' and believed that the PRC government was not 'as cook-a-hoop as they would like to appear'. The Foreign Office also reminded the Hong Kong government to cancel the NCNA's registration if it 'misbehave[d] again'.[139] In the meantime, Grantham's government continued to tackle many other instances of 'misbehaviour' on the part of the Hong Kong press, editors and mass media employees whom it believed to be under the control of the CCP in its attempts to engage in overt and covert subversive activities against colonial rule.

'Your Paper Is an Influence for Evil': Suppressing *Ta Kung Pao*

A serious fire that broke out on 21 November 1951 in Tung Tau Village in Kowloon, destroying over 3,000 huts and rendering more than 15,000 squatters

---

[136] Letter from Leo Lamb to Chang Han-fu, Vice Minister for Foreign Affairs of the PRC, 6 June 1952, FO 371/99362.

[137] Telegram from Commonwealth Relations Office to the UK High Commissioner in Canada, Australia, New Zealand, South Africa, Indai, Pakistan and Ceylon, 5 June 1952, FO 371/99362; telegram from the Chargé d'Affaires in Beijing to the Foreign Office requesting the draft letter to be passed to Washington, 30 May 1952, FO 371/99362.

[138] Telegram from the Secretary of State for the Colonies to Grantham, 28 May 1952, CO 371/99362; note on 'New China News Agency in Hong Kong' by J. O. Lloyd of the Foreign Office, 3 June 1952, FO 371/99362.

[139] A note on 'New China News Agency in Hong Kong' by C. H. Johnston and the response by R. H. Scott, 26 June 1952, FO 371/99362.

homeless, exposed not only the Hong Kong government's inability to cope with the unexpected magnitude of the housing needs of a huge number of migrants but also the ability of the 'communists to cash in on the situation and to stir up trouble'.[140] Many of the squatters were mainlanders who had fled from China since the late 1940s. As they had been unable to 'crowd into the congested slum dwellings', they had 'established themselves in flimsy shacks in bombed-out areas in the town or on the adjacent hill-sides', with many building themselves a 'house – if a structure of a few square feet, made of beaten-out kerosene tins, old pieces of discarded match-boarding or old sacking can be called a house'.[141] After the fire, the leftist press, describing the fire that had devastated an area of over three square kilometres as the biggest one in the last 100 years, published a number of reports criticising the colonial government for its delay in releasing money donated by community leaders to fire victims, forcing them to resettle in remote districts, and further for the lack of social care and welfare for the Chinese in Hong Kong. Published alongside these reports were stories of the leftist HKFTU organising the free distribution of rice and clothing to the victims.[142] A fire victims' office under the support of labour unions was also established to organise petitions to the government against the removal of victims and the clearance of squatters' areas and calling on it to coordinate the distribution of donations from leftist organisations to the victims. In January and February of 1952, a number of the office's officials were arrested by the Hong Kong Police and deported for 'endangering Hong Kong's peace and order'.[143] After Liu Qin, the chief officer of the fire victims' office, was arrested and deported on 5 February, sixteen social organisations in Guangzhou City met and resolved to organise a comfort mission to Hong Kong to visit the fire victims. Members of the meeting welcomed the deportees from Hong Kong, condemned the Hong Kong government for deporting them and announced their firm support for 'the righteous anti-persecution struggle of the Chinese in Hong Kong'.[144] When the mission arrived in Shenzhen on 1 March, the Hong Kong government announced in a press conference that it would be refused entry to the colony.[145] Meanwhile, thousands of supporters organised by a reception committee had gathered at Kowloon Train Station, waving the national flags of the PRC and singing to greet the mission that was expected to be arriving from Guangzhou.[146]

---

[140] SCMP, 22 November 1951; Grantham, *Via Ports*, 158; Chi-Kwan Mark, 'Everyday Propaganda: The Leftist Press and Sino-British Relations in Hong Kong, 1952–67', in *Europe and China in the Cold War: Exchanges Beyond the Bloc Logic and the Sino-Soviet Split, New Perspectives on the Cold War*, ed., Janick Marina Schaufelbuehl, Marco Wyss and Valeria Zanier (Leiden: Brill, 2019), 156.

[141] Grantham, *Via Ports*, 154–5.

[142] *Ta Kung Pao*, 10 and 13 December 1952; Mark, 'Everyday Propaganda', 156.

[143] *Wah Kiu Yat Po*, 12 January 1952.   [144] *Ta Kung Pao*, 7 February 1952.

[145] SCMP, 2 March 1952.

[146] *Ibid.*; *Wah Kiu Yat Po*, 2 March 1952; *Ta Kung Pao*, 2 and 5 March 1952.

When these supporters left the train station after learning that the mission could not cross the border, they clashed with Hong Kong police officers who had been ordered to disperse the crowd. The confrontation turned into a riot involving over 10,000 Chinese and hundreds of police during which '198 tear gas shells, one round of Greener gun [ammunition] and two rounds of revolver ammunition' were fired.[147] The March First Riot, as it later came to be called, resulted in one death, tens of injuries and over a hundred arrests. Of those arrested, eighteen were convicted and twelve were expelled from Hong Kong.[148]

Vociferously protesting the Hong Kong government's actions against the comfort mission supporters, the *People's Daily* in Beijing published a commentary on 4 March that was reprinted the following day in three major leftist newspapers in Hong Kong: *Ta Kung Pao*, *Wen Wei Po* and the *New Evening Post*. Calling the actions 'barbarous, wicked and criminal acts of arresting, killing and persecution' in pursuit of the 'pernicious and wicked plots of the American and British Imperialists' to carry out a 'secret plan to convert Hong Kong into a base for ... imperialist aggression' against China, the commentary warned that the Hong Kong and British governments would 'bear the whole responsibility for any grave consequences in connexion with provocative outrage' against the Chinese in Hong Kong, promising that their 'head would bleed for having knocked it against the great force of the Chinese People'.[149]

This belligerent commentary gave Grantham's government an opportunity to demonstrate how the newly passed CPCO could keep the press within legal–political limits. On 19 March, the publishers, printers and editors of the three offending newspapers were prosecuted for publishing seditious material that was intended to 'bring the Government into hatred and contempt or create dissatisfaction against the Government or raise discontent among the inhabitants of the colony'.[150] If the papers were convicted on this charge, they could be suspended under the ordinance.[151] During the trial of *Ta Kung Po*, the government's counsel opened his case by stressing the usual apolitical freedom rhetoric: 'Freedom of speech and of writing are very dear to us wherever the British flag flies. It is no aim of the prosecution to stop a man having any political beliefs he may have. The Prosecution is by no means aimed at Communism.' Nevertheless, he continued, the law 'took care that these freedoms were not abused'. In particular, the law forbade 'writings and speeches likely to cause breaches of the peace and to promote insurrections, or promote

---

[147] SCMP, 6 May 1952.

[148] FO 371/99243, as quoted in Mark, 'Everyday Propaganda', 157; SCMP, 6 May 1952.

[149] *Fei Yi Ming and Lee Tsung Ying* v. *R* (1952) 36 Hong Kong Law Report 133.

[150] Sedition Ordinance 1938, ss. 3 and 4; SCMP, 6 May 1952.

[151] Control of Publications Consolidation Ordinance 1951, s. 4 and First Schedule; Sedition Ordinance 1938, ss. 3 and 4.

in the minds of the people discontent or disaffection against the local Government'.[152] *Ta Kung Pao*'s editor, one of the defendants, testified from the dock that the paper had simply done its duty in publishing facts about the March First Riot and had criticised the government without any seditious intent. He also stated that the paper had published the government's version of the riot 'side by side with the subject matter' over which he was being charged to ensure a fair presentation, thereby removing any seditious intent.[153] In directing the jury, Senior Puisne Judge Williams of the Supreme Court stressed that the 'truth of the statement contained in the article was no defence' and that the jury 'was not called upon to apportion any blame or even inquire into the origin' of the riot. What it was being asked to do was determine whether the article 'had stirred up hatred and contempt for the Government'.[154] After forty-five minutes of deliberation, the jury found the publisher and editor guilty and to be sentenced to a fine or imprisonment by Judge Williams.[155] Upon the application of the prosecution under the power granted by the CPCO, Williams also ordered the suppression of *Ta Kung Pao* for six months. After handing down his sentence, Williams could not help but make sentimental remarks about *Ta Kung Pao*: 'The account you have published of the March 1 incident in your newspaper is a tissue of lies from start to finish . . .. Your paper is an influence for evil in the Colony.'[156]

This successful suppression of a major leftist newspaper in Hong Kong resulted in a strongly worded protest from the Chinese Foreign Ministry to the British chargé d'affaires in Beijing on 10 May in which it condemned the 'illegal trial' and persecution of the Chinese press, as well as Hong Kong government measures that 'trampled on the fundamental freedom and rights of the Chinese Residents in Hong Kong'.[157] The suspension order against *Ta Kung Pao* was subsequently shortened to twelve days, although the publisher's and editor's appeals against their conviction were quashed by the Full Court. The Hong Kong government also dropped the charges against *Wen Wei Po* and the *New Evening Post* owing to concerns that the hearings would provide 'a platform for left-wing propaganda by the defence Counsel' and hence be 'counter-productive'.[158] For instance, during the trial of *Ta Kung Pao* the defendants had disclosed the police tactic of deporting tens of political dissents during the midnight hours to escape public attention, as well as the location of a secret detention camp for deportees, many of them political dissidents, on Chatham Road in the Tsimshatsui area of Kowloon (near the present-day

---

[152] SCMP, 19 April 1952.   [153] SCMP, 30 April and 6 May 1952.   [154] SCMP, 6 May 1952.
[155] The publisher was fined HK$4,000 or nine months' imprisonment and the editor was fined HK$3,000 or six months' imprisonment.
[156] SCMP, 6 May 1952.   [157] FO 371/99244, as cited in Mark, 'Everyday Propaganda', 159.
[158] Transcript of interviews with Governor Robert Black by Steve Tsang in 1987 as cited in Mark, 'Everyday Propaganda', 160.

Science Museum).[159] Deportees were taken from the camp to the Chinese border in police trucks, carried off in chartered junks or towed in boats by police launches before being cut loose near mainland China.[160]

The Hong Kong government regarded deportation as its 'best trump card',[161] as it allowed it to dispose of the troublemakers who infested the colony in a quick and inexpensive manner under the power afforded by the colony's numerous deportation laws, including the Expulsion of Undesirables Ordinance.[162] Such power allowed a person to be considered undesirable and deported if he or she was 'suspected of being likely to promote sedition or cause a disturbance of the public tranquillity' unless he or she was a British subject or had been resident in Hong Kong for ten years or more.[163] It was a tool regularly used to get rid of 'undesirable' journalists, editors and media workers. On 10 January 1952, eight film industry workers who were suspected of taking part in leftist propaganda were arrested at midnight and deported to the mainland the following morning. Amongst them were a number of actors, actresses and directors, as well as Szema Man-shum, a famous scriptwriter, a high-profile writer for *Wen Wei Po* and a leading figure in the CCP's united front work for film workers in Hong Kong.[164] In addition, despite protests from Beijing, more than fifty left-wing labour unionists, some of whom were believed to have been involved in organising the comfort mission and in the March First Riot, were deported over the next few months. An editorial published in March 1952 in the SCMP, the colony's major English-language paper, gives a flavour of the way that some Europeans, or government officials at least, thought about eliminating opposition through deportation: 'Any who will not serve the essential interests of this Colony must be invited to leave. This is not 'oppression': it is a simple safeguard.'[165]

Patriotism as a State Security Threat

In addition to suppressing the local left-wing media and deporting its workers, Grantham also suggested prohibiting the importation of newspapers from the

---

[159] *Ta Kung Pao,* 22 and 29 April 1952, as cited in Mark, 'Everyday Propaganda', 159; also see Zhou, 香港左派鬥爭史, 92–3.

[160] For origin, source of legal powers and use of deportation in Hong Kong history, see Munn, 'Our Best Trump Card'.

[161] Badeley to Colonial Office, January 1904, CO 129/327, 23–5, as cited in Munn, 'Our Best Trump Card', 26.

[162] The Expulsion of Undesirables Ordinance (Cap. 242) was enacted on 2 September 1949, less than a month before the formal establishment of the PRC; see also Munn, 'Our Best Trump Card'.

[163] Expulsion of Undesirables Ordinance (Cap. 242), ss. 3 and 4.

[164] *Ta Kung Pao,* 12 January 1952; Zhou, 香港左派鬥爭史, 102–3.

[165] SCMP, 3 March 1952; also Richard Klein, 'The Empire Strikes Back: Britain's Use of the Law to Suppress Political Dissent in Hong Kong', *Boston University International Law Journal* 15.1 (1997): 18.

mainland under the power afforded by the CPCO owing to their 'particularly obnoxious reporting of 1 March disorders and other recent events'. Without such a prohibition, he advised the Colonial Office, the 'usefulness of prosecutions' against the leftist press in Hong Kong would be 'largely offset, if publications from the mainland, containing similar objectionable materials, are allowed to circulate in Hong Kong'.[166] This proposed action was held back, however, again because of worries over possible retaliation from Beijing and the inherent contradiction with the free-world rhetoric that London had been publicising. In a letter responding to Grantham's suggestion, Leo Lamb, the British chargé d'affaires in Beijing, argued that prohibiting the importation of Chinese newspapers into Hong Kong would be 'a flagrant denial of the rights and freedoms which we *pretend* to uphold' [emphasis added]; hence, such a measure 'would be easily exploited by Chinese Government propaganda to our disadvantage'. In addition, the proposed prohibition 'might give the Chinese Government [a] welcome pretext for preventing the delivery [of newspapers from Hong Kong and the UK]' to the British chargé d'affaires in Beijing.[167]

Despite Grantham's unsuccessful attempt to stop the importation of materials from the mainland, forcing the NCNA to register under Hong Kong press law, suppressing *Ta Kung Pao* and convicting its publisher and editor, and deporting leading leftist film workers were believed to have set clear limits 'to the virulence of propaganda which may be disseminated locally'.[168] The Korean armistice in 1953 and the establishment of diplomatic relations between Britain and the PRC following the Geneva Conference in 1954 also relaxed the international tensions that had escalated during the Korean War.[169] The next couple of years saw a period of moderation in tone in the attacks of the left-wing press on the Hong Kong and British governments.[170] Leftists in Hong Kong, following the CCP's foreign policy of 'peaceful co-existence', began concentrating on 'peaceful penetration', of which Hong Kong students and youths remained the 'primary target'.[171] Communist propaganda made strong appeals to the nationalist feelings of these two groups by praising

---

[166] Letter from Grantham to the Secretary of State for the Colonies, 8 April 1952, FO 371/99362.

[167] Letter from Leo Lamb to the Foreign Office, 9 April 1952, FO 371/99362.

[168] Extracts from a Survey of Subversive Communists Activities in the Far East, 1 July – 30 September 1952, CO 968/259; also Grantham, *Via Ports*, 149.

[169] James T. H. Tang, *Britain's Encounter with Revolutionary China, 1949–54* (London: Macmillan, 1992), 115–25.

[170] Florence Mok, 'Chinese communist influence in Chinese left-wing press in Cold War Hong Kong, c. 1949–1970' (unpublished manuscript).

[171] 'Hong Kong: Implications of Recent Chinese Policy', document from A. Grantham to Secretary of State, 2–3, 25 June 1956, CO 1030/203, cited in Mok, 'Chinese Communist Influence'; extract from a Survey of Subversive Communist Activities in the Far East, 1 July – 30 September 1952, CO 968/259.

China's achievements since the PRC's establishment.[172] Not only did the CCP promote such feelings amongst students and the working class, but KMT supporters in Hong Kong, with the support of the United States, also promulgated their own patriotic, anti-communist propaganda amongst the Hong Kong Chinese. Anglo-American solidarity against communism notwithstanding, the Hong Kong government did not see completely eye-to-eye with London regarding Hong Kong's use as a base for US anti-PRC initiatives.[173] With Hong Kong stuck in the middle of the evolving and sometimes embarrassing Cold War relationship amongst Britain, the PRC and the United States, Grantham's government had to be highly sensitive to the co-existence of propaganda from the two opposing Chinese regimes in Hong Kong, and it took action when it was thought that the 'patriotic' activities of the two camps might cause trouble.[174] The commemoration and celebration of events of a political nature made the Hong Kong government particularly anxious. For example, Special Branch and the director of education were asked to monitor how many schools displayed the PRC's national flag on the PRC's national day (1 October), International Children's Day and Labour Day.[175] Schools were warned of a potential breach of the Education Ordinance, which disallowed the display of flags of a political nature. Police officers sometimes even searched schools and interrogated teachers when they discovered the schools to be flying the PRC's national flag.[176] At the same time, the public display of the flag of the Republic of China (ROC, i.e. Taiwan) in the streets and outside shops during its national day on 10 October in competition with the display of PRC flags a week earlier also worried the government. On 10 October 1955, the ROC's national flags were hoisted in 'many streets, especially in Wan Chai, Shau Ki Wan, Diamond Hill and industrial areas in Kowloon' and were also seen 'flying from the windows

---

[172] 'Chinese Communist Press Machine in Hong Kong: Its Scope and Its Impact', by Hong Kong Special Branch, 4, 21 November 1968, FCO 40/222; 'The Vulnerability of Hong Kong to Non-Military Aggression', by Local Intelligence Committee, 2, (date missing) June 1955, CO 1035/78, both cited in Mok, 'Chinese Communist Influence'.

[173] For the United States's involvement in anti-communist activities in Hong Kong and the Hong Kong government's reactions, see Mark, *Hong Kong and the Cold War*, chapter 5, and Xun Lu, 'The American Cold War in Hong Kong, 1949–1960: Intelligence and Propaganda', in *Hong Kong in the Cold War*, ed. Priscilla Roberts and John Carroll (Hong Kong: Hong Kong University Press, 2016).

[174] The embarrassing relationship refers to the disagreement between Britain and the United States regarding the recognition of and the pace of developing a normal relationship with the PRC, despite overall solidarity; see Mark, *Hong Kong and the Cold War*, chapter 3.

[175] Savingram from the Governor to the Secretary of State for the Colonies, 26 June 1953, CO 968/259.

[176] *Ta Kung Pao*, 18 February 1952.

or roofs of residences, resettlement flats and junks in Causeway Bay, Yau Ma Tei and Cheung Chau'. Amidst KMT supporters renewing their allegiance to Chiang Kai-shek in mass rallies and rightist leaders toasting US Consul General in Hong Kong Everett Drumright in a celebration cocktail party, a team of police officers dismantled, with little opposition, several large ceremonial arches built by KMT supporters at an amusement park at Lai Chi Kok in Kowloon using the legal excuse that the structures were 'illegally erected on Crown land'.[177]

A year later, however, the removal of signs of patriotism on the ROC's national day did not meet with the same level of tranquillity and cooperation. On 10 October 1956, the Double Tenth celebration day, the tearing down of Nationalist flags posted on the walls of Block G of the Li Cheng UK public housing estate in Kowloon by a junior staff member of the Resettlement Office triggered one of the most serious riots in Hong Kong history and gave birth to the notorious legal measure of detention without trial for 'undesirables'.[178] A small crowd of KMT supporters initially gathered to demand an apology and then assaulted Resettlement Office staff. During the night, riots broke out in other parts of Kowloon, with roughly 5,000 rioters, many of them KMT supporters, setting fire to and looting leftist schools and shops.[179] The disturbance spread and intensified over the next two days. In response, the military was called onto the streets, a curfew was imposed, and the governor warned citizens of the risk of being shot. The riots resulted in at least sixty deaths, forty-three of which were caused by gunshot wounds.[180] The Emergency (Detention) Regulations were put in place on 14 October 1956, allowing anyone arrested in connection with what became known as the Double Tenth riots to be detained for up to fourteen days.[181] Detention for further fourteen-day periods could be authorised by the governor if he was satisfied that 'any person... already in custody ought to be detained in order that further inquiry may be made'.[182] The following month, the even more draconian Emergency (Detention Orders) Regulations entered into force on 13 November. The new regulations, which permitted the *indefinite detention* of any arrestee against whom the governor in council found

---

[177] SCMP, 11 October 1955.
[178] Carol Jones and Jon Vagg, *Criminal Justice in Hong Kong* (London: Routledge-Cavendish, 2007), 319.
[179] *Ibid.*, 294.
[180] There were no published figure as to how many were killed by the army or police, and there was disagreement in the total deaths described in earlier works; see Jones and Vagg, *Criminal Justice in Hong Kong*, 299 and 301; also Klein, 'The Empire Strikes Back,' 21; and Carroll, *A Concise History*, 146.
[181] Emergency (Detention) Regulations (G.N.A. 99 of 1956), reg. 2(1).   [182] *Ibid.*, reg. 2(3).

it impracticable to enforce a deportation order, were partly in response to the PRC government's increasing reluctance to accept deportees from the mid-1950s.[183] More than 1,200 people were detained for involvement in riots under the regulations in 1956, but their use did not stop there after Grantham left office in 1957.[184]

---

[183] Emergency (Detention Orders) Regulations (G.N.A. 104 of 1956); Jones and Vagg, *Criminal Justice in Hong Kong,* 317; Munn, 'Our Best Trump Card'.
[184] For the total number of persons held in detention, see Jones and Vagg, *Criminal Justice in Hong Kong,* 236.

4 'Patriotism to You Can Be Revolutionary Heresy to Us': Hardened Control of Media, Schools and Entertainment

Grantham's successor, Robert Black, who had previously served as colonial secretary under Grantham before being appointed governor of Singapore during the Malayan Emergency, supported the retention of the draconian regulations allowing detention without trial even in a period without major civil unrest. Between 1956 and 1960, more than 32,000 people were detained in the name of controlling the activities of criminals and triad members. Most of them were locked up in the detention centre in Tsim Sha Tsui.[1] The practice attracted criticism from the press in both Hong Kong and the UK, as well as from such pressure groups as the London-based section of the International Commission of Jurists (commonly known as JUSTICE). It was even criticised by the chief justice of the Hong Kong Supreme Court as 'unwelcome and repugnant to the ideas prevailing in any British community'.[2] The Colonial Office also expressed its concern about the extraordinarily wide discretion against individual liberties given to the Hong Kong government. It admitted that 'Hong Kong ... is the only colonial territory which gives such powers to the Governor without first requiring him publicly to declare a state of emergency' and confessed that it was 'uneasy about the situation'.[3] In response, Governor Black committed to possibly dispensing with such a 'temporary' measure when the opportunity was ripe but made it clear that he regarded the immediate repeal of the regulations as 'politically unwise' because their purpose was to destroy 'alien secret organisations'.[4] He agreed only to 'improve'

---

[1] Jones and Vagg, *Criminal Justice in Hong Kong*, 319.
[2] Extract of Ceremonial Opening of the Supreme Court Assizes, 19 January 1961, CO 1030/1427. For the frequent use of emergency regulations against political dissents in colonial Hong Kong and the extraordinary wide power allowed under these regulations in comparison with powers under emergency regulations of other British colonies, see M. Ng, Zhang and Wong, "Who But the Governor in Executive Council Is the Judge?'
[3] Note of J. C. Burgh dated 4 May 1960, CO 1030/1427.
[4] Letter from the Governor of Hong Kong to the Secretary of State for the Colonies, 10 September 1962, CO 1030/1427.

the regulations by establishing a tribunal to review detention decisions.[5] However, the reality is that the 'temporary' Emergency (Deportation and Detention) Regulations were repealed only in 1995, more than thirty years after their passage and two years before Hong Kong was handed back to China.[6]

Seeing China turn from wearing a 'smiling mask of good neighbourliness towards Hong Kong' in the mid-1950s to wearing a 'scowling mask' to confront 'an old-fashioned imperialist country', Black tightened surveillance over and hardened his approach towards two major disseminators of communist propaganda: schools and the media. Propaganda put out by both was seen as being used by the CCP to 'keep the Hong Kong Government on the defensive and to deter the [UK] from alienating China by the threats of political trouble over Hong Kong'.[7] Black faced an even more challenging situation with respect to curbing the communist activities of schools and suppressing communist propaganda in the media than Grantham had. Widespread famine in China sparked an unexpected rise in the number of immigrants in the late 1950s, increasing the population of Hong Kong from 1.8 million in 1947 to over 2.9 million in 1958, of whom more than 1 million were immigrants.[8] More than 10,000 people crossed the border into Hong Kong every month with the intention of staying for the long term to escape from 'a totalitarian proletariat as long as they [could] make a tolerable existence outside it'.[9] The influx of immigrants created a huge gap in the provision of education to children who took refuge in Hong Kong with their families. CCP-affiliated organisations in Hong Kong took advantage of that gap to establish numerous new schools for the children of immigrants. Although the Education Ordinance empowered the government to close down 'unregistered' schools with political affiliations, it was difficult, Black explained, 'to justify too rigid an enforcement' as long as 'vacancies were not available in registered schools'.[10] How to keep such

---

5   Emergency (Deportation and Detention) Regulations (G.N.A. 50 of 1962); see also Emergency (Deportation and Detention) (Forms) Order (G.N.A. 67 of 1962); Emergency (Deportation and Detention) (Amendment) Regulations (G.N.A. 68 of 1962); Emergency (Deportation and Detention) (Advisory Tribunal) Rules (G.N.A. 69 of 1962).

6   See Emergency (Deportation and Detention) (Forms) (Repeal) Order 1995 (L.N. 252 of 1995); Appointment of Places of Detention (Consolidation) (Repeal) Notice 1995 (L.N. 253 of 1995); Emergency Regulations (Repeal) Order 1995 (L.N. 254 of 1995); Emergency (Deportation and Detention) (Advisory Tribunal) (Repeal) Rules 1995 (L.N. 255 of 1995).

7   'Hong Kong: Review of Developments during 1958' from Black to the Secretary of State for the Colonies, 1, 21 January 1959, CO 1030/581.

8   'Hong Kong: Review of Developments during 1958', 2–3; population figures recorded in Census & Statistics Department, Hong Kong, *Hong Kong Statistics 1947–67* (Hong Kong: Hong Kong Government, 1969), 14; for the great famine of China in the late 1950s, see Frank Dikötter, *Mao's Great Famine: The History of China's Most Devastating Catastrophe, 1958–62* (London: Bloomsbury, 2010).

9   'Hong Kong: Review of Developments during 1958', 2–3.

10   Savingram from Black to the Secretary of State for the Colonies, 12 August 1960, CO 1030/1107.

much-needed unofficial schooling within ideological limits remained a headache for the Hong Kong government for the next decade. By necessity, the government engaged in 'more of a holding action than a positive attempt at clearing Communist influence away from schools'.[11] As we will see, such action included striking hard at high-profile educators of the best-known CCP-dominated schools to make other schools aware of the legal consequences of overstepping the political red lines.

With respect to the media, in addition to newspapers, radio broadcasting had become an increasingly popular information and entertainment channel for Chinese people in Hong Kong, especially for the illiterate. By the late 1950s, there were three radio stations operating in Hong Kong. Radio Hong Kong (RHK) had been established by the government in 1928 as a public radio station. Rediffusion (RDF), operated by a British corporation, and Commercial Radio (CR), operated with investments from local Chinese businessmen, were licensed in 1949 and 1959, respectively, to operate as privately run commercial radio stations.[12] The vast amount of information communicated over the airwaves at all hours of the day made it very difficult for the government to ensure the 'political correctness' of that information. To make matters worse, the radio sets used in Hong Kong were able to receive radio broadcasts from the mainland. The spill-over of communist propaganda from radio stations in China was a serious matter of concern for both the Hong Kong government and the Colonial and Foreign Offices in London. Other forms of media and entertainment such as films and live performances also caused concern when the Hong Kong government discovered that many film studios and performance troupes had communist affiliations.

Complicating matters was the role that Hong Kong played as a useful proxy for the US in its foreign policy towards Communist China during the Cold War era. Formally disengaging from and isolating China after the Korean War, the US established its espionage centre in Hong Kong and continued over the years to use the colony as a listening post for information about and intelligence on China, with the overt consent of the UK.[13] The PRC also attempted to 'exploit the peculiar situation of Hong Kong' to widen 'the gap between British and American foreign policies in relation to China' as part of its divide-and-conquer strategy to weaken Anglo-American anti-communist solidarity.[14] Moves to suppress communist propaganda in Hong Kong were readily

[11] 'Hong Kong: Review of Developments during 1958', 3.
[12] RTHK, 從一九二八年說起: 香港廣播七十五年專輯 [Since 1928: Broadcasting for seventy-five years in Hong Kong] (Hong Kong: RTHK, 2004), 137.
[13] Ye Lin, 在中國的影子下: 美國對香港的外交政策 1945–1972 [In China's shadow: US foreign policy towards Hong Kong 1945–1972] (Hong Kong: Chung Hwa, 2018), 135.
[14] 'Hong Kong: Review of Developments during 1958', 1. For UK–US disagreement regarding the roles of Hong Kong in their respective China strategies, see Ye, 在中國的影子下, 96–101.

publicised by the communist media as part of the US game plan against China. As we will see, Black's government needed to expand its surveillance network over media and schools not only so that it could take quick action to suppress covert subversive communist propaganda and political activities in schools but also so that it could sometimes limit US anti-communist propaganda activities in Hong Kong to avoid unnecessarily provoking local communists in Hong Kong and the Beijing government for the sake of internal security. The overarching aim was to avoid materially embarrassing London's relations with Washington and Beijing.

New Education Law against Schools, Teachers and Principals

Upon his return to Hong Kong as the colony's twenty-third governor, Black took stock of leftist schools in Hong Kong. It was estimated that there were forty-one 'communist controlled' schools with over 14,000 students and 130 'communist penetrated' schools with close to 60,000 students.[15] Black envisioned the situation 'becoming very serious' and initiated a series of quick and heavy-handed measures to set a strong tone for educators in an attempt to 'recover some of the ground that [had] been lost or at least to hold the situation in check'.[16] On 31 January 1958, just a week after being appointed governor, Black put the Education (Amendment) Ordinance and Education (Amendment) Regulations into effect. This new set of laws and regulations greatly expanded the government's power to close a school or remove a school manager, principal or teacher. In addition to the power to approve the appointment of school managers and teachers under the former Education Ordinance of 1952, the appointment of school principals was made subject to the approval of the director of education under the revised ordinance, and approval could be withdrawn if a principal was, in the director's opinion, no longer fit to do his or her job.[17] A teacher's registration could also be cancelled if the director was satisfied that 'the environment in which that person received his education or any part thereof has been such as to make him unsuitable as a teacher in the Colony'.[18] This new provision posed a serious threat to teachers at leftist schools in Hong Kong because a teacher's education background in mainland China could result in deregistration even if he or she was competent and had not breached any law while teaching. A school could be closed if the director of education was of the opinion that the conduct of its managers, teachers or pupils was or had been 'unsatisfactory'.[19] Over and above these wide powers granted to the director, the governor was empowered to cancel the registration of

---

[15] Telegram from Black to the Secretary of State for the Colonies, 21 June 1958, CO 1030/581.
[16] Telegram from Black to the Secretary of State for the Colonies, 21 June 1958.
[17] Education Ordinance 1952, as amended in 1958, s. 28A.   [18] *Ibid.*, s. 32A.
[19] *Ibid.*, s. 42B.

a school, a school manager or a teacher if he considered their continued registration 'prejudicial to the public interest or the welfare of the pupils or of education generally'.[20] Control over expression inside schools and student activities was further tightened so that 'no salutes, songs, dances, slogans, uniforms, flags, documents or symbols' of a political nature could be practised, displayed or worn in schools without the director's permission, and student associations could not be formed within schools without government approval.[21] The director of education now had the absolute discretion to expel from school any students who participated in processions, propaganda, political activities or labour disputes.[22]

The 1958 amendment to the Education Ordinance also introduced extensive regulations by which a school could be closed if the government was not satisfied that the premises were in sound structural condition, such as having adequate floor strength.[23] Inspectors were authorised to inspect schools and to request that they carry out structural improvements. If a school did not comply with such a request, it could be closed, with police officers authorised to enter the premises to effect closure if necessary.[24] Although the government claimed that the new regulations had been passed to ensure the safety of students, the left-wing press criticised them as covert measures against the numerous smaller leftist schools that were operating in tenement buildings owing to a shortage of suitable school premises.[25] In response to such criticisms, the government and Legislative Council argued that the regulations constituted a sound measure to protect students from physical and educational hazards and to guard against 'indoctrinated teachers and pupils' and 'underhand methods of [the] infiltration of political propaganda'.[26]

As we will see, instead of using the new powers to target smaller leftist schools, Governor Black took aim at the largest and best known to 'strik[e] at the heart of the trouble, namely at one of the main personalities engaged in organizing the communist indoctrination of students'.[27] In June 1958, he sought approval from the Colonial Office to take action against a 'leading communist school', Pui Kiu Middle School, and its Chinese principal Parker Tu. Pui Kiu Middle School, which had fifty-seven staff members and approximately 1,000 students, held the number two position in Special Branch's list of communist-controlled schools.[28] Tu was described by Black as 'probably the most influential personality in communist educational circles'.[29] Earlier,

---

[20] *Ibid.*, s. 37. [21] Education Regulations 1952, as amended in 1958, regs. 71, 72 and 88.
[22] *Ibid.*, reg. 87D. [23] Education Ordinance 1952, as amended in 1958, s. 12.
[24] *Ibid.*, ss. 42B and 47C.
[25] For criticism of the leftwing press, see *Ta Kung Pao*, 3 January 1958.
[26] Official Report of Proceedings of Hong Kong Legislative Council, 8 January 1958.
[27] Telegram from Black to the Secretary of State for the Colonies, 21 June 1958.
[28] 'The Chinese Communist Party in Hong Kong'; telegram from Black to the Secretary of State for the Colonies, 21 June 1958.
[29] Telegram from Black to the Secretary of State for the Colonies, 21 June 1958.

during a school visit, inspectors from the Education Department had found a number of communist books in Pui Kiu's library. They reported that 'indoctrination is conducted by means of a variety of highly developed teaching techniques and by daily study of the magazine *"China Youth"*, the organ of the Young Communist League'.[30] Tu was also accused of continuing to employ two teachers from China whose registration had been cancelled based on the director's opinion that the environment in which they had received their education rendered them unsuitable to teach under the recently added section 32A of the Education Ordinance.[31] Written directions given by the director of education to Tu requested that he refrain from holding political activities, using materials of a political nature or employing unregistered teachers in Pui Kiu. He was also asked to sign an undertaking to ensure that the school remained free from political activities 'of any kind whatsoever' and submit a complete list of the names and addresses of all teachers and students at the school.[32] Tu refused to sign the undertaking. After seeking endorsement from the Executive Council and the Colonial Office, and despite warnings from Duncan Wilson, the chargé d'affaires in Beijing, about the potential adverse effects of any actions against Pui Kiu and Tu on the 'recently improved climate in Sino-British trade', Black cancelled Tu's registration as a principal and teacher under section 37 of the Education Ordinance, which empowered the governor to take such action in 'the public interest'.[33] To prevent Tu from continuing 'to exercise influence over Pui Kiu School and other schools and to foment student reaction to his de-registration', Black asked the police to deport him to the mainland on 6 August, the day after his deregistration, using the power granted under the Deportation of Aliens Ordinance to summarily deport non-British subjects for 'the public good'.[34]

About two weeks after Tu's deportation, police action was used against another 'hardcore Communist middle school': Chung Hwa Middle School.[35] On 26 August, approximately seventy police officers went to Chung Hwa Middle School, located on Robinson Road, to enforce a closure order against the school under the new building regulations of the Education Ordinance on the grounds that its 'roof timbers had rotted and the floor joists had been eaten

[30] *Ibid.*

[31] *Ibid.*; Zhou, 香港左派鬥爭史, 173–4; Education Ordinance, as amended in 1958, s. 32A.

[32] Telegram (no. 564) from Black to the Secretary of State for the Colonies, 8 July 1958, CO 1030/581.

[33] Telegram from Black to the Secretary of State for the Colonies, 5 July 1958, CO 1030/581; Education Ordinance 1952, as amended in 1958, s. 37.

[34] Telegrams from Black to the Secretary of State for the Colonies, 8 July (no. 563 and 564), 1 August 1958, CO 1030/581; Zhou, 香港左派鬥爭史, 175–6; Deportation of Aliens Ordinance (Cap. 240), s. 3(1)(c).

[35] Telegram (no. 718) from Black to the Secretary of State for the Colonies, 26 August 1958, CO 1030/581.

away by white ants' and was thus unsafe for students. Although pro-government newspapers portrayed the closure as quick and smooth, with 'no attempt to interfere with the police while they were sealing the building', the left-wing press reported police brutality against students, teachers and reporters, and provided pictures of the confrontations (see Figure 4.1).[36] It was reported that during the eviction process, more than twenty students and teachers had been injured, with journalists beaten and their cameras smashed by the police.[37]

The incident stirred up what the Colonial Office described as 'an unusual degree of publicity' and generated propaganda of 'unprecedented violence'. On its front page, the *People's Daily* condemned the Hong Kong government's action against students and teachers. The left-wing International Organisation of Journalists protested to the Hong Kong government about police violence

Figure 4.1 Confrontation between policemen and journalists during the eviction process. Source: *Ta Kung Pao*, 27 August 1958, courtesy of *Ta Kung Pao*.

[36] Telegram (no. 719) from Black to the Secretary of State for the Colonies, 26 August 1958, CO 1030/581; SCMP, 27 August 1958; *Ta Kung Pao*, 27 August 1958
[37] SCMP, 27 August 1958; *Ta Kung Pao*, 27 August 1958. Reuters, 26 August 1958, and *Daily Worker*, 27 August 1958, both kept in CO 1030/581.

against journalists and described the incident as a 'gross provocation aimed against the freedom of the press', a protest that Black advised the Colonial Office to ignore.[38] However, Black could not ignore the unexpected demonstrations of thousands of people that took place in Guangzhou and at the main gate of the office of the British chargé d'affaires in Beijing in the two days following the forced closure of Chung Hwa School. On 28 August, China's MFA sent a strong note of protest to the chargé d'affaires against the Hong Kong government's series of actions against educators and journalists since passage of the revised Education Ordinance in January 1958. In its 'comprehensive bill of grievances', the MFA also complained about the deportation of Parker Tu, the prohibition on flying national flags in schools (which will be discussed in greater detail in the next section), and the Hong Kong government's support of KMT-run schools in Hong Kong and its approval of the use of KMT textbooks in which Nanjing was labelled as the capital of China and Chiang Kai-shek as president. These actions were described as following 'hostile [US] policy towards China' and 'creating two Chinas'.[39] The elevation of a local incident in Hong Kong to an unexpected level of geopolitical relevance was considered a tactic by China to pressurise the UK into separating diplomatically from the US policy of support for Taiwan during the Second Taiwan Strait Crisis, with China's bombing of the offshore islands of Jinmin and Mazu having commenced just a few days before Chung Hwa School's closure.[40] This 'major fuss' ended in early October when Black's government allowed Chung Hwa to reopen in a temporary structure pending repairs to the original school premises. Admitting that the incident's outcome 'would not stop the Communists from claiming a victory for their tough methods', Black insisted that it would have been resolved in the same way even 'if there had been no fuss'.[41] In late October, the Second Taiwan Strait Crisis also cooled down.[42]

Banning Patriotic Activities in Schools

In the same period that saw measures taken against major communist schools and their key leaders, Black's government continued to keep a close eye on the activities of students in other leftist schools. It was especially concerned with

---

[38] Telegram from Black to the Secretary of State for the Colonies, 29 August 1958, CO 1030/581.

[39] Telegram from the Chargé d'Affaires in Beijing to the Foreign Office, 28 August 1958, 1 September 1958, CO1030/581; *Ta Kung Pao*, 28 August 1958, *People's Daily*, 31 August 1958.

[40] Telegram from the Secretary of State for the Colonies to Black, 4 September 1958, CO 1030/581. For a brief description of the Second Taiwan Strait Crisis that lasted for two months from 23 August until late October 1958, see Mark, *The Everyday Cold War*, 61–2.

[41] Telegram from Black to the Secretary of State for the Colonies, 3 October 1958, CO 1030/581.

[42] Mark, *The Everyday Cold War*, 62.

students' expression of patriotism and allegiance to Communist China during festive events. Back in April, the director of education had sent a circular to schools reiterating the regulations under the revised Education Ordinance that prohibited the display of symbols or flags of a political nature.[43] Upon further enquiry, leftist schools were told not to hoist the PRC flag during the forthcoming Labour Day on 1 May.[44] Eight leftist schools defied the instruction and flew the five-star flag on their school premises on Labour Day. The Education Department sent warnings to the schools and asked their principals to provide an explanation and take disciplinary action. A week later, another leftist school, Xin Qiao Middle School, was banned from flying the national flag, having the national anthem sung and paying respect to a portrait of the leader of Communist China during the school's anniversary celebration.[45] Protests by leftist educators and over twenty local leftist labour unions finally led to a note of protest being sent by China's MFA to the British chargé d'affaires in Beijing. The ministry regarded the prohibition on flying the national flag and singing the national anthem as an unfriendly action towards the Chinese government and as depriving the 'sacred inviolable right of Chinese living in Hong Kong' to patriotic expression.[46] As a result of this challenge at the diplomatic level, the under-secretary of state for the colonies had to answer enquiries about the prohibition on celebrating International Labour Day in Hong Kong from a Labour Party member of parliament in London, and the Hong Kong government also issued a statement in response.[47] The statement admitted prohibiting the flying of the national flag on both International Labour Day and Xin Qiao Middle School's anniversary. However, although 'there is in the ordinary way no prohibition on the flying of the national flags of any country in Hongkong', it explained, the government 'discourages the extensive or frequent flying of national flags in such a way or on such occasions as may tend to provoke incidents or a breach of peace'. Accordingly, International Labour Day was 'not regarded by the Director of Education as suitable for celebration by schools'.[48] For Black, this bureaucratic response was just a courteous way of answering a 'difficult point' raised by Beijing, that is, why Chinese school children in Hong Kong did not enjoy 'complete liberty to sing Chinese songs, fly the Chinese flag and read up-to-date Chinese text books on history, philosophy and economy'. If he had been less courteous, he might have said, as he did say in his explanation to the secretary of state for the colonies, 'What is patriotism to you can be revolutionary heresy to us.'[49]

---

[43] *Ta Kung Pao*, 1 June 1958, translated and kept in HKRS 163–1–2201.
[44] Zhou, 香港左派鬥爭史, 171.
[45] *Hong Kong Standard*, 2 and 3 August 1958, kept in HKRS 163–1–2201.
[46] *Wen Wei Po*, 7 June 1958, *Ta Kung Pao*, 8 June 1958, *New China News Agency*, 10 June 1958, translated and kept in HKRS 163–1–2201.
[47] SCMP, 18 June 1958.   [48] SCMP, 12 June 1958.
[49] 'Hong Kong: Review of Developments during 1958', 3–4.

Given the Hong Kong government's increased vigilance towards leftist schools' activities, such schools sometimes organised activities to express their patriotism covertly under the guise of normal school events, which put the government in a guessing game as to their true objective. In the case of any doubt, it suppressed them. For example, a joint-school physical training exercise involving 4,000 students sponsored by ten leftist schools was scheduled to be held on 9 December 1958 at the stadium of the South China Athletic Association in Causeway Bay on Hong Kong Island. The commissioner of police, under the power granted him by the Places of Public Entertainment Ordinance, had approved the event in principle on 12 November. Newspaper reports and programme booklets submitted to the police a few days before the event, however, led the commissioner to think that it was not 'a gymnastic display' but 'a thinly-disguised political rally' with 'in fact a political purpose behind' it. The event was suspected of being a way to pay homage to China's achievements during the Great Leap Forward.[50] One day before the event, the government informed the organiser of its decision to withhold its permission and to broadcast to the public that the event had been cancelled.[51]

In addition to the open suppression of school activities of a suspected communist or patriotic nature, the Hong Kong government was also urged by London to strengthen its surveillance network over local communists by having Special Branch penetrate left-wing organisations because 'the activities of [Communist China's] agents outside the mainland constitute the most important of Her Majesty's Governments' intelligence targets in the Far East'.[52] The Hong Kong government received periodic reports from its local intelligence committee on sensitive information on the left-wing press and schools collected and collated by Special Branch. Such information covered a wide range of affairs ranging from how leftist newspapers struggled to increase revenue and reduce expenditure and staffing changes amongst the left-wing media and schools to the personal movements and whereabouts of targeted teachers and headmasters, what was discussed in a teachers' meeting at a particular school and what was taught in a particular lesson at a particular school.[53] Based on this information, a series of actions were taken from 1958 to 1960 to close a large number of unregistered leftist schools during a period in which China was undergoing an economic crisis following the Great Leap Forward, and hence it was anticipated that Chinese reactions to any measures taken against left-wing

[50] 'Hong Kong: Review of Developments during 1958', 4; telegram from Black to the Secretary of State for the Colonies, 9 December 1958, CO 1030/581; Zhou, 香港左派鬥爭史, 182–3.
[51] Telegram from Black to the Secretary of State for the Colonies, 9 December 1958; SCMP, 9 December 1958.
[52] Letter from Alan Lennox-Boyd, Secretary of State for the Colonies to Alexander Grantham, 30 August 1957, CO 1030/580.
[53] Various regular reports of Hong Kong Police Special Branch from 1960 to 1962 in CO 1030/1106 and CO 1030/1107.

interests in Hong Kong would be 'mild'.[54] Taking advantage of relaxed political pressure from Beijing, the Hong Kong government determined to actively
enforce the Education Ordinance unless the closure of schools 'would deprive
children of the only means of education available to them' within their neigh-
bourhoods or would be undesirable because of 'over-riding political necessity'.
As a result, only 431 (of which about 180 had left- or right-wing political
affiliations according to the government's intelligence) of the colony's 1,263
unregistered schools survived the Education Department's eighteen-month
deregistration campaign. Although the director of education had the power to
close a school on political grounds under the Education Ordinance, he chose to
close this large number of unregistered schools on such technical grounds as
fire hazards or problems with sanitation, floor stress or teachers' qualifications,
which were deemed devoid of 'political content or implications', to minimise
the negative publicity that could be expected for a campaign seen as 'aimed
at . . . left-wing or patriotic education'.[55] Suppressive actions against schools or
their key personnel were reported not only to London; the US government was
also briefed via its consulate-general in Hong Kong or the British Embassy in
Washington.[56]

Political Censorship of Radio Broadcasts

The period from the early 1960s until the beginning of the Cultural Revolution
in 1966 saw a moderation in tone against the colonial government in the left-
wing press. The economic crisis in China resulting from the Great Leap
Forward and the Sino-Soviet split made 'the economic importance of
Hong Kong to [China] as an earner of foreign exchange . . . perhaps greater
than ever', according to an observation by the Colonial Office in London.[57] The
left-wing press in Hong Kong also suffered both the loss of a financial subsidy
from Beijing and reduced circulation in Hong Kong during the period. The
decline in readership suggested that the aggressive editorial policy of left-wing
papers was no longer well-received by Chinese readers in Hong Kong. Major
left-wing papers such as *Wen Wei Po* and *Ta Kung Pao* thus modified their
strategy in 1960, no longer offering the 'most doctrinaire' content praising the
achievements of Communist China and condemning imperialists, but paying
greater attention to local news, crime, sport and even the occasional salacious

---

[54] Extract of secret despatch from Black (date missing, likely in 1960), CO 1030/1107.
[55] Savingram from Black to the Secretary of State for the Colonies.
[56] Letter from P. G. F. Dalton, Foreign Office, to K. G. Ashton, Colonial Office, 20 August 1958;
letter from W. I. J. Wallace, British Embassy in Washington, to C. B. Burgess, Colonial
Secretary of Hong Kong, CO 1030/580.
[57] Telegram from the Secretary of State for the Colonies to Black, 4 September 1958, CO
1030/581.

story.[58] Left-wing press 'criticism of Western foreign policy tended to concentrate on the US rather than Britain' during this period.[59]

Nevertheless, the softening of tone in the left-wing press did not make the tasks of censoring and policing the media and the dissemination of hostile ideologies any easier for Black's government. A huge influx of immigrants from the mainland, bringing with them capital, managerial skills, craftsmanship and a cheap labour force, led to the booming of Hong Kong's industrial economy from the 1960s onwards amidst economic disaster and famine in mainland China. A growing workforce and rising wages rendered newspapers inadequate as the major source of ideas, information and entertainment for the people of Hong Kong. Cheaper radio sets produced by Asian exporters such as Japan incentivised growing numbers of people, whether literate or not, to look to radio broadcasts in addition to the print media as an instantaneous source of news, as well as such entertainment as music and radio dramas.[60] At the same time, films, live drama and opera performances also became an increasingly trendy way for citizens to spend leisure time with friends and family. The vibrant development of the mass media and conduits of communication and information in Hong Kong in the late 1950s and 1960s was of interest not only to ordinary people but also to the major Cold War rivals looking to turn the cinemas, theatres and airwaves of Hong Kong into important battlefields of political propaganda in 'Asia's cultural Cold War'.[61] We will see how the Hong Kong government policed and censored the emerging mass media and walked a tightrope during this cultural cold war amongst the forces of Communist China, London, the US and KMT agents in Hong Kong.

Hong Kong did not have a free-to-air television service until 1967. Until that year, radio broadcasts were the only aural media in Hong Kong, save for the 'expensive and culturally moribund' cable television service introduced in 1957, which was accessible to only a few well-off households.[62] RHK was established in 1928 by the Hong Kong government in response to a call by the Colonial Office in

---

[58] Mok, 'Chinese communist influence'.

[59] Extract from Local Intelligence Committee Monthly Report, February 1960, CO 1030/1106, cited in Mok, 'Chinese communist influence'.

[60] David Clayton, 'The Consumption of Radio Broadcast Technologies in Hong Kong, c. 1930–1960.' *Economic History Review* 57.4 (2004): 691–726; Shi Wen-hong, '香港的大眾文化與消費生活' [Popular culture and consumption in Hong Kong], in 香港史新編/*Hong Kong History: New Perspectives*, ed. Wang Gung-wu (Hong Kong: Joint Publishing, 2017), 2:665–71.

[61] A term used in Po-shek Fu, 'Entertainment and Propaganda: Hong Kong Cinema and Asia's Cold War', in *The Cold War and Asian Cinemas*, ed., Po-shek Fu and Man-Fung Yip (London: Routledge, 2019), 238–62.

[62] Clayton, 'The Consumption of Radio Broadcast Technologies' 697; Zhang Zhen-dong and Li Chun-wu, 香港廣播電視發展史 [The history of broadcasting in Hong Kong], (Beijing: Zhongguo guangbo dianshi chubanshe, 1997), 71–2.

the 1920s to 'establish a direct channel of political communication between colonial state and local society'.[63] RHK was Britain's second colonial broadcasting station, being preceded by one established in Kenya two months previously.[64] Established subsequent to the disastrous Canton–Hong Kong Strike and Boycott supported by the united front of the CCP and KMT to challenge Britain's legitimacy to rule Hong Kong, RHK had a politically driven content strategy from the outset. The aim was to strengthen colonial rule by enhancing 'appreciation and understanding of the British system as exemplified in Hong Kong', as an internal government document on the development of broadcasting in Hong Kong put it in late 1950.[65] In 1947, a wired radio service licence was granted to RDF, a UK-based media conglomerate closely connected to the political establishment in London that operated radio stations in Malta, Trinidad, Venezuela, Jamaica, Barbados, British Guiana and Singapore.[66] The colonial government hoped to use RDF to strengthen mass electronic communication without having to invest any of its already tight public budget, which was to be allocated to more urgent post-war reconstruction projects.[67] At the end of the 1950s, it was estimated that roughly 775,000 adults and 390,000 children regularly listened to radio broadcasts in Hong Kong, approximately two-thirds of whom were RHK listeners.[68]

Government's Control of News Broadcasts

To ensure that this expanding audience received politically 'desirable' messages, the content of the English and Chinese channels of both RHK and RDF were highly regulated and subject to political censorship as far as was practicable. Despite the controller of broadcasting having overall responsibility for all RHK programmes and operations, the content of RHK's programmes was in fact subject to the control and censorship of various other government departments before they could be aired. The scripts of RHK radio dramas and Chinese operas were pre-censored before airing by staff members of the secretary for Chinese affairs, whose office was also responsible for the 'pre-censorship of plays given

---

[63] S. H. King to Colonial Office, 7 December 1927, CO 129/506/10, cited in Clayton, 'The Consumption of Radio Broadcast Technologies', 712.

[64] 'The Future of Broadcasting in Hong Kong', a statement (Sessional Paper No. 2 of 1956) prepared by the Colonial Secretariat for Legislative Council, para. 1, 11 January 1956, HKRS 41–1–8882.

[65] 'The development of broadcasting', November 1950, HKRS 163–1–1178, cited in Clayton, 'The Consumption of Radio Broadcast Technologies', 712.

[66] Clayton, 'The Consumption of Radio Broadcast Technologies', 698.   [67] Ibid., 713–14.

[68] Notes for the meeting of the ad hoc committee of communist activities, 7 May 1958, HKRS 952–1–1. Note that the total population of Hong Kong by the end of 1959 was approximately 3 million, according to Census & Statistics Department, Hong Kong, Hong Kong Statistics, 14.

for public performance by trade unions and by schools', 'plays in Chinese theatres' and Chinese scripts of public talks.[69] The government's Information Services Department (ISD) had 'a monopoly' over news supplied to RDF and RHK (and subsequently also to CR, as will be seen later in this section).[70] The ISD collected local news stories, purchased news reports from Reuters and provided official news scripts to radio stations for their announcers to read during news bulletins and programmes.[71] Radio stations had to work closely with the Radio News Room of ISD on a day-to-day basis to obtain up-to-date 'official' news bulletins for broadcasting for each timeslot of news programmes. Of course, government documents on how such a system of official monopoly and political censorship operated are extremely difficult to locate in the archives, and yet there is correspondence between RHK and the ISD that proves the existence of the latter's supply of 'official news' for daily radio broadcasts. For example, in 1962, when RHK planned to increase the frequency of its Cantonese news programmes, it had to request that the ISD supply it with additional news bulletins to cover three main news periods with ten-minute bulletins and short five-minute bulletins during the day.[72] The ISD also admitted in its annual report that preparing daily news bulletins for electronic media in Hong Kong was one of its normal daily duties. The report stated that the ISD's Radio News Room 'continued to operate on a round-the-clock basis, producing news bulletins, summaries and headlines for the English and Chinese networks or Radio Hong Kong, Commercial Radio, Rediffusion [Radio] and Rediffusion TV'.[73] The ISD also had the power to restrict political expression on the radio, as well as responsibility for providing 'guidance on all talks or features concerning

---

[69] For pre-censorship responsibilities of the Office of the Secretary for Chinese Affairs, see Xiao-jue Wang, 'Radio Culture in Cold War Hong Kong', *Interventions*, 20.8 (2018): 1157, and memo from J. C. McDouall, Secretary for Chinese Affairs, to Colonial Secretary, 11 October 1957, HKRS 163–1–2035, and notes for the meeting of the ad hoc committee of communist activities, 7 May 1958, HKRS 952–1–1. Au Wai-sum, Assistant Secretary for Chinese Affairs, was responsible for 'pre-checking of Chinese scripts' of plays and public talks, per the description of internal allocation of duties of the Secretariat for Chinese Affairs contained in a circular from Secretary for Chinese Affairs to heads of government departments, 3 January 1958, HKRS 1448–2–53.

[70] Acting Financial Secretary to Deputy Colonial Secretary, 16 October 1959, HKRS 163–1–1695; see also Clayton, 'The Consumption of Radio Broadcast Technologies', 714–15.

[71] Clayton, 'The Consumption of Radio Broadcast Technologies', 715. The decision to monopolise news outputs of RHK, RDF and the newly licensed CR by distributing the same sets of news bulletins to these stations was reached in these correspondences: Deputy Colonial Secretary to Colonial Secretary, 20 October 1959; Acting Colonial Secretary to Deputy Colonial Secretary, 21 October 1959, Deputy Financial Secretary to Deputy Colonial Secretary, 23 October 1959, HKRS 163–1–1695; such power to provide news bulletins to radio stations was also reiterated in 'The Future of Broadcasting in Hong Kong', a statement prepared by the Colonial Secretariat for the Legislative Council, paras. 19 and 47, 11 January 1956, HKRS 41–1–8882.

[72] Memo from Director of Broadcasting to Director of ISD, 4 August 1962, HKRS 41–1–8524.

[73] Annual Departmental Reports of the IRD for 1962–3.

governmental activities'.[74] RDF's licensing conditions compelled it to air programming produced by RHK, BBC and other public sector broadcasters elsewhere in the British Empire for a quarter of its total airtime.[75] RDF had never failed to relay 'special talks and features considered to be in the public interest and put out by RHK', according to a colonial secretariat report praising the company's 'utmost cooperation'.[76]

In 1957, the Hong Kong government decided to establish another commercial radio station to meet rising public demand for entertainment content of a higher standard and greater diversity, as well as to increase government income from the licence fees on radio receiver sets to meet RHK's expanding expenditure. An equally important reason was that failure to raise the standard of radio content would likely prompt more people to listen, via signal spill-over, to such nearby radio stations as Radio Villa Verde in Macau and Guangzhou Radio in China, which could broadcast unregulated CCP or anti-British propaganda.[77] Despite the aggressive pitching of RDF and pressure from the Colonial Office, the Hong Kong government decided to favour a consortium known as Hong Kong Commercial Broadcasting Co., Ltd (CR) led by George Ho, a Chinese investor in Radio Villa Verde and a member of the prominent Ho Tung family, with backing from Jardine Matheson and 'leading Chinese citizen[s]' such as famous businessman and philanthropist Tang Shiu-kin.[78] Based on intelligence suggesting that the CCP 'were keenly interested in Hong Kong's plan for a new commercial service', all applicants for the tender to establish a new commercial radio station were referred to Special Branch for political vetting.[79] Under pressure from RDF in London, the Colonial Office referred the matter to the ministers in London to decide whether to grant a commercial radio licence to RDF or to a group of

---

[74] Clayton, 'The Consumption of Radio Broadcast Technologies', 715; 'The Future of Broadcasting in Hong Kong', paras 19 and 47.

[75] Clause 4(11) in the Licence to RDF, 9 December 1955; also see Clayton, 'The Consumption of Radio Broadcast Technologies', 715.

[76] 'The Future of Broadcasting in Hong Kong', para. 26.

[77] 'The Future of Broadcasting in Hong Kong' and 'Resolution regarding the Future of Broadcasting in Hong Kong', Hong Kong Legislative Council, HKRS 41–1–8882; also minute by John Martin, Colonial Office, advising the ministers on the tender for the commercial broadcasting service in Hong Kong, 20 November 1957, CO 1027/283. Listeners in Hong Kong could receive radio signals spilled over from Guangzhou and Macau. For criticisms of the standard of programs and operations of RDF in Hong Kong by local elites and businessmen, and background of Radio Villa Verde, see Clayton, 'The Consumption of Radio Broadcast Technologies', 714–18.

[78] Letter from the Governor of Hong Kong to E. Melville, Colonial Office, 16 October 1957, CO 1027/283. CR's annual return filed on 22 January 1960 showed that its shareholders include Jardine Matheson & Co., Tang Shiu-kin and Shum Wai-yau, the founder of *Wah Kiu Yat Po*, HKRS 2139–16–3. The Hong Kong government also reported in the letter that George Ho would 'sever his connection with Radio Villa Verde' should he be granted the licence and that Radio Villa Verde might 'founder as a result'.

[79] Telegram from the Secretary of State for the Colonies to the Governor of Hong Kong, 5 April 1957, and the Governor's reply, 10 April 1957, CO 1027/283.

Chinese businessmen in Hong Kong. Despite their concern that 'at some future date control [of the radio station] might pass to undesirable hands', the ministers in the end accepted the strong recommendation of the Hong Kong government and unofficial members of the Executive Council to grant the licence to CR after receiving 'definite assurance' that the Hong Kong government would retain complete control over the content of the programmes broadcast by the new licensee, as well as the power to terminate the licence if CR's operation became 'in any way ... prejudicial to the public interest'.[80]

In response to the ministers' request, the fifteen-year commercial broadcasting licence issued to CR in August 1959 contained stringent terms and conditions that gave the government 'effective control of [the] licensee' and the programmes it aired.[81] It also empowered the director of the ISD to 'determine [the] choice of news broadcasts'.[82] Clause 7(3) of CR's licence stipulated that the licensee broadcast such news bulletins as the ISD director 'may require' and should not relay the news bulletins of any other radio stations except the BBC or RHK.[83] The director was also authorised to pre-censor any programme scripts he or she wished.[84] Further, the government could request that CR refrain from broadcasting 'any matter' and cease to 'employ any particular person or class of persons'.[85] The licence conditions also prohibited 'undesirable propaganda being knowingly transmitted' without the government's permission.[86] The breach of any of these conditions could result in revocation of the licence by the government.[87] The Telecommunication Ordinance also empowered the governor to cancel a radio station's licence or prohibit transmission of radio content if in his view 'the public interest' so required. Again, we can today trace the actual operation of the government's news control system only from correspondence between CR and the ISD. Similar to the need for RHK to coordinate with the ISD to obtain official news bulletins for daily broadcast, the archived documents shown in Figure 4.2 show that in April 1967, CR also requested that it be sent 'extra news headlines' to feed its extending broadcasting until 1 a.m. on certain days, a request to which the director of the ISD agreed.[88]

---

[80] Telegram from the Secretary of State for the Colonies to the Governor of Hong Kong, 4 December 1957, CO 1027/283.

[81] Telegram from the Governor of Hong Kong to the Secretary of State for the Colonies, 5 December 1957, CO 1027/283.

[82] *Ibid.*

[83] Clause 7(3) of the signed 'Licence to Establish a Commercial Broadcasting Service', 28 August 1959, HKRS 2139–16–3.

[84] Clause 7(8) of the signed 'Licence to Establish a Commercial Broadcasting Service'.

[85] Clauses 7(9) and 22(1) of the signed 'Licence to Establish a Commercial Broadcasting Service'.

[86] Telegram from the Governor of Hong Kong to the Secretary of State for the Colonies, 5 December 1957, CO 1027/283; Clause 7(10) of the signed 'Licence to Establish a Commercial Broadcasting Service'.

[87] Clause 12 of the signed 'Licence to Establish a Commercial Broadcasting Service'.

[88] Letter from CR to Director of ISD, 17 April 1967, and letter from Director of ISD to CR, 22 June 1967, HKRS 2139–16–3.

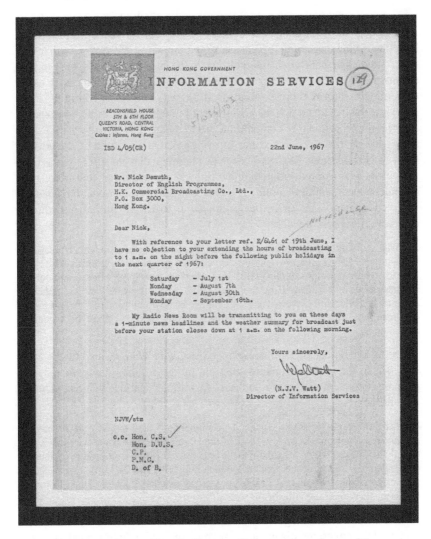

Figure 4.2 Letter from the director of information services to CR on
22 June 1967 agreeing to provide extra news headlines for CR's
broadcasting. Source: HKRS 2139–16–3, courtesy of Public Records Office,
Government Records Service of Hong Kong.

Such day-to-day control of radio news bulletins did not operate unnoticed by
the public, although the English press was more vocal than its Chinese coun-
terpart in criticising the 'government's control and manipulation of news and

news sources within the Colony'.[89] From the mid-1960s, the government found itself under continual attack from the English press for 'hand[ing] out news bulletins' to the three radio broadcasters and the wired TV station with a very limited audience that RDF had established in the late 1950s. In response to such criticism, Nigel Watt, the director of the ISD (also commonly referred to as the Government Information Services, or GIS), was quoted as admitting in an interview the fact that it was the government's intention that 'radio news should not become an element of competition' between the three broadcasters. At the same time, he defended that stance by saying that news issued by the government to broadcasters was not censored, claiming that the ISD 'had trained journalists who worked within their own ethics' and that these 'journalists have an independent editorial policy'.[90] This bureaucratic explanation not only failed to convince the press but prompted it to reveal further government obstruction of press freedom:

Mr. Watt will find it hard to persuade any that there is no censorship here. Denials will fool no-one . . .. How often are reporters denied direct access to Government officers and have to summit questions through GIS? How often are newspapers forced into quoting an anonymous spokesman? How often does GIS send out pre-written items that are blatantly angled to suit Government? . . . Let there be no doubt about it – there is a strict censorship of official news sources in this Colony, and it cannot be denied or camouflaged.[91]

An op-ed in another English newspaper, the *China Mail*, echoed the SCMP's criticism of the news censorship practised by the colonial government, complaining that it was 'boring to hear on various stations almost identical newsflashes'[92]:

It may be a surprise, but Radio Hongkong, Commercial Radio and RTV [RDF] have no control over their own news . . .. Most of the [foreign news] agency wire news goes directly to GIS and is then passed on [to the broadcasters] after scrutiny and, sometimes, censorship . . .. Local news is written completely by GIS and the local stations are not allowed to change or update it, unless by courtesy of GIS . . .. Radio Hong Kong and others must cut their unbiblical cord with GIS.[93]

The influential news magazine *Far Eastern Economic Review* (FEER) also criticised the government-supplied news bulletins as 'ungrammatical travesties of journalism, totally lacking in any "news sense" or skill in presentation' and

[89] SCMP, 10 January 1965.   [90] SCMP, 31 July 1968; SCMP, 10 January 1965.
[91] SCMP, 10 January 1965.
[92] 'Out Come the Answers to Radio HK', *China Mail*, July 1968 (date of report missing), HKRS 70–1–230–1. It was written by Vincent Shepherd, a TV personality and commentator and one of the first full-time law teachers in Hong Kong. See Christopher Munn, *A Special Standing in the World: The Faculty of Law at the University of Hong Kong, 1969–2019* (Hong Kong: Hong Kong University Press, 2019), 50.
[93] *China Mail*, July 1968 (date of report missing), HKRS 70–1–230–1.

denounced the GIS, 'whose dead hand also falls heavily on other communications media'.[94] FEER editor Derek Davies also wrote that it was not only news bulletins that were suspected of being subjected to political censorship but also RHK's public affairs programme. As evidence, he reported that a discussion on the problems of the minority peoples of Asian countries, including India and Burma, and their independence movements that had been scheduled to air on the programme had been dropped. Davies quoted the programme's producer as explaining that it had been dropped because the topic was 'too delicate politically'. Davies was very unhappy that political censorship was operating beyond the limit of 'anti-Communist propaganda' to restrain 'balanced and informed discussion of local and regional interests'.[95]

Although the media's critical commentaries and complaints should not be taken as reflecting proven facts, it is truthful to say that the GIS was widely perceived by the media community of 1960s Hong Kong as an autocratic censorship machine that deprived citizens of free speech and a free press, values that the media community of the day were keen to speak up for, as 1965 commentary in the SCMP demonstrates:

In the past years, empire-building bureaucrats in the Information Services [Department] have turned the official propaganda machine into an autocratic censorship body that has been too inclined to treat the Colony's press, radio and television outlets as servants rather than masters. As it is presently conducted, the 'S' in GIS should stand for service to the press media and not to Government departments. Its rigid control of the flow of information – or the non-flow as is the case far too often – has all but snuffed out the life of such concepts as the press's freedom to inquire and it intrudes deeply into the public's right of free and proper access to information.[96]

Whilst journalists and outspoken citizens were criticising the government's policy of controlling the news content of broadcasters, many of them may have been unaware that the non-news entertainment programmes aired by radio stations, especially those featuring Chinese content, were also monitored by the police on a daily basis and subject to the control, censorship and manipulation of the colonial government to serve its political ends.

'Watching' Entertainment

In the late 1950s, the increase in the number of broadcast hours and programme genres of Hong Kong's radio stations rendered the workload of pre-censoring non-news radio programmes by the secretary for Chinese affairs' 'Chinese writer who [was] heavily employed on other duties' too overwhelming to handle. The shortage of manpower and difficulty in finding reliable expatriates

---

[94] *Far Eastern Economic Review*, 18 July 1968, HKRS 70–1–230–1.
[95] SCMP, 21 July 1968, HKRS 70–1–230–1. [96] SCMP, 3 January 1965.

with 'a high standard of Chinese' prompted the secretary for Chinese affairs to admit in 1957 that the pre-censorship of Chinese scripts for RHK and RDF was 'more a matter of form than of real censorship'.[97] Yet, a lack of resources to pre-censor radio programmes did not mean the loosening of government control over the broadcasters' output. The Hong Kong government strategised and stream-lined its control over RHK's output to ensure that it did not broadcast anything that had a political bias, and nor was RHK to allow any 'speakers to broadcast on innocuous subjects in such a way that political capital [could] be made', particu-larly those of a left-wing bent, because they were broadcasting on a 'government station'. There were two methods of control. First, the government exercised 'direct control of output, whereby a satisfactory and above all swift system [was] evolved for checking ideas, performers and materials, in such a way that there [would] not appear in fact to be any control'. Second, the government put in place 'a considered approach' to guard against 'political capital being made out of the context in which non-political material was broadcast'.[98]

A note from a meeting entitled 'Monitoring of Broadcasts' records a discussion held in February 1958 between Alastair Todd, acting defence secretary, and Donald Brooks, controller of broadcasting (who also headed up RHK), on how political control over the content of radio broadcasting could be effectively carried out despite limited resources, particularly once the new commercial broadcaster CR commenced operations in 1959. Both Todd and Brooks believed that it would not be technically difficult to cut off a programme if the officers responsible for political monitoring noticed undesirable content. Nonetheless, they agreed that the political monitoring of the broadcasts of numerous radio channels would not be possible owing to the lack of a 'sufficient number of Europeans capable of speaking Cantonese and Putonghua' such as the 'Jesuits of Wah Yan College', whom they considered possible candidates.[99] Neither man considered it desirable to employ Chinese people for the job 'because of either political alignment or reluctance to undertake what [would] in fact be a very grave responsibility'.[100] At the end of the meeting, they agreed that Special Branch officers should be responsible for the political monitoring of radio content to 'ensure [the] non-recurrence' of undesirable live radio announcements and that the 'announcer[s] concerned

---

[97] Agenda item for Finance Committees Meeting of 17 July 1957, HKRS 163-1-2035; minute by S. T. Kidd, Colonial Secretariat of Hong Kong, 8 July 1957, HKRS 163–1–2035; memo from J. C. McDouall, Secretary for Chinese Affairs, to Colonial Secretary, 11 October 1957.

[98] Hong Kong government's internal note marked as 'Top Secret' on aims, strategies and methods to control RHK's output, 19 June 1957, HKRS 952–1–1.

[99] Note of discussion between Acting Defence Secretary and Controller of Broadcasting, 15 February 1958, HKRS 952-1-1. Wah Yan College was a Catholic secondary school run by the Jesuit Society in Hong Kong from 1932.

[100] Note of discussion between Acting Defence Secretary and Controller of Broadcasting, 15 February 1958, HKRS 952–1–1.

could be removed fairly speedily from duty and not readmitted'.[101] It was not only announcers who were monitored; the Chinese programme staff of RHK had 'naturally been security-checked' despite the difficulty of ascertaining their true political aspirations through the vetting system.[102]

In addition to pre-censoring the scripts of radio dramas and operas and monitoring live announcements, the colonial government was also concerned about communist propaganda infiltrating into another major genre of content broadcast via radio, that is, Chinese folk music and songs. Gramophone records kept by and Chinese songs played by radio stations were subject to control and regulation by a high-level group headed by political advisor R. T. D. Ledward.[103] For instance, the controller of broadcasting was asked to work with the office of the secretary for Chinese affairs to transcribe and scrutinise the lyrics of politically questionable Chinese songs played during RHK programmes. Figure 4.3 shows the notes of correspondence on such political scrutiny among the senior programme assistant at RHK, the controller of broadcasting and the secretary for Chinese affairs. Two Chinese songs, namely, 小河淌水 (the flowing water of a river) and 百靈鳥,你這美妙的歌手 (the lark, such a wonderful singer), had been passed to the office of the latter. 小河淌水 was a folk song from Yunnan province describing how two lovers living in the mountainous area missed each other. 百靈鳥,你這美妙的歌手, a folk song from Xinjiang province, described the sweet song of a flying lark. Despite the lyrics of both songs being found not to have politically sensitive content, the secretary for Chinese affairs advised the controller of broadcasting not to include them in RHK programmes because they had 'only become well-known since being regularly plugged... by the C.P.G. [Chinese Central People's Government]'.[104] Figure 4.4 shows another note on censorship written by Samuel S. Chen, apparently a Chinese censor working for the secretary for Chinese affairs, who was reporting to the secretary about the gramophone records he had been asked to 'listen to and scrutinize'. Chen reported that eight folk songs featured on the records might have 'potential[ly] provocative and/or political substance'. One of them was the well-known patriotic song 滿江紅 (the whole river is red), which describes how the famous Song dynasty general Yue Fei 岳飛 had taken 'a vow to re-occupy the lost land intruded upon by the Huns'. The times are different now, Chen explained to the secretary, noting that although the song concerned historical events, it could be 'misinterpreted' by anyone unfamiliar with those events. These notes were subsequently passed on to the controller of broadcasting for action.[105] In

---

[101] *Ibid.*   [102] Hong Kong government's internal note marked as 'Top Secret', 19 June 1957.

[103] Letter from Ledward to Brooks, Controller of Broadcasting, 30 April 1958, HKRS 952–1–1.

[104] Note from J. C. McDouall, Secretary for Chinese Affairs, to Controller of Broadcasting, 17 May 1958, HKRS 952–1–1.

[105] Note (date missing, likely in 1958) from Samuel S. Chen to Secretary for Chinese Affairs marked with a message from Secretary for Chinese Affairs to Controller of Broadcasting, HKRS 952–1–1.

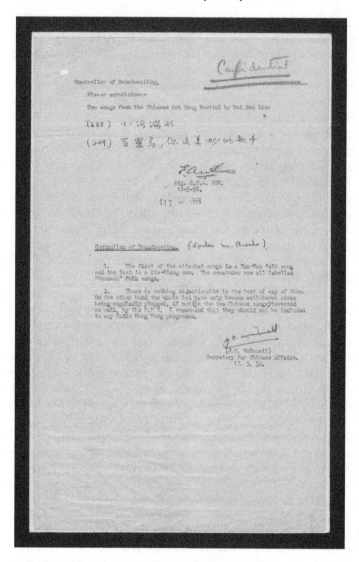

Figure 4.3 Notes of correspondence between the senior programme assistant at RHK, the controller of broadcasting and the secretary for Chinese affairs on political censorship of Chinese songs played by RHK. Source: HKRS 952–1–1, courtesy of Public Records Office, Government Records Service of Hong Kong.

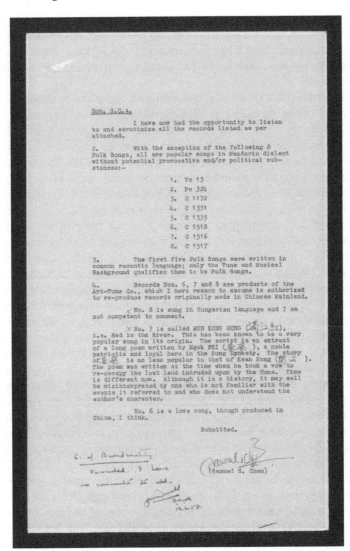

Figure 4.4 Note submitted by a Chinese censor to the secretary for Chinese affairs (and subsequently forwarded to the controller of broadcasting) reporting the result of political censorship of Chinese songs and gramophone records played by RHK. Source: HKRS 952–1–1, courtesy of Public Records Office, Government Records Service of Hong Kong.

another memo from the secretary for Chinese affairs to the controller of broadcasting, the former returned the scripts of two other songs and recommended their 'outright deletion' from RHK programmes.[106] All of these empirical examples usefully demonstrate how far the red lines on politics could be stretched by the government.

Furthermore, out of political concerns over the use of gramophone records produced in the mainland in RHK broadcasts, the political advisor of the Hong Kong government in 1958 discussed their regulation and censorship with the controller of broadcasting, the secretary for Chinese affairs and senior officials of the Colonial Secretariat. As of that year, RHK had purchased 556 gramophone records produced in mainland China, most of them containing either folk songs or operas in various Chinese dialects.[107] The folk songs that had been written to extol 'the improvement in living and working conditions since liberation' created particular anxiety for this group of senior officials. If RHK were to broadcast these songs, they argued, 'then by implication the British Government is giving positive support for the Chinese People's Republic'. It was thus suggested that their broadcasting be banned, although it was resolved that the controller of broadcasting would work closely with the secretary for Chinese affairs in screening mainland-produced folk songs, with 'discrimination' exercised where necessary. Such songs would not be banned completely, only those 'which had definitely unpleasant political overtones'. Non-folk recordings from the mainland could be used 'unless again there were any political implications'.[108] At the same time, the officials suggested that the broadcasting of classical operas not be entirely banned, as they were 'of a higher artistic standard than can be produced in Hong Kong'. Again, though, if their content was politically undesirable, it was a different story. To ensure the politically correct assessment of opera content, the censors of the secretary for Chinese affairs should not only censor opera scripts, as per usual practice, but should also listen to operas before they were broadcast.[109]

In practice, this censorship system was unable to prevent all suspicious content from being broadcast on RHK. It was particularly difficult for the controller of broadcasting to make a political assessment of apparently non-political interviews with film stars or singers known to be affiliated with left-wing organisations. Special Branch officers, who were responsible for monitoring such interviews, were to notify the controller when 'left-wing personalities' featured

---

[106] Memo from Secretary for Chinese Affairs to Controller of Broadcasting, 17 March 1958, HKRS 952–1–1.

[107] Purchase record of mainland made Chinese gramophone records, 7 February 1958, HKRS 952–1–1.

[108] Notes for the Meeting of the Ad Hoc Committee of Communist Activities, 7 May 1958; Minutes of the Meeting of the Ad Hoc Committee of Communist Activities, 7 May 1958, HKRS 952–1–1.

[109] Notes for the Meeting of the Ad Hoc Committee of Communist Activities, 7 May 1958,.

in Chinese broadcasts on RHK.[110] The controller also sometimes wrote to the government to seek instruction on whether he was allowed to broadcast the soundtracks of filmed opera performances by famous Chinese films stars such as Ma Tse-tsang and Hung Hsin-nu but produced and distributed by well-known left-wing film studios.[111]

In addition to preventing objectionable content, primarily communist propaganda, infiltrating into radio broadcasting, the Hong Kong government also used RHK to create positive propaganda to instil 'a feeling of belonging to Hong Kong' and 'a sense of pride in the Colony' and to promote British 'industrial achievements and links with the Colony'.[112] RHK was also useful in reassuring the Chinese population in Hong Kong that Britain was not 'losing interest' in the colony despite its unfriendly attitude towards the Hong Kong textile industry and the apparent disunity in diplomatic policies towards the PRC between the UK and the US. It was suggested that the station interview students from Hong Kong who were studying in Britain and present a feature on an exchange programme with Sarawak and North Borneo to emphasise 'the continuation of British interest in the Far East'. Further, to highlight how 'British industrial achievement' benefitted Hong Kong, a joint committee of senior government officials advised it to produce a piece about the new radar navigation systems at Kai Tak Airport because such a story 'would be useful as a peg on which to hang a talk describing the invention of radar' by Britain. All of this 'trumpet blowing', the joint committee suggested, 'had to be done carefully' so that the people of Hong Kong would be convinced that the UK was 'a first rate and not a fourth rate power'.[113]

RHK was also used as a vehicle for the soft publicity of government policies, with several popular programmes, including *Family Chit Chat* and *Family Diary* scripted to explain government measures. The Chinese scriptwriters of these programmes were 'supervised' to ensure that they knew what topics to avoid, as they were felt to lack a 'sense of politics'.[114] Another popular radio programme known as *Teahouse*, which took the form of a fictional, lively conversation between three to four regular customers in a teahouse, was used

---

[110] Note by Controller of Broadcasting on the call from Special Branch, 19 December 1958, HKRS 952–1–1.

[111] Memo from Controller of Broadcasting to Public Relations Officer, 12 June 1957, on whether to broadcast the soundtrack of a filmed opera entitled 搜書院 [Searching the study], which starred famous Chinese artists Ma Tse-Tsang and Hung Hsin-nu, HKRS 952–1–1. The film was produced by Union Film Enterprise and distributed by Southern Distributions, both entities are well-known left-wing movie studios/distributors. See Fu, 'More than Just Entertaining', for activities of these movies studios in Hong Kong during the Cold War era.

[112] Minutes of the Meeting of the Ad Hoc Committee of Communist Activities, 7 May 1958.

[113] Notes for the Meeting of the Ad Hoc Committee of Communist Activities, 7 May 1958.

[114] Note from Senior Program Assistant of RHK to Controller of Broadcasting on background checking of the script writers of 'Family Chit Chat' and 'Family Diary', 26 April 1958, HKRS 952–1–1.

as 'a defence programme'. The fabricated discussion was 'useful in putting the Government's points of view on subjects which have been unpopular, or which have been inflamed by the Left Wing'.[115]

Censoring Films and Live Performances

In addition to aural entertainment, visual entertainment such as films and live performances was also a target of political censorship by the colonial government. It has been amply demonstrated in recent research by Po-shek Fu and other scholars that Cold War geopolitics drove the Hong Kong government's strategies, particularly its anti-communist propaganda policies, and criteria in censoring and banning sensitive films from screening in Hong Kong cinemas.[116] This book will therefore not labour the details. Suffice it to say that the political censorship of films in Hong Kong had been operating since the early twentieth century and was formalised by the Film Censorship Regulations of 1953.

The broad yet ambiguous power of the political censorship of films under the Film Censorship Regulations continued to be wielded until the substantial amendment of those regulations in 1988, as Chapter 6 will show. Before the amendment, a film could be banned (or have scenes excised) if, in the opinion of the censor appointed by the governor, it would provoke racial hatred, hatred or contempt of the Hong Kong government, damage the colony's good relations with other territories or encourage public disorder, in addition to such usual grounds for censorship as sex, violence and moral decency.[117] The public was unaware of how these principles were applied and interpreted until 1973, when censorship guidelines were published.[118] Yet declassified documents reveal how the government applied the principles in practice. It censored films to as far as possible prevent Hong Kong from becoming a site of cultural and ideological Cold War tensions in Asia. It banned or cut films from the mainland that were 'of anti-Nationalist significance' or 'anti-foreign significance' or that 'eulogised' Mao Zedong. The government also censored films from Taiwan that called Chinese communists bandits or made any reference to the 'recovery of [the] Mainland'.[119] Not only were films from mainland China

---

[115] Notes for the Meeting of the Ad Hoc Committee of Communist Activities, 7 May 1958.

[116] For recently published works, see Fu, 'More Than Just Entertaining'; Lee Shuk-man, 冷戰光影: 地緣政治下的香港電影審查史 [Screens of the Cold War: History of film censorship in Hong Kong under geopolitics] (Taipei: Jifengdaiwenhua, 2018); and Ying Du, 'Censorship, Regulations, and the Cinematic Cold War in Hong Kong (1947–1971)', *China Review* 17.1 (2017): 117–51.

[117] *Film Censorship Standards: A Note of Guidance*, issued by Television and Films Division, Secretariat for Home Affairs of the Hong Kong Government, May 1973, HKRS 313-7-3.

[118] Lee Shuk-man, 冷戰光影, 197–8.

[119] Notes and comments on 'A statement of the general principles as adopted on 20 November 1965 by the Film Censorship Board of Review', by William Hung, Chief Film Censor, 1 December 1970, HKRS 508–3–3.

and Taiwan censored, but so too were anti-communist films produced in the US.[120] This practice reflected Hong Kong's Cold War policy of combatting the spread of communist propaganda in Asia according to the UK–US consensus while not provoking Beijing in order to safeguard Hong Kong's security. The following examples of censorship demonstrate the Cold War geopolitical considerations that underpinned film censors' decisions in the 1950s and 1960s.

In 1965, the censors banned the screening of a film called *Waves on the Southern Shores*, which revolves around a family of boat people living in Nan Wan, a fishing village in South China. In a flashback, a female character relates the bitter experience of an old man who was victimised by a villainous owner of farms and fishing boats named Kao, a protégé of KMT army officers, and tells the ill-fated story of a boat girl who was forced to serve as the chambermaid of Kao's daughter-in-law, who was from Hong Kong, as a means of liquidating her father's debt. While being pursued by armed officers of the local KMT government sent at Kao's request, the girl jumps into the sea. The film further portrays the cruelties of Japanese military officers and features the mistreatment and murder of women and children. It was banned in Hong Kong because the film censor considered it to be 'ridiculing the KMT administration, glorifying the underground Communist elements ... and showing Japanese atrocities during their military occupation'. Censorship was also warranted because 'Communists [were] referred to throughout the film as invulnerables [and] good shooters' who kept everyone 'in awe'.[121]

Censorship policies in Hong Kong during the post-war era reflect the British Empire's anxiety about not only the growing popularity of the CCP amongst the Chinese population in Hong Kong, but also geopolitical collaboration with powers friendly to Britain, including the US. In a letter the ISD sent to the Southern Film Corporation, a major Hong Kong-based film studio, concerning the panel of censors' decision about a documentary called *Peking Scientific Symposium*, the film studio was asked to 'agree to the excision from the speeches and the commentaries of words and sentences about colonialism, imperialism and American imperialism as well as the excision of pictures, speeches and commentaries referring to the war in Vietnam'. Otherwise, the ISD official warned, the film would be banned from exhibition.[122]

Archival evidence also shows that the US government exerted diplomatic pressure on London to tighten its censorship measures against any Hong Kong media thought to be sponsored or used by Chinese communists. A telegram from

---

[120] See censorship of US films in Du, 'Censorship, Regulations, and the Cinematic Cold War'.

[121] 'Films: Waves on the Southern Shores', memo from R. S. Barry, for Secretary, Panel of Censors, to Board of Review (Hon. S. C. A., Hon. D. of E, Commissioner of Police, S. of S. W.), 6 March 1965, in HKRS 394-26-14.

[122] 'Peking Scientific Symposium', letter from R. S. Barry of ISD and as the Secretary to the Panel of Film Censors, to Southern Film Corporation, 18 May 1965, HKRS 394–26–14.

the British Foreign Office to the Colonial Office dated 5 February 1958 reveals such pressure. The Foreign Office referred to its recent discussion in Washington on Anglo-American cooperation in information work abroad and asked the Colonial Office, on behalf of the US, whether it would not be possible for the Hong Kong Government to take some action to impede the production in Hong Kong of Chinese Communist films, books and periodicals.[123]

Table 4.1 lists films that were banned for political reasons from the 1970s until the regulations were relaxed in the late 1980s.

It was not only motion pictures that were policed and politically censored; the long arm of government censorship in colonial Hong Kong also extended to theatrical performances. Both the Hong Kong government and the Colonial Office in London closely monitored the frequency of visits by theatrical and musical performance troupes from China and subjected the content of their

Table 4.1 *Films banned for political reasons from the 1970s to the late 1980s and the reasons cited for the ban*

Title of films (origin of production and year of censorship)	Reasons for banning for 'political overtone'
Battle of Algiers (Italy, 1970, 75)	The film depicts how the Algerian National Liberal Front struggled against the French for independence and 'the ruthless French reprisals'.
Savage Action and Strick Punishment (North Vietnam, 1975)	'It portrays [the] US and President Nixon in the worst possible light.'
The Sand Pebbles (USA, 1967, 74, 75)	The film describes how students in China demanded the treaty powers to leave China and killed an American sailor who had tried to rescue American missionaries.
The Boxer Rebellion (Taiwan, 1975)	The film depicted how Chinese patriotic youths went to stop 'ruthless treatment given by the allied troops, but were killed'.
Great Victory of Highway 9 (North Vietnam, 1975)	The film shows 'an American defeat' and 'laid the blame of the Vietnamese war squarely onto the Americans'.
Mao by Mao (France, 1977)	It is a short documentary on the life of Mao Ze-dong and 'featured many personalities in China who were unacceptable to the Communist Party at the time'.
The Fisher Boy (China, 1977)	This cartoon made in 1959 carried messages 'that the Communist Party has successfully got rid of the foreign powers'.
The Battle of Ku Ning Tou (Taiwan, 1981)	The film depicts Chinese communists being beaten back by Taiwan in its attack on the Island of Kinman.

[123] Telegram from P. G. F. Dalton, Foreign Office, to W. I. J. Wallace, Colonial Office, 5 February 1958, CO 1030/582.

Table 4.1 (*cont.*)

Title of films (origin of production and year of censorship)	Reasons for banning for 'political overtone'
If I Were for Real (Taiwan, 1981, 85)	It could be 'seen as anti-mainland propaganda'.[124]
The Coldest Winter in Peking (Taiwan, 1981)	It portrays 'the existence after 1976 of an underground movement' in mainland China.[125]
The Anger (Taiwan, 1983)	The film featured 'lifestyles of corrupt [CCP] bureaucrats and caders' during the Cultural Revolution.
Twilight in Geneva (Taiwan, 1986)	The film criticised 'the Chinese Government, its policies, the lack of human rights, favoritism, and feud between rightists and Leftists among Party members'.

Source: Letter from J. Michie for Secretary for Administrative Services and Information of Hong Kong Government to C. E. Leeks of FCO, 28 April, 1987, FCO 40/2338; letter from Governor Wilson to FCO, 30 January 1989, 26 May, 1989, FCO 40/2823.

performances to censorship before they were permitted to enter Hong Kong. Also, under the Places of Public Entertainment Ordinance, the scripts of all plays and lyrics of all songs had to be sent to government authorities, including but not limited to the Secretariat for Chinese Affairs and Police Special Branch, for censorship before a public performance permit could be granted. As a result, politically undesirable titles were filtered out from the stage.[126] In a telegram sent to the Colonial Office in 1962, Hong Kong government officials summarised their monitoring of performance troupes from China since 1956. The various troupes mentioned, which performed in a variety of genres, came from provinces across China. They included the Chinese Folk Artists Group, Swatow Opera Group, Shanghai Shaoshing Opera Group, Shanghai Youth Opera Group, Shanghai Vocalist Troupe and Kwantung (North-Eastern China) Acrobatic Group. The Hong Kong government was of the view that it was not

---

[124] 'If I Were for Real' was banned five times since 1981. It was approved for showing in May 1989, after the passing of a new Film Censorship Ordinance in 1988 (which will be discussed in Chapter 6), as explained in a letter from Governor Wilson to the FCO, 30 January 1989, FCO 40/2823.

[125] The film was approved for showing in May 1989 after the passing of a new Film Censorship Ordinance and partly because of the 'low-key Chinese response' to the showing of 'If I Were for Real', as explained in a letter from Governor Wilson to the FCO, 26 May 1989, FCO 40/2823.

[126] For the law under the Places of Public Entertainment Ordinance (Cap. 172) on theatrical censorship, see Johannes Chan, 'Freedom of Expression: Censorship and Obscenity', in *Civil Liberties in Hong Kong*, ed. Raymond Wacks (Hong Kong: Oxford University Press, 1988), 208–9; for archival evidence of censorship of theatrical performances in practice during the 1950s and 1960s, see Cheung Chui-yu, '香港政府治理戲劇的策略, 1945–1997' [Hong Kong government's strategies in governing theatres' (MPhil diss., Chinese University of Hong Kong, 2013), chapter 2.

desirable to prevent 'these Communist ventures in the entertainment field altogether'. Yet 'it is not in [the government's] interests that they should be too frequent and successful or that the Communists should secure a monopoly of popular culture'. It also worried that 'if such performances became too regular a feature in Hong Kong they might become a target for right-wing [KMT-backed] demonstrations'. Therefore, the Hong Kong government had set internal limits on the number of visits per year by such groups and requested that they follow 'the various conditions laid down by the Commissioner of Police regarding the approval of scripts [and] avoidance of propaganda'.[127]

Such a fine balancing act of controlling and censoring the cultural activities of leftist groups without banning them entirely did not always satisfy Britain's Cold War partners, most notably the US, however, as shown by a telegram from the British Embassy in Washington to the Foreign Office in 1958. In the telegram, P. L. Carter of the British Embassy requested that the Foreign Office 'consider the feelings of the Americans in putting their efforts against Communist opposition on the truly formidable scale'. He suggested that the media activities of communists be further curtailed by manipulating such municipal regulations as those pertaining to sanitation and fire precautions if overt political suppression was undesirable from Hong Kong's point of view.[128] The balancing act also did not prevent Hong Kong from becoming a useful hub of political propaganda by the CCP, KMT and the US, as well as an important market for the trading of political intelligence amongst the Cold War powers.[129] Behaving largely within the confines of political censorship, left-wing trade and labour unions, media groups, and schools continued to grow in scale and membership in the 1960s, and their potential influence on the masses was painfully felt by the colonial government in a violent show-down in 1967.

The 1967 Riots and Hard Strike on the Left-Wing Press

In May 1967, serious disturbances again broke out in Hong Kong, this time driven not by Nationalist supporters but by local communists who had infiltrated trade and labour unions, schools, and cultural and media organisations during the 1950s and 1960s. The resulting territory-wide anti-imperialist riots, which lasted for seven months and caused 51 deaths, 848 injuries and nearly

---

[127] Telegram from E. G. Willan, Colonial Secretariat, to J. D. Higham of Colonial Office, 17 October 1962, CO 1030/1108.

[128] Top Secret telegram from P. L. Carter, British Embassy in Washington, to Donald Hopson, Foreign Office, 27 May 1958, CO 1030/583.

[129] The colonial government did monitor the 'activities of intelligence peddlers in Hong Kong' who, for example, sold intelligence regarding CCP to the US; see CO 968/226 for details of these activities. See also Lu, 'The American Cold War in Hong Kong', 117–40.

4500 arrests,[130] began with an industrial dispute at an artificial flower factory in Kowloon in early May 1967.[131] The riots were led by the self-proclaimed Leftist All Circles Anti-Persecution Struggle Committee, apparently with the support of state organs in Beijing, where the Cultural Revolution was falling into the hands of radicals.[132] The large-scale anti-colonial campaign led to demonstrations, strikes, food supply stoppages, violent confrontations between the police and protesters, and the explosion of bombs.[133] Governor David Trench, who had succeeded Black in 1964, responded, with London's support, by swiftly deploying coercive measures to 'strike hard' at the leftists, despite the usual concerns and warnings of the Foreign Office that Beijing might retaliate against provocative actions in Hong Kong.[134] In addition to the replacement of Commissioner of Police Edward Tyrene on 12 July 1967 because he was thought to have shown 'reluctance to commit his forces to firm action' and 'anxiety about the use of excessive force'[135] and reinforcing the British military force in Hong Kong, numerous emergency regulations were brought into effect from 23 May 1967 onwards to cope with the civil unrest. The colonial government was granted wide powers to promulgate provisions on detention and offences relating to sabotage and the possession of offensive weapons and inflammatory publications. Freedoms had no place when state security was considered to be at stake. Although neither Trench nor his colleagues in London believed that Beijing would move to recover Hong Kong immediately, London made plans for an evacuation from Hong Kong in the event of an emergency.[136]

---

[130] Serial no. 115, June 1968, FCO 40/53, cited in Ray Yep, '"Cultural Revolution in Hong Kong": Emergency Powers, Administration of Justice and the Turbulent Year of 1967', *Modern Asian Studies* 46.4 (2012): 1010.

[131] For detailed accounts of the riots, see Gary Ka-wai Cheung, 六七暴動：香港戰後歷史的分水嶺/*Hong Kong's Watershed: The 1967 Riots* (Hong Kong: Hong Kong University Press, 2012); Mark, *The Everyday Cold War*, chapter 4; for a recollection of events by a local leftist and former deputy general manager of *Wen Wei Po*, see Zhou, 香港左派鬥爭史, chapters 20–7.

[132] It was believed that radicals led by Jiang Qing took over from Premier Zhou En-lai the power to direct the Cultural Revolution from January 1967, see G. K. Cheung, 六七暴動, 33–4. One major turning point in escalating leftist riots in Hong Kong was the statement issued by the MFA on 15 May 1967 and successive and supportive editorials of *People's Daily* from 3 June to 5 July 1967; see Ray Yep, 'The 1967 Riots in Hong Kong: The Domestic and Diplomatic Fronts of the Governor' in *May Days in Hong Kong: Riot and Emergency in 1967*, ed. Robert Bickers and Ray Yep (Hong Kong: Hong Kong University Press, 2009), 22–3, and G. K. Cheung, 六七暴動, 55 and chapter 4; Carroll, *A Concise History*, 153–6.

[133] Yep, 'The 1967 Riots in Hong Kong', 22–3.

[134] Ray Yep and Robert Bickers, 'Studying the 1967 Riots: An Overdue Project', in *May Days in Hong Kong: Riot and Emergency in 1967*, ed. Robert Bickers and Ray Yep (Hong Kong: Hong Kong University Press, 2009), 9. For concerns about provoking Beijing and conflicting views between Trench and the Foreign Office, see Mark, 'Everyday Propaganda', 163, and G. K. Cheung, 六七暴動, chapters 7–8.

[135] Top Secret telegram from Hong Kong (O.A.G.) to the Commonwealth Office, No. 1046, 16 July 1967, FCO 40/112, cited in Yep, 'Cultural Revolution in Hong Kong', 1010.

[136] Commonwealth Office, 'Feasibility Study on Evacuation of Hong Kong', 6 September 1967, FCO 40/92, used in G. K. Cheung, 六七暴動, 141–2, footnote 8.

Police powers to raid, arrest and detain were expanded, thereby enabling the police to carry out large-scale arrests of activists.[137] One of largest raids was of a building in North Point on Hong Kong Island. It involved more than 1,000 policemen and soldiers, who were supported by three helicopters from HMS *Hermes*.[138] To facilitate the extended interrogation of those arrested, the governor/colonial secretary was empowered to detain any persons, whether aliens or British subjects, for any period up to one year without trial and for any reason.[139] Many of the leftist detainees were kept at the Victoria Road Detention Centre at Mount Davis in the south-western district of Hong Kong Island (now used as the University of Chicago's Hong Kong campus), which was operated by Special Branch. To avoid organised protests during court hearings, judges were also empowered to exclude members of the public from court.[140] The district court's sentencing limitation was increased from five to ten years of imprisonment.[141]

In addition to mobilising left-wing schools and trade unions, the Anti-Persecution Struggle Committee, together with the NCNA, directed leftist newspapers in Hong Kong, which were selling more than 350,000 papers per day, to engage in propaganda warfare to support the anti-imperialist struggle.[142] The papers published 'patriotic' editorials and reports featuring such sensationalist headlines as 'Dying British-Hong Kong imperialism uses Chinese against Chinese',[143] 'The white-skinned pigs are furious',[144] 'Young students pioneer the anti-British movement',[145] 'Using violence against violence to punish white-skinned pigs and defeat the [yellow-skinned] dogs',[146] 'Chinese policemen said they would battle against the violence of British Hong Kong'[147] and '[Chinese policemen should] disobey orders, let the cat out of the bag [and] refrain from beating up or arresting people'.[148] Needless to say, all of these pieces were regarded by the colonial government as highly inflammatory, provocative and libellous, and thus as warranting suppression.[149] The political censorship laws used to prosecute *Ta Kung Pao* in 1952 were once again used against leftist

---

[137] Emergency (Prevention of Inflammatory Speeches) Regulations (L.N. 80 of 1967), reg. 3.
[138] Carroll, *A Concise History*, 155; Zhou, 香港左派鬥爭史, 278.
[139] Emergency (Principal) Regulations (Commencement) (No. 3) Order (L.N. 118 of 1967); Emergency (Committee of Review) Rules (L.N. 119 of 1967).
[140] Emergency (Courts) Regulations (L.N. 79 of 1967), regs. 3 and 4.
[141] Emergency (Principal) (Amendment) (No. 2) Regulations (L.N. 120 of 1967), reg. 4.
[142] For the role of the NCNA, see Mark, 'Everyday Propaganda', 162; circulation figures of nine leftist newspapers are reported in 'Chinese Communist Press Machine in Hong Kong: Its Scope and Its Impact', prepared by Special Branch, 21 November 1968, FCO 40/222.
[143] *Tin Fung Daily*, 1 July 1967, reported by WKYP, 24 August 1967.
[144] *Hong Kong Evening News*, 4 August 1967, reported by WKYP, 25 August 1967.
[145] *Tin Fung Daily*, 7 July 1967, reported by WKYP, 24 August 1967.
[146] *Tin Fung Daily*, 31 July 1967, reported by WKYP, 25 August 1967.
[147] *Afternoon News*, 6 August 1967, reported by WKYP, 25 August 1967.
[148] SCMP, 11 August 1967.   [149] Mark, 'Everyday Propaganda', 162.

newspapers. Extensive communication between the colonial government in Hong Kong and the Commonwealth Office in London culminated in a decision that it was hoped would strike a balance between teaching the local leftist press a serious lesson and minimising the risk of Beijing being provoked into retaliating on the diplomatic front. It was decided that prosecution should target not the leaders of the three mainstream left-wing newspapers, *Ta Kung Pao*, *Wen Wei Po* and *New Evening Post*, but those of three fringe papers: *Tin Fung Daily*, *Afternoon News* and *Hong Kong Evening News*.[150] On 9 August 1967, five senior executives responsible for publishing and printing these three papers were arrested and charged with ninety-nine criminal offences, including publishing seditious material in contravention of the Sedition Ordinance, publishing 'fake news which is likely to alarm public opinion or disturb public order' in contravention of the CPCO, and inciting disaffection amongst members of the police force in contravention of the Incitement to Disaffection Ordinance, based on twenty-one articles.[151] Using the power to suspend the press afforded by the CPCO, the government also successfully obtained a court order on 17 August to have the three papers suspended pending the outcome of the trial hearing.[152] The suspension order was followed by the raid of the papers' offices by a police team armed with shotguns (Figure 4.5). Over thirty staff members were arrested in the raid.[153] The accused publishers and printers of the three papers, similarly to those accused in the *Ta Kung Po* case in 1952, used the trial hearing to protest from the dock against 'political persecution' by the British authorities and the deprivation of press freedom. The trial judge, Magistrate E. Light, responded by reiterating that 'freedom of the press is limited'. If it were not, he added, then the result would be 'terrorism' and 'no freedom at all'.[154] After a four-day trial, the five leaders of the newspapers were sentenced to three years' imprisonment, and the three newspapers were ordered to shut down for six months.[155]

---

[150] Communication between Hong Kong and London on the choice of papers for prosecution; see G. K. Cheung, 六七暴動, 155–7; Mark, 'Everyday Propaganda', 163–4.

[151] 'Prosecution of the *Afternoon News*, *Hong Kong Evening News* and *Tin Fung Yat Pao*', memo from D. R. Harris, Commissioner of Police, to Director of Information Services, 2 September 1967, memo prepared by Senior Information Officer (press enquiries), 19 December 1967, HKRS 70–1–313B; SCMP, 11 and 25 August 1967; Klein, 'The Empire Strikes Back', 51; Mark, 'Everyday Propaganda', 163–4; G. K. Cheung, 六七暴動, 157; Yep and Bickers, 'Studying the 1967 Riots', 9.

[152] Memo from D. R. Harris, Commissioner of Police, to Director of Information Services, 2 September 1967, HKRS 70–1–313B; *Kung Sheung Daily*, 18 August 1967.

[153] *Kung Sheung Evening News*, 19 August 1967; Mark, 'Everyday Propaganda', 164; G. K. Cheung, 六七暴動, 157.

[154] *Hong Kong Star*, 3 September 1967, HKRS 70–1–313B.

[155] For verdict and sentencing, see SCMP, 30 August, 5 and 8 September 1967. A weekly magazine 'Youth's Garden Weekly' and its supplement, the 'New Youth', were also suspended in November. Their publisher, proprietor and editor, Chan Tsui-tsun, was prosecuted for publishing a seditious publication and for publishing a publication containing writing

Figure 4.5 Raid of three newspapers' offices by a police team armed with shotguns. Source: *Kung Sheung Evening News*, 19 August 1967, courtesy of Robert H.N. Ho Family Foundation.

According to government archival records, twenty-two employees of the left-wing press, including reporters and editors of *Ta Kung Pao*, *Wen Wei Po*, *Hong Kong Commercial Daily* and the NCNA, were also arrested and charged, and some of them were convicted and jailed for between three and five years for a wide range of offences, including taking part in an intimidating assembly, uttering inflammatory speech and assaulting a police officer during the seven months of disturbances.[156] One reporter was sentenced to two years' imprisonment for passing a note to one of the convicted printers during the aforementioned trial hearings. The note, according to the convicted reporter, was

calculated or tending to persuade or induce persons to commit an offence, per memo prepared by Senior Information Officer (press enquiries), 19 December 1967, HKRS 70-1-313B.

[156] 'Jailed Communist Newspapers Employees in 1967 Civil Disturbances', 24 November 1968, and memo prepared by Senior Information Officer (press enquiries), 19 December 1967, HKRS 70-1-313B. Some of these arrests and trials were reported in SCMP, 11 June and 8, 14 and 15 September 1967; for a leftist's recollection, also see Zhou, 香港左派鬥爭史, 276-8.

a reminder to the person in the dock to protest loudly against his illegal conviction.[157] In sentencing some of the convicted reporters, District Court Judge R. O'Conner said that they had manufactured news for their employers, that they did not have 'the stuff of martyrs and heroes' and were 'a disgrace to their profession'.[158]

These actions against the left-wing press and journalists, perhaps to the surprise of London, met strong retaliatory actions from Beijing. After Xue Ping, an NCNA editor and reporter, was sentenced to two years' imprisonment for taking part in an unlawful assembly that Xue claimed to have been covering with his colleagues, Beijing placed Anthony Grey, a British correspondent of Reuters in China, under house arrest.[159] Grey was not released until October 1969 after Wong Chak, the last journalist of the left-wing press jailed during the riots, had been released.[160] Even worse, on 22 August, following the arrest of executives from the three aforementioned left-wing newspapers, as well as the forced suspension of these papers and the raid of their offices, a crowd of more than 10,000 radical Red Guards in Beijing protested outside the office of the British chargé d'affaires before breaking in and setting it on fire. Twenty-three Britons, including diplomats and their family members, were beaten up, some struck on the head with bamboo poles, forced to their knees and photographed in humiliating postures. Amongst them was Percy Cradock, the then political counsellor who later became one of the most important advisors to Prime Minister Margaret Thatcher during the Sino-British negotiations over Hong Kong's handover. In four hours of appalling rampage, the British office was ransacked and burnt to the ground, although fortunately all of the Britons inside were rescued by Chinese soldiers and plain-clothes policemen without serious injury.[161]

Citizens Jailed for Inflammatory Speeches

Returning to Hong Kong, freedom of speech for both the press and citizens was placed under strict control, with the Emergency (Prevention of Inflammatory Speeches) Regulations prohibiting the distribution of anti-government materials and allowing anyone who uttered inflammatory speech to be sentenced to prison for up to ten years.[162] Inflammatory speech was extremely broadly defined to mean any speech, address, slogan or words that contained

---

[157] SCMP, 6 September 1967.   [158] SCMP, 14 September 1967.

[159] SCMP, 20 July 1967; Mark, 'Everyday Propaganda', 118–19.

[160] The governor of Hong Kong reduced the sentence of certain prisoners (including journalists of the left-wing press) jailed during the 1967 riots to enable their early release; see GIS's press release, 9 May 1969, HKRS 70-1-313B; for the release of Grey, see Mark, *The Everyday Cold War*, 143–8; also Carroll, *A Concise History*, 156.

[161] Mark, *The Everyday Cold War*, 118–24; Carroll, *A Concise History*, 156.

[162] Emergency (Prevention of Inflammatory Speeches) Regulations (L.N. 80 of 1967), reg. 5.

'inflammatory matter' and might incite violence, encourage disobedience of the law, lead to a breach of the peace, promote feelings of ill will and hostility between different races in Hong Kong, or cause disaffection towards the police force or government. A week after the regulations' passage, to extend the prohibition to the non-verbal dissemination of undesirable ideas, the governor formulated another set of regulations known as the Emergency (Prevention of Inflammatory Posters) Regulations. They punished anyone who posted a poster or photograph containing 'inflammatory matter' with up to two years of imprisonment.[163] Furthermore, the police were authorised to break into any premises they believed to have been used to utter inflammatory speech.[164] Many teenagers were jailed for possessing communist or anti-colonial leaflets as a result of these anti-free speech regulations. For example, Tsang Tak-shing, an eighteen-year-old secondary school student who became the secretary for home affairs of the Hong Kong Special Administrative Region (SAR) in 2007, was arrested for placing posters condemning the colonial government as 'fascists' in classrooms at St Paul's College where he studied and sentenced to two years' imprisonment on 9 October 1967, as reported in the SCMP.[165] A seventeen-year-old printing worker was arrested for possessing 120 inflammatory posters and jailed for two years and eight months.[166] One student was jailed for six months for putting up an inflammatory poster on the wall of his middle school, and another was prosecuted after a piece of paper on which inflammatory words had been written was found in his drawer.[167] Two fifteen-year-old boys were charged with possessing and putting up inflammatory posters in a staircase in a resettlement area.[168] Some of these teenagers were even deported after their convictions. According to Rey Yap's research, offences relating to inflammatory materials or speech accounted for 11 per cent of the 121 persons convicted during the riots and recommended for deportation under the Deportation of Aliens Ordinance. The average age of these 'speech' offenders was just twenty-five.[169]

Left-wing schools, or communist-controlled schools as the colonial government called them, were also engineered to disseminate ideas on patriotism, anti-imperialism, and anti-colonialism and to take students and teachers to the streets. Students were seen parading in the streets, waving red books and flags and chanting slogans and putting up posters.[170] Director of Education W. D. Gregg warned in a radio interview that he would close any schools that

[163] Emergency (Prevention of Inflammatory Posters) Regulations (L.N. 83 of 1967), reg. 4.
[164] Emergency (Prevention of Inflammatory Speeches) Regulations (L.N. 80 of 1967), reg. 3.
[165] Yep, 'Cultural Revolution in Hong Kong', 1015; SCMP, 10 October 1967; WKYP, 10 October 1967.
[166] SCMP, 12 September 1967.
[167] Klein, 'The Empire Strikes Back', 50; 'Around Hongkong', SCMP, 12 November 1967.
[168] SCMP, 8 December 1967.   [169] Yep, 'Cultural Revolution in Hong Kong', 1022.
[170] SCMP, 12 July 1967.

engaged in 'activities that were considered to be subversive'.[171] Nine leftist schools subsequently received warning letters from the Education Department laying down thirteen conditions with which they were to comply. Failing such compliance, the schools would be closed. These conditions included prohibition of the manufacture, display and dissemination of inflammatory materials.[172] They led to a student demonstration involving over 1,000 young people, who were dispersed by the police using tear gas.[173] A large number of teachers and students, as well as headmasters, were also arrested during protests, police raids of their schools or simply after being found in possession of inflammatory posters.[174] Students found to have taken part in anti-government activities were also dismissed by government and government-subsidised schools.[175] The leading leftist school Heung to Middle School was raided by the police near midnight on 24 July with the assistance of a company of Gurkha Rifles. The school was forced open and searched. The police, who discovered a blackboard on which was written 'Lay down your weapons and return home', took 'one of the biggest haul of inflammatory posters' (as shown in Figure 4.6) found so far, leading them to believe that the 'school was being used as a distribution centre for this material'.[176] Some leftist schools were believed to be organising violent resistance and manufacturing bombs for use against the police in anti-government demonstrations. Chung Wah Middle School was closed and subsequently deregistered by the government using the power of the Education Ordinance after an explosion inside the school led to the serious injury of an eighteen-year old student. The police believed that the explosion had occurred during the manufacture of a bomb, whilst leftists insisted that it had occurred during a school laboratory experiment.[177] Following the explosion, four leftist schools were raided and more than 100 teachers and students were taken to the police station, where sixteen of them were charged with obstructing the police and uttering inflammatory speech.[178]

Freedom of entry and mobility was also curtailed. The Emergency (Prevention of Intimidation) Regulations made the assembly of three or more persons unlawful if any person in the said assembly did or said anything likely to alarm or intimidate another person, with those in breach liable to a maximum of five years' imprisonment.[179] The Emergency (Closed Areas) Regulations

---

[171]   SCMP, 7 July 1967; Klein, 'The Empire Strikes Back, 46.
[172]   *Ta Kung Pao*, 19 August 1967; SCMP, 19 August 1967.   [173]   SCMP, 27 August 1967.
[174]   For some of the many newspaper reports on arresting and charging young people for possessing inflammatory posters during the seven months of disturbances, see SCMP, 9 September, 12 and 30 November, 8 December 1967. Sixteen teachers and a schoolmaster were arrested and charged for taking part in an intimidating assembly during a demonstration held outside Government House on 15 July; SCMP, 21 July 1967.
[175]   *Ta Kung Pao*, 19 August 1967.   [176]   SCMP, 25 July 1967.
[177]   SCMP, 30 November 1967; Zhou, 香港左派鬥爭, 304.   [178]   SCMP, 29 November 1967.
[179]   Emergency (Prevention of Intimidation) Regulations (L.N. 98 of 1967), reg. 4.

Figure 4.6 Cartons of 'inflammatory posters' removed by plain-clothes policemen during the raid of Heung to Middle School, a well-known leftist school in Hong Kong. Source: SCMP, 25 July 1967.

made one's presence in any area declared a 'closed area' by the governor, such as communist labour union buildings, unlawful and liable to three years of imprisonment.[180] Many of the protesters, including students and journalists, were prosecuted under these regulations for taking part in an 'intimidating assembly'. Similar to many of the emergency regulations promulgated from the 1920s to the 1950s, the emergency powers used to tackle the 1967 riots remained on the statute books long after the riots had lost steam in late 1967, although some of the Emergency (Principal) Regulations were gradually discontinued by orders in council from 1968 to 1970. Nevertheless, they could be

---

[180] Emergency (Closed Areas) Regulations (L.N. 99 of 1967); Emergency (Closed Areas) (North Point Power Station) Order (L.N. 100 of 1967); Emergency (Closed Areas) (Hok Yuen Power Station) Order (L.N. 101 of 1967); Emergency (Closed Areas) (Hong Kong Tramways Limited Depot, Workshops and Welfare Centre) Order (L.N. 107 of 1967).

reinstated at any time if deemed necessary by the governor in council. A small number were repealed, whilst others were incorporated into permanent legislation such as the Public Order Ordinance, which remained a source of controversy and criticism for the remainder of the colonial era.[181]

'Distillation' of the News

Not only were newspapers and their journalists prosecuted under censorship laws during the 1967 riots, but news broadcasts on the riots were also carefully censored. During this period, a 'special publicity unit' was established within the GIS, which worked with the police and RHK to wage a propaganda campaign designed to win the hearts and minds of Hong Kong citizens.[182] The GIS also withheld from broadcasting news about police raids and searches and bomb reports from communist newspapers because it believed that such information was being misused by the communist press for 'violent propaganda purposes'.[183]. The task was a 'clear-cut one – to expose the disruptive and violent efforts of the communists, to support the police and to rally public opinion'.[184] RHK's Chinese channel aired a special daily programme called *Indisputable Facts* to 'ridicule, expose and counter communist tactics, action and propaganda'.[185] The scripts of the programme were written by the GIS and RHK, and 'an authoritative tone' was used to read them. Director of Broadcasting Donald Brooks, in a 1969 *China Mail* interview, did not shy away from admitting that 'it was embarrassing, highly embarrassing' during the 1967 riots when newscasts relayed from the BBC, the news agency most trusted by the Hong Kong government, were giving a very different picture of the situation from that presented by RHK, whose news bulletins were 'prepared' by a unit of eight subeditors under the GIS. Brooks defended this practice of 'editorial discretion' by arguing that it constituted a 'distillation' of the news.[186] The *China Mail* was sceptical: 'The word 'censorship' is a word

---

[181] For example, Public Order Ordinance (No. 64 of 1967). For regulations repealed, see Emergency Regulations (Repeal) Order (L.N. 39 of 1970); Emergency Regulations (Repeal) (No. 2) Order (L.N. 56 of 1970); Emergency (Principal) Regulations (Discontinuance) Order (L.N. 42 of 1970); Emergency (Principal) Regulations (Discontinuance) (No. 2) Order (L. N. 52 of 1970).

[182] Annual Departmental Report by the Director of Information Services for the financial year 1967–8, para. 12; Yep and Bickers, 'Studying the 1967 Riots', 11; Ching Cheong, 香港六七暴動始末：解讀吳荻舟 [1967 riots in Hong Kong: Reading from Wu Di-zhou] (Hong Kong: Oxford University Press, 2018), 199–208.

[183] Memo entitled 'Teleprinter Service to Newspaper' prepared by N. J. V. Watt, Director of Information Services, 19 December 1967, FCO 40/115.

[184] Annual Departmental Report by the Director of Information Services for the financial year 1967–8, para. 15.

[185] *Ibid.*, para. 28; Chen Yun, 一起廣播的日子：香港電台八十年 [Broadcasting together: The 80th anniversary of RTHK] (Hong Kong: Ming Pao, 2009), 108.

[186] *China Mail*, 24 May 1969, HKRS 70–1–230–1.

Mr. Brooks would like to see censored as far as Radio Hongkong is concerned.'[187] Brooks, in response, further justified such editorial discretion:

A newspaper editor doesn't print everything he receives – he has his own reasons for publishing things or otherwise and not necessarily because any pressure is put on him. The same applies to radio. I think it unfortunate that the press refers to control of radio as censorship.[188]

Interestingly, when asked by the *China Mail* reporter if he had ever been asked not to run a programme, Brooks said 'no', claiming that the government did not exert pressure on him, 'it merely expresse[d] its likes and dislikes'.[189]

Although it is difficult to locate declassified files that document how such likes and dislikes, and so-called editorial discretion, influenced and censored the programme content of broadcasters in colonial Hong Kong, particularly with respect to reporting news and current affairs, one point is clear: the government maintained control on a day-to-day basis over the news content of all three radio stations (RHK, CR and RDF), the one wired television station (Rediffusion TV) and the newly licensed wireless television broadcaster (TVB) until the early 1970s by supplying them with news bulletin scripts.[190] To differentiate themselves in presenting the same set of daily news as other broadcasters, television stations often used not journalists but celebrities as news announcers.[191]

---

[187] *Ibid.*   [188] *Ibid.*   [189] *Ibid.*

[190] The 'Radio News Room' section of the Annual Departmental Report by the Director of Information Services prior to 1972 did not shy away from detailing such control, see such reports from 1960 to 1971.

[191] For example, TVB used artists such as Josiah Lau and Chu Wai-tak to host the news bulletins; see TVB, *TVB* 開心三十年 [TVB 30th anniversary] (Hong Kong: TVB, 1997), 152.

5 Preparing to Negotiate with China: Overt Loosening and Covert Control

Back in the driver's seat of the country's foreign affairs, Chinese Premier Zhou En-lai in December 1967 ordered local leftists in Hong Kong to stop planting bombs and reviewed their movements in the colony. In early 1968, Zhou passed the message to leftist organisations in Hong Kong that the 'anti-persecution struggle' had taken a wrong turn.[1] The loss of Beijing's support put an end to the seven-month riots, which left local leftist organisations with serious financial and manpower losses owing to government suppression, as well as the mass-scale arrest, deportation and detention of communist supporters, including teachers, students, workers and journalists. The party-line content of left-wing newspapers also lost them nearly half their daily readership over the seven-month period.[2] Workers belonging to left-wing trade unions that had participated in the territory-wide strikes had difficulty finding new employers, many of whom were wary of their potentially violent behaviour. The late 1960s and early 1970s thus saw the toning down of direct confrontation by the leftist press and schools. Leftist newspapers became 'less doctrinaire' and devoted increasing space to 'non-political local news, sports items and spicy stories' in an attempt to regain credibility and revenue from Hong Kong readers.[3]

After a painful victory in suppressing the riots, David Trench proposed that a harsher approach be taken towards communist schools and local leftists going forward, but was pulled back by the Foreign Office in London and British chargé d'affaires in Beijing, with debates subsequently taking place between those two entities and the governor over the dilemma that had been facing Hong Kong and London since the 1950s:

There are two areas of particular sensitivity for the communists in Hong Kong: the press and education . . . .. The question, as always, is to balance the need to take firm action to maintain the Government's authority and public confidence in Hong Kong against the

---

[1] G. K. Cheung, 六七暴動, 73–174; Jin Ruoru, 中共香港政策秘聞實錄：金堯如五十年香江憶往 [Secrets of CCP's Hong Kong policies: Jin Ruoru's fifty years of recollection] (Hong Kong: Tianyuan 1998) 147–8.

[2] Mok, 'Chinese communist influence'; Jin, 中共香港, 142–4.

[3] Paper entitled 'Chinese Press Machines in Hong Kong: Its Scope and Its Impact', prepared by Police Special Branch, FCO 40/222, cited in Mok, 'Chinese communist influence'.

risk to Sino-British relations in general, and to Hong Kong in particular, of a strong C.P. G. [Chinese Central People's Government] reaction to any measures we may take.[4]

The Foreign Office emphasised that a balance needed to be struck between suppressing local communists in Hong Kong and maintaining workable Sino-British relations. The Foreign Office and British chargé d'affaires were also very concerned about how a worsening Sino-British relationship might harm the ongoing diplomatic communications over the release of dozens of Britons detained in China.[5] The chargé d'affaires also expressed concerns about the UK's export trade with China, which had fallen significantly, and would likely continue to fall if the relationship between the two countries worsened owing to confrontations in Hong Kong.[6] The foreign secretary thus implored Trench to take into account the effect on British subjects held hostage in China when considering any further actions.[7]

In Trench's view, the poor Sino-British relationship was due to a number of factors, none of which were the fault of the British side. The most fundamental cause of the poor relations, he informed London, was the CPG's lack of success in imposing its will in Hong Kong. That lack of success was compounded by revolutionary fervour in China, ideological opposition to the British Hong Kong government and the 'necessity' of protesting against the UK's solidarity with the US government in Hong Kong. From this perspective, a major concession from Hong Kong would most likely encourage further aggression from the CPG, whereas a small concession might reduce the stridency of the CPG's propaganda attacks but would not change the funda-mentals of Sino-British relations. The governor thought that improved relations might be better achieved via alternative means such as an 'effective diplomatic offensive' or 'publicity'.[8]

Nevertheless, Trench was bound by London's instruction to not take further actions against local communists unless developments in Hong Kong made actions 'unavoidable', in which case the governor should provide advance notice and allow time for ministerial consultation.[9] . Vilification of the Hong Kong government and the publishing of what it regarded as seditious material continued through until the end of Trench's governorship in 1971, although the intensity of both diminished. Yet Hong Kong was 'inhibited' by

[4] 'Notes on item for discussion with the Governor of Hong Kong', prepared by Hong Kong Department of FCO, 15 October 1968, FCO 40/212.
[5] Briefing note on 'Visit of Minister of State (Lord Shepherd) to Hong Kong May/June 1969', prepared by Hong Kong Department of FCO, 21 May 1969; letter from J. B. Denson, British Chargé d'Affaires in Beijing, to J. O. Moreton, FCO, 6 May 1969, FCO 40/212.
[6] D. Hopson, British Charge d'Affaires in Beijing, to FCO, 8 July 1968, FCO 40/88.
[7] Commonwealth Office to Hong Kong, 25 August 1967, FCO 40/88.
[8] Governor Trench to Commonwealth Office, 12 July 1968, FCO 40/88.
[9] Foreign Office's paper entitled 'Communist Schools in Hong Kong' from James Murray to Sir Denis Allen, 30 September 1968, FCO 40/89.

London from prosecution partly because of the dreadful memory of the burning and sacking of the office of the chargé d'affaires in Beijing. Reserving prosecution for the most 'blatantly seditious and inflammatory' publications was, in the opinion of the Foreign and Commonwealth Office (FCO), the 'best course to adopt in the interests of Sino/Hong Kong/British relations generally'.[10]

At the same time, the leftist press also adopted a new approach. Instead of inciting rebellion against 'British fascist imperialism', it would criticise 'the [Hong Kong] authorities on the ground of real or alleged deficiencies in the administration of the Colony's affairs', particularly 'in the spheres of public transport, crime, labour disputes, hawkers and resettlement schemes'.[11] There were also fewer displays of overt hostility from teachers and students in communist-controlled schools towards the government's school inspectors.[12] The relative peace in Hong Kong at the turn of the decade also coincided with a calmer geopolitical climate globally, with the gradual improvement of the relationship between the Chinese and Anglo-American camps eventually leading to the recognition of PRC's membership of the UN in 1971, President Nixon's historic visit to China in 1972 and the exchange of diplomats between China and the UK in 1972.[13]

Behind MacLehose's 'Golden Era': Britain's China Strategy

It was against this geopolitical backdrop that Murray MacLehose succeeded Trench as governor of Hong Kong in late 1971. Unlike previous governors, who had a career background in the colonial service, MacLehose was the first to be a career diplomat in the Foreign Office.[14] He thus had a nuanced understanding of how Hong Kong should be run in light of the likely diplomatic change in China's relationship with the 'principal Pacific powers and with the rest of the world' in the near future.[15] Unlike Trench, whom MacLehose regarded as having prioritised 'security risks' over forward planning for Hong Kong, he saw the advantage of 'initiating a highly secret but thorough look' at Hong Kong's future. In MacLehose's top-secret 'business plan'

---

[10] Briefing note on 'Visit of Deputy Under-Secretary of State (Sir Leslie Monson) to Hong Kong October 1969', prepared by Hong Kong Department of FCO, October 1969 [exact date of note missing], FCO 40/212.

[11] Briefing note on 'Visit of Deputy Under-Secretary of State (Sir Leslie Monson) to Hong Kong October 1969'.

[12] Letter from J. A. Harrison, Colonial Secretariat, to A. G. Gaminara, FCO, 11 March 1969, enclosing a report entitled 'Inspections of Communist-controlled Schools' prepared by Education Department of Hong Kong on 26 February 1969, FCO 40/212.

[13] See Mark, *The Everyday Cold War*, chapters 5 and 6 on normalisation of relations between China and the UK.

[14] Carroll, *A Concise History*, 161.

[15] MacLehose to Leslie Monson, Wilford, Morgan, Laird, 'Guidelines for the Governor Designate of Hong Kong: Paper C: Hong Kong & China', 18 October 1971, FCO 40/329.

outlining what would guide his governorship, which was submitted to the FCO in October 1971, he emphasised the work that needed to be done in Hong Kong to increase Britain's 'bargaining power' with China in negotiations over the future of Hong Kong when 'a more favourable' Chinese government had emerged.[16] He divided the twenty-six-page policy paper he submitted to the secretary of state into three parts: the first on long-term planning, the second on domestic policies and the third entitled 'Hong Kong and China'. MacLehose's suggested policies were predicated on the proposition that Britain would have to negotiate with China over the future of Hong Kong before 1997. In the long-term planning section, he emphasised the need to 'work out policies in Hong Kong consciously designed to prolong confidence and so gain all possible time for conditions to emerge in China in which a favourable negotiation would be possible'.[17] He contended that the 'successful manipulation' of policies 'might gain us a few years and might improve our bargaining position'. To that end, the now fondly remembered housing and education reforms implemented during his governorship were listed under 'Domestic Policies' in this governing thesis paper. They fit in with what MacLehose considered to be 'a basic condition for the continuation of the Colony, namely that a wide margin over the standard of living in China must be maintained'. In MacLehose's view, that had to be accomplished 'against the background of the end of the lease in 26 years', and the stresses and strains that prospect would start to generate 'comparatively soon'.[18]

One should not overstate MacLehose's foresight in situating Hong Kong's development in its inevitable return to China. He was simply following what had been thoroughly studied and concluded by ministers in London through the series of secret studies on the future of Hong Kong prepared after the 1967 riots. Those studies concluded that Hong Kong had no hope of gaining independence because of China's explicit opposition and it being militarily indefensible. The UK's view on its control over Hong Kong's future beyond or even before 1997 had been quite pessimistic in 1969, given that 'China could take Hong Kong at any time of her choosing either as a result of a direct military attack or by making our position in the colony untenable through organised internal uprisings'. 'Hong Kong's future must eventually lie in China', one study concluded, noting that the British objective 'must be to attempt to negotiate its return, at a favourable opportunity, on the best terms obtainable for its people and

---

[16] See MacLehose to Leslie Monson, Wilford, Morgan, Laird, 'Guidelines for the Governor Designate of Hong Kong: Paper A: Long Term Planning', 18 October 1971, FCO 40/329.

[17] MacLehose to Leslie Monson, Wilford, Morgan, Laird, 'Guidelines for the Governor Designate of Hong Kong: Paper A'.

[18] Maclehose to Leslie Monson, Wilford, Morgan, Laird, 'Guidelines for the Governor Designate of Hong Kong: Paper B: Domestic Policies', 18 October 1971, FCO 40/329.

for our material interests there'.[19] Such pessimism underwent a slight shift
when Premier Zhou En-lai informed Malcolm MacDonald, a former British
commissioner-general for Southeast Asia, that China would not seek to get
Hong Kong back until the expiry of the lease on the New Territories.[20] In
a new paper on the future of Hong Kong prepared by Alec Douglas-Home,
secretary of state for foreign and commonwealth affairs, for the Cabinet's
Defence and Oversea Policy Committee in December 1971, although it was
still acknowledged that 'if the Chinese Government is determined to expel
us at any time there is little we can do to prevent this', London now viewed
retaining control of Hong Kong beyond 1997 as not entirely impossible.[21]
The paper set out the advantages and disadvantages of doing so. The
advantages included keeping the UK's 'commitment to the 2 million inhabitants who are citizens of the UK' and would otherwise find themselves
under PRC rule, using Hong Kong 'as a base and source of intelligence'
and maintaining the UK's balance of payments. The paper also argued that
keeping a colony would run counter to the UK's post-war colonial policy
and that the UK's membership of the European Economic Community
might make Hong Kong 'an increasingly embarrassing political anachronism'. It nevertheless recommended – and ministers endorsed – three
options with respect to strategies pertaining to the future of Hong Kong.
While maintaining the status quo, the UK would take 'preliminary informal
soundings with Peking' nearer to 1997 with a view to 'negotiat[ing] new
terms of lease' or, securing an indication from the Chinese that they would
'not interfere with the present arrangements after 1997' or to negotiating
'an orderly withdrawal in 1997' if the first two options failed to
materialise.[22]

It was in this strategic context that Governor MacLehose devised plans to
maximise Britain's bargaining power with China by meeting the material
demands of the people of Hong Kong, who were transitioning through a state

---

[19] See the following documents cited in Mark Chi-kwan, 'Development without Decolonisation?
Hong Kong's Future and Relations with Britain and China, 1967–1972', *Journal of the Royal
Asiatic Society* 24.2 (2014): 323–5; Godden to Moreton, 22 April 1969, FCO 40/160; memorandum by Stewart for MCHK, K(69)1, 'Hong Kong: Long Term Study', 28 March 1969, CAB
134/2945; memorandum, Wilford to Monson, with Annex: draft paper for ministers,
9 December 1970, FCO 40/265.

[20] Mark, 'Development without Decolonisation?', 332.

[21] Memorandum on 'The Future of Hong Kong' by the Secretary of State for the FCO to the
Cabinet's Defence and Oversea Policy Committee, 13 December 1971, CAB 148/117. The view
that 'Hong Kong could not be defended against a Chinese military' was re-affirmed repeatedly
over the next decade; see meeting minutes of Defence and Oversea Policy Committee: Sub-
Committee on Hong Kong, 17 November 1983, CAB 148/230.

[22] Memorandum on 'The Future of Hong Kong'. For impact of British entry into the EEC and
withdrawal from the East of Suez on the future planning of Hong Kong, see Mark,
'Development without Decolonisation?'

of 'semi-destitution to semi-affluence', thereby 'securing the loyalty of the potential demandeurs' while rejecting the need to democratise Hong Kong constitutionally.[23] Yet both the FCO and MacLehose agreed that there was no rush to negotiate with the Maoist regime, preferring to wait until 'a more favourable [Chinese] Government emerged'.[24] To give Britain time to improve its bargaining position, MacLehose advised London that, in addition to making life in Hong Kong 'so superior in every way' to that in China so that the Chinese government would 'hesitate before facing the problems of absorption [of Hong Kong]', Hong Kong should not obstruct communist China from making legitimate profits and absorbing foreign exchange from Hong Kong, should not permit 'unnecessary friction' with China and should not give an 'impression of any move towards representative or independent government'.[25] The 'status quo' – a key word repeated in a UK Cabinet memorandum on 'The Future of Hong Kong' written by the secretary of state for foreign and commonwealth affairs – was to be maintained skilfully to meet both the political wish of London and the economic need of Beijing.[26]

Coinciding with this strategic direction for Britain, a few months after the reaching of an agreement to exchange ambassadors between Britain and China on 13 March 1972, the UN General Assembly overwhelmingly adopted a resolution regarding China's request to exclude Hong Kong and Macao from the list of colonial territories in November, thereby paving the path for the return of both to China.[27] At almost the same time, MacLehose in his policy review to the secretary of state reiterated the strategic importance of placing Hong Kong's domestic policies against the odds of future negotiations with China about Hong Kong: 'to tackle the domestic problems of the Colony so vigorously during the next 10 years that they would be eliminated to a point at which by Western standards there was nothing to be ashamed of anywhere, and by Chinese standards much to spur civic pride and a sense of achievement everywhere'.[28] The broad aim was to foster civic pride as a 'useful substitute'

---

[23] MacLehose to Leslie Monson, Wilford, Morgan, Laird, 'Guidelines for the Governor Designate of Hong Kong: Paper B'. For MacLehose's reluctance against democratisation, see Ray Yep and Tai-lok Lui, 'Revisiting the Golden Era of MacLehoseand the Dynamics of Social Reforms,' *China Information* 24.3 (2010): 249–72, and Tai-lok Lui, '"Flying MPs" and Political Change in a Colonial Setting: Political Reform under MacLehose's Governorship of Hong Kong', in *Civil Unrest and Governance in Hong Kong: Law and Order from Historical and Cultural Perspectives*, ed. Michael Ng and John D. Wong (London: Routledge, 2017), 76–96.

[24] 'Guidelines for the Governor Designate of Hong Kong: Paper A & Paper C'. For the FCO's studies, see Mark, 'Development without Decolonisation?'

[25] Minute from E. O. Laird to Sir Leslie Monson, 29 November 1971; 'Guidelines for the Governor Designate of Hong Kong: Paper A & Paper C'.

[26] Memorandum on 'The Future of Hong Kong'.

[27] Mark, 'Development without Decolonisation?', 333.

[28] MacLehose to Douglas-Home, 5 May 1972, FCO 21/1023, cited in Mark, 'Development without Decolonisation?', 333–4.

for 'national loyalty', make the people of Hong Kong feel that 'Hong Kong is an entity to which they belong, and the place they wish to live in', and avoid 'actions and administrative procedures in Hong Kong which tend to highlight the diminishing term of the Lease', thereby maximising Britain's leverage in negotiating with China over Hong Kong's future. MacLehose oversaw a series of socioeconomic reforms that resulted in his eleven-year governorship being fondly remembered as Hong Kong's 'golden era' characterised by benevolent colonialism.[29] Yet, recent studies by Lui Tai-lok and Ray Yep reveal that in the FCO's eyes MacLehose was a reluctant reformer who refused or resisted many of London's requests for a more progressive overhaul of Hong Kong's social and political systems to address London's strategic and political concerns. MacLehose was particularly opposed to the idea of introducing a more representative legislature in Hong Kong because he placed 'over-riding importance' on keeping the Legislative Council's membership 'constructive and co-operative'. He also believed that the people of Hong Kong had 'little interest' in representative government owing to their 'authoritarian tradition of government' and China's inherent opposition to such ideas.[30] Recent studies have also revealed that many of the reform projects in the MacLehose era, such as the construction of public housing estates and measures to combat corruption, were built on foundations laid by his predecessors.[31]

Nevertheless, compared with the miserably over-crowded squatter slums scattered across the territory, severe shortage of school places as a result of child migration from China, meagre social welfare and medical provision to the general public, and hopelessly corrupt public service and police force at the end of 1960s, MacLehose's reforms in the economic, housing, education and social welfare arenas did indeed both impress and benefit the people of Hong Kong, who were the carefully planned secondary beneficiaries of the socioeconomic

---

[29] MacLehose to Monson et al., 16 October 1971, FCO 40/329 cited in Yep and Lui, 'Revisiting the Golden Era,' 253 . Not only the general public, earlier works of historians also joined this celebratory narrative of the 'MacLehose years', without much study of his underlying strategic intention (partly perhaps owing to the fact that colonial files documenting such intention were not yet opened for public access). See such narrative, for example, in Roger Buckley, *Hong Kong: The Road to 1997* (Cambridge: Cambridge University Press, 1997), chapter 4. For a recent 'revisiting' of such a narrative, see Yep and Lui, 'Revisiting the Golden Era', and Ray Yep, 'The Crusade against Corruption in Hong Kong in the 1970s: Governor MacLehose as a Zealous Reformer or Reluctant Hero?' *China Information* 27.2 (2013): 197–221.

[30] For MacLehose's reluctance in democratising legislature, see Lui, '"Flying MPs"'; for MacLehose's negotiation with London for socioeconomic reforms in Hong Kong, see Yep and Lui, 'Revisiting the Golden Era', and Yep, 'The Crusade against Corruption'. For Maclehose's initial response to the idea of a more representative legislature in Hong Kong, see paras 4 and 6 of MacLehose to Leslie Monson, Wilford, Morgan, Laird, 'Guidelines for the Governor Designate of Hong Kong: Paper B'.

[31] On Trench's proposals of anti-corruption, Yep, 'The Crusade against Corruption', 198; on housing, see Steve Tsang, *A Modern History of Hong Kong 1841–1997* (London: I. B. Tauris, 2004), 205.

reforms that took place under the masterplan for future negotiations with China,[32] another beneficiary envisaged by MacLehose in his grand scheme. Building a strong economy would not only support 'decisions on the biggest expenditures in [Hong's Kong's] history', but would also provide a reason for China to continue its status quo policy regarding Hong Kong, whose value lay largely with its position as the mainland's major source of foreign exchange obtained from selling products in or via Hong Kong. 'So long as this situation persists, Hong Kong's usefulness to the Chinese will remain', MacLehose explained to the FCO. 'Conversely if this situation changed we might be in for trouble.'[33] As Carroll noted, MacLehose 'happened to be in Hong Kong during a period of remarkable economic growth' that made his grand welfare plan possible. Hong Kong's gross domestic product increased at an average of 10 per cent from the 1960s through to the 1970s thanks to the influx of immigrant workers, producers and consumers from China, as well as industrialisation and trade networks developed in the 1960s.[34] As an experienced diplomat and former political advisor to Governor Black from 1959 to 1962, MacLehose knew well that feeding China economically might not necessarily guarantee ample time for Britain to improve its bargaining position with China in the foreseeable future. He was well aware that 'one cannot interpret Communist Chinese history in economic terms'. It was 'not at all clear what the features of the new era' (i.e. that following China's isolation by the US) would be, nor what effect they would have on 'China's willingness to tolerate a colony on her doorstep – however profitable its existence may be'. All that the Hong Kong government could do was 'to ensure that the advantages China obtains are maximised and the disadvantages and loss of face are minimised'. 'If the Chinese choose to play against us', MacLehose admitted, 'such gambits would be nullified.'[35]

The fact that Hong Kong's gross domestic product grew fivefold from the early 1970s to the early 1980s, combined with the less intense co-existence of local leftists and the left-wing press with the colonial government, improving geopolitical relationship amongst China, Britain and the US following the China–USSR split, and the petering out of the Cultural Revolution in the mainland, made it possible for MacLehose to implement his grand plan in the next decade without too much disruption from social unrest or global tensions. Putting aside the underlying geopolitical objectives of this plan and the fact that some of his planned projects failed to achieve their claimed

---

[32] For the widespread corruption, social problems and injustices in the housing and education sectors in Hong Kong during the 1950s and 1960s, see Elsie Tu, *Colonial Hong Kong in the Eyes of Elsie Tu* (Hong Kong: Hong Kong University Press, 2003).

[33] 'Guidelines for the Governor Designate of Hong Kong: Paper C'.

[34] Carroll, *A Concise History*, 162–3.

[35] 'Guidelines for the Governor Designate of Hong Kong: Paper A & Paper C'.

objectives, he met the Hong Kong people's expectations in education, housing, social welfare, healthcare and anti-corruption to an extent entirely unprecedented in colonial rule.[36] Whilst much scholarly focus has been placed on MacLehose's social reforms (which this book is not going to repeat), his strategies and policies concerning the politically sensitive issues of freedom of speech and the press have largely been neglected. This book argues that in order to cultivate 'civic pride', maintain 'a wide margin over the standard of living in China' and strengthen the Hong Kong people's identification with and loyalty to the colonial government, MacLehose tried not only to build a superior Hong Kong by materialistic standards but also to create a public image of Hong Kong as a much more liberal society than the communist mainland, thereby maximising Britain's leverage in its future negotiations with China. The next section tracks the beginnings of the liberation and de-silencing of Hong Kong by its last few governors as London counted down the remaining twenty-six years of its hold on Hong Kong.

Making Hong Kong a 'Free Society': Overt Liberalisation, Covert Control

Described by historians as 'a master of publicising his programs with bold promises' and skilful in his 'astute publicity campaign', MacLehose was highly sensitive to his government's public image.[37] In a section entitled 'Government's image with the people' contained in his governorship guidelines submitted to London, he expressed his unhappiness about the 'singularly fragmented and badly staffed press' in Hong Kong and the Hong Kong government's failure to improve the lines of communication with the people. He promised to look into the issue 'as a matter of priority' and search for a 'government spokesman of sufficient calibre'[38] to handle the press in a different manner to ensure that his strategic aim to create an image of colonial benevolence before Britain's negotiations with China over the future of Hong Kong could be achieved.

---

[36] MacLehose's ten-year housing plan, for example, failed to build enough housing units as scheduled, leaving 750,000 people still living in squatter areas when MacLehose left office in 1982; see Andrew C. K. Yu, 'Was Governor Maclehose a Great Architect of Modern Hong Kong?', *Asian Affairs* 51.3 (2020): 485–509. MacLehose was also criticised in recent studies as a reluctant crusader in the anti-corruption campaign, and a reluctant reformer in social welfare reform who ignored London's calls for a minimum wage and statutory hours of work, and a contributory scheme for social security; for such criticism, see Yep and Lui, 'Revisiting the Golden Era', and Yep, 'The Crusade against Corruption'.

[37] See descriptions by Carroll, *A Concise History*, 161, and Tsang, *A Modern History of Hong Kong*, 205.

[38] MacLehose to Leslie Monson, Wilford, Morgan, Laird, 'Guidelines for the Governor Designate of Hong Kong: Paper B', para 14.

MacLehose's disappointment with the professionalism of the press and the government's relations with the press was not unjustified. Even though electronic media such as radio and wireless television broadcasts were gradually taking over from newspapers as the major source of daily news and government announcements for the people of Hong Kong in the late 1960s and early 1970s, radio and television stations did not even employ their own news teams to cover local and international news. Senior broadcasters at RHK have admitted that in the early 1970s RHK did not have skilled journalists capable of covering daily news, even though the station had been in operation for more than forty years.[39] As mentioned in Chapter 4, daily news bulletins on RHK, CR and RDF were 'fed' by the GIS every hour and read by news announcers who were sometimes not professional journalists but radio hosts and TV celebrities. TVB, the first wireless television broadcaster, which began operations in late 1967, was also on the feeder list of GIS news bulletins until approximately 1969–70. As the GIS (under Trench's governorship) stated in its annual report for that year: 'H. K.T.V.B. operates its own news service and both T.V. stations [TVB and Rediffusion TV] obtained their filmed news material from their own sources.'[40]

Building upon Trench's unprecedented step of granting TV broadcasters freedom (the limitation of which will be discussed in the paragraphs to follow) in covering and reporting news stories, MacLehose's government further purported to liberate radio broadcasters in Hong Kong. Some of these liberalising steps came as a surprise even to senior broadcasting officials in Hong Kong. As a first step, shortly after MacLehose's arrival in Hong Kong as its new governor, the directors of the most important departments for controlling views and information broadcasts on air were replaced, namely, those of RHK and the GIS. James Hawthorne from the BBC was appointed director of broadcasting, replacing Donald Brooks, who had led RHK for sixteen years. In 1973, the government then decided that RHK should compile its own news bulletins[41] Hawthorne found the lifting of government control over the news quite a surprising decision, as it led to a sudden shortage of experienced journalists capable of covering daily news: 'Suddenly . . . the rules were changed. But the problem was that for years, [journalists] had been working in a particular way and they had no real experience in following up a good news story.' Immediately after the establishment of RHK's newsroom, the GIS had to second information officers to work with and train up RHK

[39] RTHK, 從一九二八年說起, 88–91.
[40] Annual Departmental Report by the Director of Information Services N. J. V. Watt for the financial year 1969–70.
[41] RTHK, *RTHK–50 Years: Broadcasting in Hong Kong from 1928–1978* (Hong Kong: Government Printer, 1978), 13, 19, 20. RHK was renamed RTHK (Radio Television Hong Kong) 'to reflect the station's ever increasing involvement in locally produced [TV] programmes' since 1970. RTHK, *RTHK–50 Years*, 13.

journalists before the newsroom could operate on its own.[42] In 1974, CR's licence was extended for another fifteen years, and it was allowed to produce and broadcast its own news bulletins instead of relaying RHK's news bulletins or reading GIS news scripts.[43] The 'independence' of their news desks was proudly remembered as a milestone of 'editorial autonomy' in publications commemorating the anniversaries of RHK and CR, and yet the reality was that the autonomy to produce programmes, including news bulletins and current affairs programmes, was in fact subject to the political restrictions contained in the Radio Programme Standards issued by the Hong Kong government.[44] A radio programme was considered 'objectionable' according to the standards if it contained matters that, amongst other things, 'provoke[d] hatred of the Government, the laws or the administration of justice in Hong Kong', was 'undesirable in the public interest' or 'damage[d] good relations with other territories'. Similar state-security buzz phrases such as 'hatred of the Government', 'public interest' and 'good relations with other territories' could be found in the censorship regulations of the Emergency Regulations Ordinance, Sedition Ordinance, Education Regulations and Film Censorship Regulations, where they were left vague and undefined, as was usual in colonial laws and regulations.[45] These ambiguous political red lines remained on the statute book to impose political restraints on radio programming in Hong Kong until 1995, just two years before Hong Kong was handed back to China.[46] MacLehose's strategy for controlling the electronic media was similar to Governor Grantham's passing of the CPCO to control Chinese newspapers in the early 1950s. As the number of electronic media players increased, the colonial government chose not to spare limited manpower to prepare or pre-censor the huge amount of programming produced by radio and TV stations every day; rather, it imposed strict but vaguely defined political boundaries for media players to comply with, failing which they could be fined, prosecuted and suppressed according to the law. Special Branch was responsible for monitoring radio programmes and issuing warnings to programme hosts, as one former RTHK host recalled, if they were found to be close to stepping outside the political boundaries.[47] Otherwise, journalists and programmers were basically left alone in terms of content creation. Within these political boundaries, the news teams of radio and TV stations expanded, and many famous current affairs programmes were launched and became popular in the

---

[42] RTHK, 從一九二八年說起, 88–91.

[43] Huang Yong, Feng Zhi-feng and Huang Pei-feng, 十八樓C座為民喉舌卅年 [18/F Flat C, thirty years of broadcasting for the people] (Hong Kong: Liangguang wenhua, 2008), 98–9.

[44] RTHK, 從一九二八年說起, 89–90; Huang, Feng and Huang, 十八樓C座.

[45] Television and Entertainment Authority, Radio Programme Standards, 1984, 1992.

[46] Broadcasting Authority, Radio Code of Practice on Programme Standards, 1995.

[47] The former news programme host recollected that he had been warned by Special Branch after he had interviewed a Marxist supporter; see Chen Yun, 一起廣播的日子, 112.

mid-1970s.[48] In the first two years of his governorship, MacLehose granted licences to two additional wireless TV stations, in addition to extending TVB's existing licence. Whilst all of these stations were 'free' to produce their own news bulletins and entertainment programmes, they were subject to the political boundaries of another state-security buzz phrase, 'peace and good order', set by the Television Ordinance, which empowered the government to set and publish boundaries as the Television Regulations and Television Programme Standards.[49] It also empowered the government to prohibit the broadcasting of any programme if it threatened 'the peace or good order of the Colony'. If the government considered that any programme intended for broadcast by a licensed TV station might affect the peace or good order of Hong Kong, it could require that station to supply to the government 'on demand any material, including the script thereof, which is intended for broadcasting'[50] or 'pre-record the programme and submit it … for approval before it is broadcast'.[51] TV stations were also required by the Television Regulations to include 'a reasonable proportion' of materials that are 'wholly of British or Commonwealth origin' in their programme line-up.[52] The regulations also required stations to obtain news 'from sources or services approved by the Director of Information Services'.[53] MacLehose's government further amended the 1964 Television Ordinance to make it a statutory responsibility for TV stations to include news programmes and announcements of public interest and 'other materials supplied' by the government.[54] In addition to mandating what materials could be included in TV programmes, the law also empowered the government to demand the pre-censorship of programmes on political grounds, requiring TV stations to exclude any material likely to encourage civil disobedience, discredit or bring into disrespect the law, or serve the interests of a foreign political party.[55] The Television Programme Standards also stipulated that no TV programme should contain any matter that was 'undesirable in the public interest' or that might 'deride or otherwise discredit the law and its enforcement'. Failure to comply with these rules could result in the revocation of broadcasting licences. These political limitations remained largely in place until the last few years of the colonial era, as we shall see in the next chapter.

'Promoting' Press Freedom

Liberating radio and TV stations from having to 'announce' news bulletins prepared by the GIS coincided with a change of directorship at the GIS. David

---

[48] *Ibid.*, 115–17.   [49] Television Ordinance (No. 32 of 1964), ss. 27–9.
[50] *Ibid.*, ss. 33 and 35(3).   [51] Television (Amendment) Ordinance (No. 7 of 1973), s. 16.
[52] Television (Standards of Programmes) Regulations 1964, reg. 3.   [53] *Ibid.*, reg. 5.
[54] Television (Amendment) Ordinance 1973, s. 15.
[55] Television (Standards of Programmes) Regulations 1964, reg. 4.

Ford, a former British military officer who had served in seventeen different outposts of the empire and been seconded to Hong Kong during the 1967 riots, took over from Nigel Watt in 1974. Reading the annual departmental reports of the GIS under Watt and Ford reveals a distinct difference in how the roles of the GIS were packaged and presented to the public. Watt's report was politically outspoken and boasted about the GIS's counter-communist propaganda, with one report stating: 'Communist loudspeakers installed at the Bank of China building were countered by rival and more powerful loudspeakers set up in buildings in the vicinity which regaled the public with the music of Cantonese opera and effectively drowned the stream of communist propaganda.' Watt also detailed how diligent the GIS's Radio News Room was in 'serving' radio and TV stations with 'fourteen news bulletins and summaries in English and Chinese ranging from two to ten minutes [that] are prepared daily by radio news room staff who work in shifts, manning the news room throughout the day and night'.[56] He did not shy away politically from naming the newspapers that voiced 'orthodox Chinese communist policies' or spoke for the 'Nationalist regime in Taiwan'.[57] The annual reports of the GIS under Watt and his predecessors were published as a ten-plus-page booklet containing more than sixty paragraphs of descriptions of the GIS's daily work and responsibilities. The organisation's main task prior to Ford's arrival was 'to keep both the people of Hong Kong and people overseas accurately informed of Government's achievements and aims'.[58] It needed to 'cope with the increasing need for positive publicity to retain and fortify public confidence in Government both locally and overseas'.[59]

In contrast, the GIS under Ford toned down its role as a colonial propaganda machine, instead positioning itself as 'a major link between the government, the people of Hong Kong and the rest of the world'.[60] Ford trimmed down the GIS's annual departmental report into fewer than four pages and scrapped many of the details that had been reported under Watt, such as descriptions of the daily news bulletins fed by the Radio News Room to radio and TV stations and the number of films censored each year by the GIS. Ford reorganised the department into three divisions, namely, a Public Relations Division to 'promote, understand and improve the relationship between the government and the

---

[56] Annual Departmental Report by the Director of Information Services for the financial year 1967–8, para. 8, 57–9.

[57] Annual Departmental Report by the Director of Information Services for the financial year 1965–6, para. 8.

[58] Annual Departmental Report by the Director of Information Services for the financial year 1960–1, para. 2.

[59] Annual Departmental Report by the Director of Information Services for the financial year 1967–8, 1.

[60] Annual Departmental Report by the Director of Information Services for the financial year 1976–7, 3.

people'; a News Division responsible for producing daily information bulletins that give factual information on official policies and public projects and routine notices to newspapers and broadcasters in Hong Kong; and a Publicity Division responsible for producing government publications and films and promoting official campaigns and events such as the Festival of Hong Kong and Clean Hong Kong Campaigns.[61] The Film Censorship Section was hived off from the GIS and transferred to the Secretariat for Home Affairs.[62] Outside the GIS office, Ford and senior government officials began to disseminate to the public a new official discourse on press freedom and the role of the mass media in Hong Kong. Shortly after taking up the GIS directorship, Ford addressed journalism students on the role of the GIS in publicising and explaining government policies in areas that were 'non-controversial and unquestionably for the good of the community'. He explained that the GIS was 'not used in a political way to influence public opinion in controversial issues'.[63] The GIS, he continued, 'would strongly resist any attempt to promote Government interference in the media' and would not 'muster support in a political way for itself on controversial policies'.[64] He encouraged the press to voice opposition on behalf of the people of Hong Kong and to stimulate discussion and debate on public affairs because Hong Kong had 'no elected official opposition to the Government'. He disagreed with press complaints that it was very difficult for journalists to access government officials for interviews. The government was, he said in response to such complaints, 'in no way staffed by gagged civil servants surrounded by an impenetrable wall of silence'.[65] Ford also rebutted the claim that freedom of the press was 'fettered by censorship and control'. In his view, the legal sanctions were 'minimal', being 'limited to such matters as the libel laws and sedition', with no other government sanctions – political or otherwise – imposed.[66]

The GIS under MacLehose's governorship overtly endeavoured to build an image of Hong Kong as a free and open society. Under Trench's governorship, the GIS had been repeatedly condemned by the press for obstructing public and press access to information. Newspaper editors complained that with the exception of government-friendly newspapers, journalists were not allowed to 'develop direct press-Government relations', such as contacting government

---

[61] Annual Departmental Report by the Director of Information Services for 1973–4, 1. For Festival of Hong Kong and other major 'civic-pride-building' campaigns of the MacLehose period, see Hong Kong Memory Website: www.hkmemory.hk/MHK/collections/festival_of_hong_kong/about/index.html (Hong Kong Festivals) and MacLehose's interview with RTHK broadcast on 31 October 1972 and archived at RTHK website: https://app4.rthk.hk/special/rthkmemory/details/innovation/136/111 (Clean Hong Kong Campaign).

[62] 'Film Censorship in Hong Kong', enclosed in memo from Fred Ting, Assistant Director, to Directorate Members, 28 June 1978, HKRS 313/7/3.

[63] SCMP, 30 January 1975.   [64] SCMP, 4 February 1975.   [65] SCMP, 3 February 1975.

[66] SCMP, 4 February 1975.

officials for press interviews, without going through the GIS, which acted as 'the sole door between the press and Government'.[67] GIS director David Ford opened that 'door' by organising an unprecedented 'Meet the Media' session for members of the press to directly meet and pose questions to senior government officials, including the directors of Social Welfare, Labour, and Medicine and Health. In the press notification for the first 'Meet the Media' session in 1973, the GIS under its new directorship explicitly highlighted the change in style in comparison with the past government: 'In the past newsmen have said that it is not always easy for them to make direct contact with department heads. We hope that these sessions will provide the opportunity to put this right.'[68]

The press generally welcomed this new arrangement, which broke the monopoly that certain papers had enjoyed in having exclusive access to senior government officials. The left-wing press, however, took a highly sceptical view. Commenting on the first session held in February 1973, the left-wing *Wen Wei Po* criticised the half-an-hour 'Meet the Media' session attended by seven senior officials as a superficial show by the government that added nothing new to what was already known about government policies. It was also pointed out that if the government really wanted to loosen the restrictive information environment, it should allow the press to interview government officials at any time, not only during pre-arranged 'Meet the Media' sessions.[69]

Official Rhetoric: 'Freedom of the Press Is Absolutely Essential'

At the same time, MacLehose worked hard to erase the draconian marks left by his predecessor, who had prosecuted and imprisoned a large number of left-wing activists and journalists during the 1967 riots. He emphasised the need to release all of these 'confrontation prisoners' without a 'grand gesture' as soon as possible because 'failure to maintain momentum on this issue might prejudice my entire governorship with Peking'.[70] A few months after the release of the two remaining prisoners in 1973, Hong Kong hosted the twelfth quadrennial conference of the Commonwealth Press Union. Addressing more than 100 journalists and press officials from seventeen Commonwealth regions during the conference's opening ceremony, MacLehose stressed that 'freedom of the press is absolutely essential, and the press in Hong Kong is as free from government restrictions on what it publishes as any in the world'.[71]

---

[67] *Post Herald*, 26 February 1967, HKRS 545-1-188.
[68] Press invitation, 20 February 1973, HKRS 70-6-879.
[69] *New Life Evening Post, Wah Kiu Man Po, Hong Kong Times* and *Wen Wei Pao,* 22–28 February 1973, HKRS 70-6-879.
[70] MacLehose to Leslie Monson, Wilford, Morgan, Laird, 'Guidelines for the Governor Designate of Hong Kong: Paper A & Paper C', para 17. For diplomatic negotiation on the release of confrontation prisoners, see Mark, *Everyday Cold War,* 184–7.
[71] SCMP, 4 October 1974.

Despite this liberal rhetoric, many of the legal provisions contained in such feared laws as the CPCO and Emergency Regulations, which had been used to sanction the press, detain journalists and suppress free speech, remained on the statute books. Rules requiring broadcasters to filter politically undesirable content, as stipulated in the Television Ordinance, Television Regulations and Codes of Practice for broadcasters, also remained in force for another two decades. Film censors still carried out their daily duties, censoring films on political or security grounds. As discussed in Chapter 4, films were banned from exhibition or excised if the censor 'in his considered opinion' thought there was a likelihood that their 'showing in a public place' would 'provoke hatred between persons in Hong Kong of different races, colours, class, nationality, creed or sectional interests', 'provoke hatred or contempt of the Government of Hong Kong' or 'damage good relations with other territories'.[72] Compared with film censorship in the 1960s, the 1970s saw a relative relaxation in the government's censoring of 'mainland film[s] of anti-Nationalist [Party] significance'. Rather, 'films in [a] modern setting showing the darker concerns of Hong Kong' and 'mainland films containing attacks on foreign powers, particularly on the U.S.A.' amidst the intensification of the Vietnam War came under stricter censorship, with such films either banned or required to cut controversial scenes. The censors were also reminded to 'bear in mind particular sensitivities ... to implied recognition of "Two Chinas"', which might provoke the PRC government.[73]

Indeed, avoiding the provocation of Beijing and developing a workable relationship with its representatives in Hong Kong was important to MacLehose. He had been endeavouring since the beginning of his tenure to build a behind-the-scenes communication channel with the Chinese government's representative in Hong Kong (mainly through his political advisor and senior officials from the NCNA's Hong Kong branch) to ensure that his grand plan of social transformation could be carried out without too many 'troubles' from Beijing and its controlled press or from communist-dominated labour unions and schools in Hong Kong. Such efforts towards the 'near normalization' of working relations between the Hong Kong government and Chinese officials in Hong Kong had borne fruit in MacLehose's view.[74] It had prevented

---

[72] 'Film Censorship in Hong Kong', enclosed in memo from Fred Ting, Assistant Director of Home Affairs Department, to Directorate Members of the same department, 28 June 1978, HKRS 313-7-3.

[73] Notes and comments on 'A Statement of the General Principles as Adopted on 20 November 1965 by the Film Censorship Board of Review', by William Hung, Chief Film Censor, 1 December 1970; 'Film Censorship: A Statement of the General Principles as adopted on 20 November 1965 by the Film Censorship Board of Review', enclosed in a memo from J. W. Sweetman, 12 January 1971, HKRS 508-3-3.

[74] 'Hong Kong: Annual Review for 1975' from MacLehose to the FCO, 23 January 1976, FCO 40/707.

'any industrial or social issues . . . from escalating into a confrontation with the Government' even during the two years of economic recession following the global oil crisis in 1973.[75] During his first five years of governorship, MacLehose repeatedly described the Chinese government as 'noticeably help-ful', 'friendly', acting with 'sympathy and restraint' and trying 'their best to cooperate to achieve friendly and constructive official relations' in his reports to the FCO.[76] In his annual review of Hong Kong sent to the FCO in 1975, while admitting that the excellent state of Anglo-Chinese relations was rele-vant, MacLehose could not help but credit his government for successfully containing political pressure from China through local working relations:

Both sides have taken advantage of [the working relations] to speak and to forewarn as well as to transact business quietly and naturally. This relationship has been built up without prior negotiation or definition, and without any official recognition of the *de facto* official status of the [NCNA] officials on the Chinese side. It has developed over the last three years as a result of the persistent design and policy of the Hong Kong Government, which has gradually come to be met with comprehension and acceptance by the Chinese – who have indeed gained much by it in Hong Kong. This evolution in local relations between the Hong Kong Government and Chinese officials has been achieved without the unsettling impact on public confidence that would have attended the dramatic innovation of official recognition of the Chinese mission.[77]

Described by the FCO as 'complacent' in tone, MacLehose's foregoing review of the Hong Kong situation may only partially explain the relatively peaceful co-existence of the colonial regime with anti-imperialist leftists in Hong Kong during the 1970s.[78]

Intelligence indicated that Beijing, under the command of Zhou En-lai, had given directives to local leftists 'that the struggle [was] to continue on peaceful lines'.[79] A study of Chinese policies towards Hong Kong entitled 'The Threat to Hong Kong' that was prepared for the Cabinet by the Ministry of Defence and FCO concluded that the economic value of Hong Kong as a market for

[75] 'Hong Kong: Annual Review for 1974' from MacLehose to FCO, 15 March 1975, FCO 40/642; 'Hong Kong: Annual Review for 1975'.

[76] 'Hong Kong: Annual Review for 1974'; 'Hong Kong: Annual Review for 1975'; 'Hong Kong: Annual Review for 1976' from MacLehose to FCO, 1 January 1977, FCO 40/758.

[77] 'Hong Kong: Annual Review for 1975'.

[78] FCO officials were not satisfied that MacLehose was inclined 'to make the most of the Chinese "dimension" as a limitation on what can be achieved' and did not fulfil its expectation on social reforms. Such 'complacency' remarks can be found in confidential note by J. A. B. Steward, FCO, 19 January 1977, FCO 40/758, and confidential note by E. N. Larmour, FCO, 18 February 1975, FCO 40/707. For conflicts of views in social reforms between MacLehose and London, see Yep and Lui, 'Revisiting the Golden Era'.

[79] See indication of CCP's 'peaceful lines' strategy in E. C. Laird (FCO) to Wilford and Logan (FCO) on Special Branch Report on the Communist Threat in Education, 13 July 1972, FCO 40/382. Such strategy continued into the 1980s; see paper for the Governor's Security Committee (No. 20/80), 28 November 1980, HKRS 935-2-1.

Chinese goods, an entrepôt linking Chinese products to global markets and a major source of foreign exchange (more than one-third) for China constituted the major reasons for China's 'status quo' policy towards Hong Kong. The Ministry of Defence summed up this view with respect to whether the Chinese would take over and run Hong Kong before the expiry of the lease: 'Yes they could, but with extreme difficulty and less profit than they presently make out of it.' Despite the pre-eminence of 'radicals' in 1975, and even more so in 1976, it was noted the Chinese policy of 'exploiting Hong Kong' had apparently hardly been affected at all, with no 'radical-inspired statements' about Hong Kong ever appearing.[80]

The restraint and pragmatism of both the colonial government and Chinese government may perhaps explain the absence of radical propaganda against continued British rule of Hong Kong in the left-wing press or large-scale confrontations between local leftists and the government during the 1970s, despite the unchanging political red lines set out in the laws and regulations for media and journalists to comply with. The quick rebound of the Hong Kong economy in 1976 also calmed down the 'querulous and nervous' population and the press, which had been, in MacLehose's view, set to 'explode' during the two-year recession. Despite the 'relaxed and effective relationship' with Chinese officials stationed in Hong Kong, as he described it in his annual reports to London, MacLehose was not entirely relaxed in keeping an eye on local political dissents, and he took action to suppress them when politically necessary. The official discourse emphasising press freedom and the relatively open media environment from the mid-1970s onwards could not entirely hide cases of journalists being beaten and arrested by the police for covering news of 'darker concerns' and of the open expression of discontent being suppressed by 'legal' means. In September 1975, for example, a journalist from Rediffusion TV was reported to have been beaten by a police inspector while covering the arrival of forty-seven refugees from Timor at Hong Kong Kai Tak Airport in late 1975. Another journalist who tried to stop the beating was also arrested.[81] Young protesters in their early twenties who engaged in an anti-unemployment and anti-inflation rally held in 1974 during the period of economic recession were arrested and prosecuted for exhibiting posters without the government's approval and obstruction.[82]

To avoid a negative portrayal in the press, police officers sometimes exercised 'restraint and [the] avoidance of fisticuffs' during rallies until the

[80] 'The Threat to Hong Kong' from Ministry of Defence to the Cabinet Office, 10 February 1978, FCO 40/958.
[81] Ng Bar-ling, ed., 香港年鑑 1976 [Hong Kong year book 1976] (Hong Kong: Wah Kiu Yat Po, 1976), 130.
[82] SCMP and WKYP, 14 September 1974.

government recognised public support for strong measures.[83] The GIS was asked to engage in covert propaganda, 'asking' radio stations to interview 'indignant parents' in order to 'persuade adults to keep their youngsters away from demonstrations'.[84] The increasing political activism of local students and youngsters became a concern for and political target of MacLehose's government. These young dissidents, mostly students at local universities or post-secondary institutions and not supervised by the CCP-dominated left-wing organisations in Hong Kong, were known as the New Left.

Surveillance of University Students and Crack Down on the New Left

The Hong Kong government believed that the open expression of discontent by the New Left had emerged in Hong Kong around 1969 when 'groups of expatriate academics, research students and clergy' had organised demonstrations against the Vietnam War outside the US Consulate.[85] The New Left shared the patriotism and anti-imperialism of the Old Left (the name given to local CCP supporters by Special Branch) but was not controlled by local left-wing organisations and often acted in association with university student unions or expatriate activists to organise protests and publish magazines critical of a wide range of domestic policies, British diplomatic policies and Cold War geopolitics. The Hong Kong government believed that Beijing had 'no overt interest' and that the left-wing press 'reported the various demonstrations factually and virtually without comment'. It was believed that China had no wish to associate with dissidents whom it could not control nor with 'any movement which might lead towards an independent status of Hong Kong'. However, by discrediting colonial rule in Hong Kong and Anglo-American foreign policies in Asia, the New Left was 'working in [China's] favour'.[86] For example, members of the New Left not only protested against the general unfairness of the economic distribution to Chinese residents under British colonial rule, but also against Japan's claim to the Senkaku Islands (known as the Diaoyutai Islands by the Chinese government) and American participation in the Vietnam War. They organised demonstrations against a wide range of social and economic issues, including rising living costs, low wages, squatter

---

[83] Minute from Denis Bray (Secretary for Home Affairs) to Colonial Secretary, 13 September 1974, HKRS 163-13-83.

[84] Minute from Colonial Secretary to Denis Bray (Secretary for Home Affairs), 13 September 1974 and from Bray to Colonial Secretary, 13 September 1974, HKRS 163-13-83.

[85] 'The New Left' paper prepared by Defence Branch / Colonial Secretariat, 3 May 1972, HKRS 890-2-36.

[86] The 'New Left' and Hong Kong, a paper prepared by the Police Special Branch enclosed in a memo from the Commissioner of Police to the Colonial Secretary, 2 August 1971, HKRS 890-2-36.

resettlement policies and increased tuition fees. They also fought to make Chinese Hong Kong's official language and protested against corruption amongst government officials. Some New Leftists founded magazines that continuously attacked the British government's support for US diplomatic policies and the inequalities of colonial rule in Hong Kong and ridiculed the British royal family.

New Left groups, led primarily by university student unions and the Hong Kong Federation of Students (HKFS), also promoted knowledge of modernising China and a Chinese identity amongst young people.[87] The HKFS publicly declared that 'Hong Kong is irrevocably part of China's territory', that it 'oppose[d] injustice in Hong Kong' and 'ruled out ridiculous statements like "Two Chinas"'. Its plan was to show concern for and deepen understanding of the 'mother country' and to 'unite with students all over the world' to support social reforms.[88] The New Left also advocated for what the Hong Kong government called the 'Know China Movement' in the form of forum discussions, exhibitions, film presentations and study tours to the mainland.[89] Lacking the support of Beijing and local CCP-controlled organisations, however, the New Left was never a major security threat to continued British rule in Hong Kong despite occasional rallies that attracted a few hundred people and the growing number of university student publications critical of the colonial government and supportive of China's rising role in foreign affairs.[90]

The New Left Movement was thought to be a natural response of Hong Kong youngsters to growing affluence and a greater amount of time to consider and speak out about social inequalities and the betterment of society. In other words, 'the living for the day which characterized the elder generation ha[d] been replaced'.[91] Nevertheless, MacLehose's government responded to the movement in serious fashion, although less violently than Trench had dealt with New Left protests in July 1970.[92] The Defence Branch of the Hong Kong

---

[87] *Ibid.*

[88] 'Declaration of Hong Kong Federation of Students', 1974 or 1975 (exact date missing), HKRS 890-2-36.

[89] 'The "Know China Movement"', memo from Special Branch, 20 August 1973, HKRS 890-2-36.

[90] The New Left Movement was described as 'centred around two small groups of young Chinese radicals', and were 'disunited and often disorganized and their hardcore strength is small', in 'the New Left in Hong Kong' paper prepared by Special Branch, 10 January 1975, HKRS 890-2-36.

[91] 'The New Left' paper prepared by Defence Branch / Colonial Secretariat, 3 May 1972, HKRS 890-2-36; 'Anti-British Movement in Hong Kong', a memo by Crowson of Hong Kong and the Indian Ocean Department of the FCO to Wilford and Logan, 31 July 1972; 'The 'Know China Movement', memo from Special Branch, 20 August 1973, HKRS 890-2-36.

[92] On 7 July 1971, twenty-one demonstrators were arrested during a demonstration organised by HKFS against the Japanese claim of Senkaku (Diaoyudao) Islands. Police brutality on protesters and journalists was widely reported in newspapers; Annex B to 'The New Left' paper prepared by Defence Branch / Colonial Secretariat; also Ng Bar-ling, 香港年鑑 *1972*, 84.

government was asked to prepare a paper on the history and development of the New Left in Hong Kong. Annexed to the fifty-nine-paragraph paper were the details and personal background of student organisations and their leading personalities. A special meeting of the governor and senior officials, including the colonial secretary, secretary for home affairs, deputy director of education, city district commissioner, defence secretary and chief information officer, was convened to discuss strategies for monitoring and containing the New Left Movement.[93] An inter-departmental Steering Group on Students Affairs was formed and met frequently from 1972 to 1978 (which is as late as declassified files disclose) to tackle 'students' activities'.[94] This high-level group tasked Special Branch with monitoring the leading student activists and collecting their personal information and information on their recent activities. City district officers were also asked to collect the details of potentially trouble-making (in the government's eyes) newspapers and magazines published by Hong Kong University (HKU), the Chinese University of Hong Kong (CUHK) and other post-secondary institutions (of which there were more than twenty in 1972). The police also arrested and prosecuted the publisher and editor of the radical magazine *70's Biweekly*, which was becoming increasingly popular in student circles, for failing to comply with administrative legal rules such as failing to print the printer's name on the magazine and failing to send the Registrar of Newspapers a copy according to newspaper regulations under the CPCO.[95] The police also curtailed the anti-colonial magazine's marketing by pulling down its posters from public places.[96] Receiving information that 'young radicals' from *70's Biweekly* and universities intended to interfere with the Queen's birthday celebration parade by putting up posters with anti-colonial slogans such as 'Down with Colonialism', a group of policemen raided a middle school, seized the posters stored inside the school and arrested eleven people, including two CUHK students and two teachers.

In reporting to the FCO about the raid and arrest, MacLehose highlighted his 'light-handedness' in dealing with youngsters: 'Though a charge of sedition might have been preferred, all are being taken before a magistrate this after-noon when an application will be made that they be bound over to keep peace.'[97] Student bodies held a press conference to denounce the government's action as 'a violation of the freedom of speech'.[98] Similar to the approach taken by previous governors in prosecuting unfriendly political activists, the

---

[93] 'Notes of G.H. [Government House] meeting to discuss "liaison with students"', 18 April 1972, HKRS 890-2-36.

[94] See minutes of the meeting of this steering group from 1972–78 in HKRS 890-2-36 and HKRS 890-2-37.

[95] SCMP, 7 December 1971, HKRS70-3-335.

[96] *China Mail*, 16 August 1972, HKRS 70-3-335.

[97] MacLehose to the FCO, 20 April 1972, FCO 40/364; SCMP, 20 April 1972.

[98] SCMP, 20 and 21 April 1972.

government mitigated the political nature of the prosecutions against the New Left by using a law unrelated to the content of the posters and speech, prosecuting instead such behaviour as unlawful assembly, using speakers without government approval, disorderly conduct or obstruction.[99] To cut local activists off from the influence of foreign New Leftists, the government also expelled expatriate dissidents from Hong Kong under the wide power granted it by the law, with such expulsions considered effective and appropriate to continue.[100]

In addition to legal sanctions, other means of covert control were employed to anticipate the complaints and actions of young people and minimise the chances of them becoming public issues. The secretary for home affairs and Special Branch held regular 'student affairs' meeting with such departments as the Education Department and Social Welfare Department to 'keep the situation under review'. University and college authorities were to be 'fully informed about any matters raised which may directly affect student discipline'.[101] The City District Office monitored student publications and held fortnightly meetings to exchange information on student activities and produce regular situation reports to keep other departments informed of 'what goes on in the student world'. Undergraduates were employed by the government to test 'the mood and aspirations' of students.[102] Government departments were reminded to keep in touch with Special Branch when dealing with 'sensitive educational issues'.[103] The secretary for the University and Polytechnic Grants Committee (UPGC), an organisation responsible for advising the government on the funding and strategic development of higher education, joined the student affairs meetings along with representatives of the Police, Education Department and Security Branch (formerly the Defence Branch until 1973) to discuss the 'potential danger of student unrest at universities and post-secondary colleges'. The secretary of the UPGC, S. F. Bailey, classified these institutions according to their potential political risk. Students at HKU were 'proud of their status and were unlikely to do anything so drastic as to jeopardise their academic pursuits', he informed the meeting. He also commended HKU's management for being 'sensible' in dealing with students

[99] See some records of arrests based on these charges in the following sources: for the arrest on 18 April 1971, see 'The "New Left" and Hong Kong,' a paper prepared by Special Branch enclosed in a memo from the Commissioner of Police to the Colonial Secretary, annexure B, 2 August 1971, HKRS 890-2-36; for the arrest on 7 July 1971, see 'The New Left' paper prepared by Defence Branch / Colonial Secretariat, annex B; for the arrest on 19 April 1972, see SCMP, 26 April 1972; for the arrest on 12 September 1974, see WKYP, 14 September 1974; for the arrest on 1 May 1977, see notes of local intelligence committee assessment for May 1977, 9 June 1977, FCO 40/757.

[100] 'The New Left' paper prepared by Defence Branch/Colonial Secretariat.   [101] *Ibid.*

[102] 'Liaison with Students' memo from City District Commissioner to Director of Home Affairs, 9 August 1974, HKRS 890-2-36.

[103] Notes of meeting of Steering Group on Student Affairs, 8 April 1975, HKRS 890-2-36.

and proving that they were able to 'stop trouble before things began to look bad'. CUHK 'was far more worrying' than HKU, according to Bailey, because its 'students were more susceptible to outside political influence' and its 'student leadership was less coherent and less competent'. The meeting also noted that CUHK students 'tended to be overtly more aggressive' than HKU students because they felt that they did not enjoy the same status in the eyes of the community and government.[104] The government obtained the minutes of student union and HKFS meetings to monitor the ongoing concerns of student bodies to 'anticipate rather than react to complaints'.[105][106] MacLehose stated that he would be 'prepared to speak to University Vice-Chancellors on specific matters'.[107]

A distinct feature of MacLehose's governance was his keen sensitivity to image and public relations. In dealing with the New Left, government departments were asked to pay particular attention 'to the need to consider the presentational aspects of what is contemplated and to handle public relations appropriately'. They were also asked to isolate moderate students from radicals and to undertake closer liaison work with the former so that 'they [are] made to believe [that the government] cares about' students' concerns, for example, in the areas of education, social reform and meaningful youth programmes. Officials were asked to keep students better informed of public issues and of the reasons for government policies and actions. Students should be shown 'a more human Government image' and made 'aware of [the] government's achievements, in which they share'. Youngsters' energies should be 'guided into useful channels, particularly voluntary work which satisfies their growing social conscience'.[108] Reasonable complaints should be addressed and remedied, albeit in an informal and low-key manner so as not to project an image of the government conceding to the radicals or losing 'room for manoeuvre' on student matters.[109] At the end of an important policy paper on the New Left, senior officials were once again reminded of the utmost importance of the government's public image and of public relations:

Government must be seen to be taking the initiative on issues like those mentioned . . . . This can make the difference between it getting credit for initiating a debate on some reform or appearing to respond lethargically to public demand. All departments should be reminded of the importance of this aspect of their work, and asked to consult GIS about particular issues at as early a stage as possible.[110]

---

[104] Notes of meeting of Steering Group on Student Affairs, 22 July 1976, HKRS 890-2-37.
[105] 'The New Left' paper prepared by Defence Branch/Colonial Secretariat.   [106] *Ibid.*
[107] Extract of record of Governor's Committee Meeting held on 19 May 1972, HKRS 890-2-36.
[108] 'The New Left' paper prepared by Defence Branch/Colonial Secretariat.
[109] Notes of G.H. [Government House] meeting held on Tuesday, 18 April 1972 to discuss 'liaison with students"; 'The New Left' paper prepared by Defence Branch/Colonial Secretariat.
[110] 'The New Left' paper prepared by Defence Branch/Colonial Secretariat.

Guiding Youngsters and Filtering the Stage

To guide youngsters' energies into 'useful channels', the government organised more recreational and cultural programmes for them. For example, the governor asked city district officers to organise a Summer Youth Programme for students to ensure, on the one hand, that they spent their off-term time in a more 'meaningful' way and, on the other, to have an opportunity to hear their thoughts. The district officers were also asked to periodically report to senior government officials on 'students' relationship with Government and their attitudes', as well as give 'a comprehensive assessment of student trends'.[111] Extending Trench's post-riots policy of promoting drama and musical performances to allow young people to let off steam and 'stage' their grievances safely, the Urban Council provided additional venues and increased its funding for local theatrical troupes to allow young people and students to perform their work. Mindful of the penetration of communist united front work, especially into the education sector and youth activities, the colonial government made these theatrical performances subject to careful political censorship to prevent theatres from becoming a state security threat. Their storylines had to pass the political censorship of the Urban Council to ensure that anti-British or communist propaganda pieces would not be staged. The popular dramas staged during the 1970s in government venues were thus concerned primarily with domestic issues such as municipal hygiene, the education system and housing problems.[112] Despite censorship, anti-government players were sometimes inadvertently sponsored by the Urban Council and allowed to stage plays in major government venues such as City Hall. In one such instance, the director of Special Branch wrote to the director of Urban Service cautioning that 'more care was needed' in approving of events to be staged and sponsored by the government.[113]

In fact, although communist-controlled organisations and their supporters in Hong Kong had been displaying cooperative/moderate attitudes since the early 1970s, their increasing penetration of the sports, recreation and cultural spheres did not go unnoticed by the governor's advisors in his Security Committee.[114] Applications from left-wing organisations such as the HKFTU to rent government venues for recreational and cultural performances were repeatedly declined, as recommended by the Security Committee.

---

[111] Notes of meeting of Steering Group on Student Affairs, 25 October 1974, HKRS 890-2-36.
[112] Cheung Chui-yu, '香港政府', 55–67.
[113] Notes of meeting of Steering Group on Student Affairs, 25 October 1974.
[114] 'Communist Influence in the Field of Physical Education, Recreation and Sport', paper prepared by Security Branch for Governor's Security Committee meeting on 4 June 1976, 24 May 1976, HKRS 935-2-1.

Explaining its recommendation, the Security Committee advised the governor:

Whilst, in accordance with policy directives from Beijing, the CCP controlled HKFTU now displays moderation and reasonableness in its handling of labour disputes and a willingness to cooperate in its attitude towards Government, its covert aims have not changed and it is as active as ever in penetration and subverting neutral organisations.[115]

The 'absolute ban on the [HK]FTU organising functions in the Government's grander centres of civic entertainment' was not relaxed until January 1980, according to a secret paper issued by the Security Committee,[116] that is, ten months after MacLehose's visit to Beijing sounding out Deng Xiao-ping on the issue of Hong Kong's future upon the expiry of the New Territories lease in 1997.

Behind MacLehose's Education Reforms: Check the Growth of Leftist Schools

MacLehose and his officials continued to keep a close eye not only on university students but also on the secondary school sector, which was traditionally the most vulnerable to the influence of left-wing propaganda. Government officials were also concerned that the emerging post-secondary student pressure groups might influence secondary students once some of the post-secondary students became teachers in secondary schools. A high-level Standing Committee on Pressure Groups (SCOPG), spearheaded by the Information Branch, Home Affairs Branch, Security Branch, Police Special Branch and the governor's political advisor, was formed to devise a 'machinery' to coordinate government surveillance of 'student activities with political overtones' and advise on counteracting measures against activities of pressure groups that would embarrass the government.[117] SCOPG was established after the Precious Blood Golden Jubilee Secondary School incident in 1977, which led to a demonstration by over 10,000 people, including teachers, secondary-school students and parents, who were protesting against financial irregularities at the church-run school and the government's decision to close the school. The demonstration and subsequent hunger strikes, which

---

[115] 'Application by Communist Hong Kong Federation of Trade Unions for Land in Sai Kung or Recreational Purposes', paper for the Governor's Security Committee (No. 20/80), 28 November 1980, HKRS 935-2-1.

[116] 'Use of the City Hall by the Federation of Trade Unions', paper for the Governor's Security Committee (No. 21/81), 12 August 1981, HKRS 935-2-1.

[117] Memo from Secretary for Home Affairs to SCOPG and SGSA members, 6 November 1978; notes of a Joint Meeting of the Standing Committee on Pressure Group (SCOPG) and the Steering Group on Student Affairs (SGSA) held on 9 November 1978 in the HAIB Conference Room, HKRS 890-2-37.

led to a reversal of the government's decision, were believed to have been supported by education pressure groups.[118] Hence, SCOPG was believed to be formed to 'undermine, co-opt or coerce' any target pressure groups or student groups.[119] In addition to this high-level surveillance group, a secret Local Intelligence Committee (LIC), headed by the political advisor and comprising the commissioner of police, director of Special Branch and 'representatives of MI5, MI6 and other bits of British intelligence', met every month to assess the political and security situation in Hong Kong. The committee's monthly assessments were sent to the Cabinet's Joint Intelligence Committee in London. Chinese communist activities and united front work in the fields of labour, education and commerce formed the bulk of the LIC's monthly assessment reports, although intelligence on the New Left, pressure groups and KMT activities in Hong Kong also appeared occasionally.[120]

Extensive political surveillance of the education sector was coupled with on-the-ground inspections by the Education Department to check the expansion of communist-controlled schools in Hong Kong. Education inspectors conducted both scheduled and surprise checks on schools to see whether communist texts and propaganda were being used in lessons or whether unregistered teachers were employed. The director of education also used the power afforded by section 68 of the Education Ordinance to refuse to register any teacher who had received education or teaching experience from China and had resided in Hong Kong for less than three years. For those resident in Hong Kong for more than three years, vetting and clearance by Special Branch was needed before their registration could be approved by the Education Department.[121]

In fact, the rapid expansion of communist-controlled schools in Hong Kong from the early 1970s alarmed the MacLehose government. Such expansion was particularly prominent in the New Territories. The student population of communist-controlled schools in the New Territories rose approximately 50 per cent from 1970 to 1975 to reach roughly 7,000 students, accounting

---

[118] For an overview of the incident from the perspective of an education academic, see Anthony Sweeting, *Education in Hong Kong, 1941 to 2001: Visions and Revisions* (Hong Kong: Hong Kong University Press, 2004), 326–7; for the Hong Kong government's view, see *Final Report of the Committee of Inquiry into the Precious Blood Golden Jubilee Secondary School* (Hong Kong: Hong Kong Government, 1978); for the university students' views, see Undergrad of Hong Kong University Students Union (HKUSU), 金禧事件特刊 [The Precious Blood Golden Jubilee Secondary School incident] (Hong Kong: Undergrad, HKUSU, 1978).

[119] *New Statesman*, 12 December 1980.

[120] *Ibid.* For monthly reports of the LIC in 1977 and 1978, see FCO 40/940, FCO 40/757.

[121] Annex B entitled 'Application of section 68 of the Education Ordinance: Miss Fung Fee-foong' to the memorandum for Executive Council for discussion on 7 May 1974 on Application of section 68 of the Education Ordinance, HKMS 189-1-373. Section 68 of the Education Ordinance (Cap. 279) empowers the director of education to refuse a permit to teach if he or she is satisfied that 'the environment in which the person has received any part of his education has been such as to make a person unsuitable as a teach in Hong Kong'.

for nearly 3 per cent of the total student population in the New Territories.[122] The government knew that checks by the Education Department could not on their own contain the increasing enrolment and influence of communist-controlled schools in the long run. It was well-known that these schools practised escape drills to 'hide excess pupils and unregistered teachers during inspections'.[123] Teachers and students were trained to read approved textbooks during government inspections and then return to left-wing materials after the inspectors had left the classroom.[124] The political climate amidst improving Anglo-Chinese relations in the early 1970s also made the adoption of 'draconian measures to eliminate communist schools' under the legal power of the Education Ordinance increasingly difficult.[125] A longer-term solution was discussed by top officials of the Hong Kong government and the FCO in London, who concurred that the most effective way to combat the threat of the continued expansion of communist-controlled schools in Hong Kong was to provide better access to free school places in government-funded secondary schools.[126] Although free primary education began in 1971, entry into government-funded secondary schools was still subject to parents' ability to pay tuition fees and children's passing of a public examination. It was noticed that particularly in the new settlement areas, communist schools were attempting to fill the gap by providing cheaper, geographically more convenient secondary school places.[127] The government originally had plans to 'provide by 1976 three years of assisted secondary education for 50% of the children in the 12–14 age group and, by the same date, to provide five years of assisted secondary education for 18–20% of the 12–16 age group'. After discussion with the FCO, the Hong Kong government's 'consensus' was that 'a more ambitious programme to provide nine years of aided education for all' should be considered seriously as 'the most effective counter measure' against the expansion of communist schools in Hong Kong.[128] This important high-level consensus to politicise education in Hong Kong as an important state security mechanism against communist propaganda provides a useful geopolitical

---

[122] Memo from Security Branch to Governor's Security Committee, 29 January 1976, enclosing a paper entitled 'Expansion of Communist Influence in the New Territories' dated December 1975, prepared by Special Branch, HKRS 935-2-1.

[123] Letter from R. F. Pierce (Defence Branch of Hong Kong) to E. O. Laird (FCO), 7 June 1972, enclosing a paper, 'The Communist Threat in Education', prepared by Special Branch, 28 April 1972, FCO 40/382.

[124] Recollection of Professor Cheng Kai-ming, who taught in a leftist school in the 1970s, in an TV interview 鏗鏘說 (Hong Kong Connection), RTHK, broadcast on 5 December 2020.

[125] Letter from A. P. B. Lambert to Kelly, 19 June 1972; letter from R. F. Pierce (Defence Branch of Hong Kong) to E. O. Laird (FCO), 7 June 1972.

[126] Letter from E.O. Laird to Wilford and Logan, 13 July 1972; letter from R.F. Pierce (Defence Branch of Hong Kong) to E. O. Laird (FCO), 7 June 1972.

[127] Letter from R. F. Pierce (Defence Branch of Hong Kong) to E. O. Laird (FCO), 7 June 1972.

[128] *Ibid.*

context for MacLehose's fondly remembered commitment to education by providing nine years of free and compulsory education to children in Hong Kong.

Less than a year after the aforementioned discussion, a government Green Paper on the proposed expansion of secondary school education in Hong Kong was released in October 1973 for public consultation. The Green Paper proposed to offer 80–100% of the children in the 12–14 age group three years of government-funded secondary education and 36–40% of the 12–16 age group five years of assisted secondary education. This was a slight step-up from the government's original plan. The Green Paper aroused considerable commentary and criticism from the public, which the government promised to heed when compiling a forthcoming White Paper that would declare the final government policy. After 'heeding' the public consultation, the governor tabled a White Paper on secondary education in Hong Kong at the Legislative Council in October 1974 to announce the offering of nine years of free education to all children from 1979 (subsequently pushed forward to 1978).[129] Although it may have looked like a major top-up to the original proposal in the Green Paper, the nine-year free education offering was in fact the consensus reached in a series of discussions between the Hong Kong government and the FCO back in June 1972 when they were strategising about how to combat the threat of communist schools. It is worth noting that nothing in either the Green or White Paper mentions the government's strategy to use free education to combat its cold-war ideological battle with such schools. Information services in Hong Kong and London cooperated to publicise 'the inadequacies of communist schools' to slow down the growth of the student population of such schools while the new government-funded schools were being built according to MacLehose's plan. The GIS was asked to covertly 'denigrate' leftist schools by publicising their students' poor performance in public examinations in newspaper reports. The Regional Information Office and Information and Research Department in London were also responsible for launching 'unattributable publicity' against communist schools. The GIS also overtly publicised the advantages of studying in a 'non-communist school' or a government-funded school.[130]

Without noticing the grand strategies and geographical underpinnings of MacLehose's education reform, that is, to prevent the expansion of communists from 'developing an impetus' in the 1970s, many historical accounts have commended the reform as a 'surprising advancement' that brought about 'a more literate, better educated community', which 'could only be in the best

---

[129] Sweeting, Education in Hong Kong, 264–8.

[130] Letter from R. B. Crowson (FCO) to R. F. Pierce (Defence Branch of Hong Kong), 17 October 1972; letter from R. B. Crowson (FCO) to Wilford and Logan, 2 October 1972; letter from R. F. Pierce (Defence Branch of Hong Kong) to E.O. Laird (FCO), 7 June 1972.

interests of Hong Kong'.[131] Some studies on the history of education in Hong Kong have associated the reform with the global trend in the 1960s and 1970s to recognise education as an important investment in the economy.[132] Although these accounts may provide part of the truth, they fail to recognise that education in Hong Kong was a strategically important site of ideological contestation in the ongoing cultural cold war in Asia during the 1970s.

Appointing the Chief Secretary as Chief Justice

In addition to extensive police surveillance efforts and the wide legal powers available, the appointment of senior judges of the court also remained an important colonial security control point that did not afford much liberalisation. In 1979, Denys Roberts, MacLehose's colonial secretary and a former attorney general, was appointed chief justice of Hong Kong. When the appointment was announced in the summer of 1978, the press expressed two worries. First, he had never been a judge, and hence lacked judicial experience in trying cases. Second, his previous role as a senior civil servant in the executive raised doubts as to the judicial independence of the court. Roberts's appointment was regarded by some members of the bar as 'a mockery of the concept of the independence of the judiciary', a feature widely advertised as a crucial component of English rule of law. One high court judge in Hong Kong was reported to have said that the appointment 'was unfortunate at the present time when there ha[s] been some discussion over the confidence of the public in the independence of the judiciary'. Another high court judge felt 'strongly [that] the Chief Justice should have been appointed from among the ranks of the present judiciary'.[133] Elsie Elliot, an urban councillor and well-known campaigner against social injustice, said that she was disappointed to see an administrator take up a judicial position.[134]

Perhaps to the surprise of the appointment's opponents, *Hong Kong Law Journal*, the flagship academic law journal edited by law lecturers in the HKU Faculty of Law, published an editorial expressing support for the appointment:

Fortunately, despite this breach of constitutional principle [of judicial independence], the next Chief Justice is a liberal, urbane and witty man, who will come to his new office with an abundance of goodwill and respect, more genuine than the traditional reverence paid to judges by lawyers and others, and bring with him inestimable administrative and

---

[131] See for example, Frank Welsh's description of the 'Golden Years' in Welsh, A History of Hong Kong, 481, and Buckley, *Hong Kong*, 93.

[132] Cheng Kai-ming, '教育的回顧(下)' [Looking back at education, II], in 香港史新編/ *Hong Kong History: New Perspectives*, ed. Wang Gung-wu (Hong Kong: Joint Publishing, 2017), 2:540.

[133] SCMP, 2 July 1978.   [134] SCMP, 1 July 1978.

other skills which should compensate for [his] inexperience in other aspects of judicial work.[135]

Ironically, the same journal, upon hearing rumours that the very same 'liberal, urbane and witty' Denys Roberts might be appointed the next chief justice in 1973, had expressed serious reservations, despite Roberts having served on its editorial board since its first issue in 1971:

A liberal, urbane and witty man, Mr. Roberts has been an energetic, reforming Attorney-General during his seven years of office. For some time it was rumoured that he might be the next Chief Justice. It is no reflection on our high opinion of Mr. Roberts if we say that the appointment of an incumbent Attorney-General, the Governor's chief legal adviser and a member of the Executive Council, to the Colony's highest judicial office would have been a most regrettable mistake, seriously damaging to that confidence, always slender in Hong Kong, which the people have in the independence of the judiciary. It is to be hoped that no such appointment will ever again be considered in future.[136]

To Roberts' surprise, rather than being offered the position of chief justice back in 1973, he was promoted from attorney general to chief secretary.[137] Whilst only future archival research can determine why legal academics became supportive of Roberts's appointment as chief justice in 1979 despite opposing it earlier, other members of the legal profession also endorsed the appointment. Urban councillor C. K. Chan, also a barrister, welcomed the appointment because Roberts was a capable and experienced administrator. Chung Sze-yuen, a senior unofficial member of the Legislative Council, commended Roberts as the 'ideal candidate'.[138] In fact, Roberts was not the first colonial administrator to be appointed chief justice of Hong Kong. The practice of such a 'connection' between the judiciary and colonial administration dated back to the late nineteenth and early twentieth centuries. William Goodman, the chief justice of Hong Kong from 1902 to 1905, had served as attorney general for thirteen years before becoming head of the judiciary. Joseph Kemp had similarly served as attorney general for fifteen years before being appointed chief justice in 1930. Michael Hogan, who was appointed chief justice of Hong Kong in 1955, had previously served as attorney general of another British colony, the Federation of Malaya.[139] Such a practice, which seems a direct contradiction of the highly praised principle of judicial independence, continued until

---

[135] 'Editorial', *Hong Kong Law Journal* 8.3 (1978): 282–3.
[136] 'Editorial', *Hong Kong Law Journal* 3.3 (1973): 254.
[137] Denys Roberts, *Another Disaster: Hong Kong Sketches* (London: Radcliffe Press, 2006), 208–9.
[138] SCMP, 1 July 1978.
[139] Albert Chen, Christopher Munn and Michael Ng, '殖民地時代香港的法制與司法' [The legal system and administration of justice in colonial Hong Kong], in 香港史新編/*Hong Kong History: New Perspectives*, ed. Wang Gung-wu (Hong Kong: Joint Publishing, 2016), 1:469–70.

1988, just nine years before the return of sovereignty to China, when Yang Ti-lang, a professionally trained judge who had commenced his career as a magistrate in the 1950s and never been an administrator, was appointed chief justice.

'Lack of Freedom Is Very Subtle Here'

A liberalising media environment enmeshed in a political surveillance machine and restrictive colonial legal and judicial infrastructure during a period of a thriving local economy and calming Cold War dynamics produces a mixed picture of freedom of expression during MacLehose's governorship. The author of an overview of newspapers in Asia commented in 1982 that Hong Kong did not have much press freedom under the law but that the law was sparingly used; accordingly, Hong Kong enjoyed an 'extent of press freedom that is equal to that in any democratic country'.[140] Meanwhile, journalists criticised the close surveillance of the press, campaigners and activists for turning Hong Kong from an 'autocracy into [a] dictatorship'.[141] In a debate about how free the Hong Kong press was, GIS Director John Slimming said that 'Hong Kong is one of the few places in the world where there is [a] completely free press and a non-elected government'. *Hong Kong Standard* Editor-in-Chief Viswa Nathan disagreed. The questions he threw back to Slimming, if read against the grain, shed light on the pressures and limitations behind the ostensibly 'free press':

Is it the duty of the Press to support everything that the Government considers 'good' for the community? Should it publish only the good and cheerful news and keep away from the public all that is unpleasant? Or is it its duty to be an impartial public witness informing the public of all matters – both good and bad – that affect their lives and thus be a mirror of the society and a fearless public commentator?

It is here that the Government, which says it allows a free press and promotes an 'open' government policy, and those who stand up for a free press and the public's right to information will disagree most vehemently . . .. Freedom to publish and a free press are not the same thing. Freedom to publish can never be meaningful if access to information and public accountability . . . are lacking.[142]

No further information can be found as to what exactly the restriction on access to information by the press Nathan was referring to, and yet there are newspaper reports from the 1970s that complain about the government's 'secret hand' in tampering with news reporting, and thus corroborate Nathan's observation. SCMP columnist Chang Kuo-sin, a senior journalist and lecturer in

---

[140] John A. Lent, ed., *Newspapers in Asia: Contemporary Trends and Problems*, (Hong Kong: Heinemann Asia, 1982), 82–4.
[141] *New Statesman*, 12 December 1980.   [142] *UK Press Gazette*, 28 May 1979, HKRS 376-8-62.

journalism who later became head of the Department of Communication at Hong Kong Baptist College, complained that the government directed television stations to broadcast government-produced propaganda.[143] Senior journalists recalled how the student journalism newspaper *Shatin News* was suppressed by CUHK, with the advising lecturers reprimanded for publishing news stories that embarrassed the university and the government.[144] Newspapers often hinted that journalists' 'appalling pay' was 'an ideal set-up' for the government to effect 'suppression of the news'.[145] MacLehose was even reported to have tried to persuade the editor of the *China Mail* and deputy editor of the influential FEER to drop their coverage of corruption in Hong Kong.[146]

In a speech delivered on Human Rights Day, urban councillor and social activist Elsie Elliot made an observation on the covertness of the control of expression in Hong Kong:

Under normal conditions here, people do not get arrested for what they say or what they print, or for assembly. But we do have framing. A person may not be arrested for what he prints, but he may be intimidated by being arrested for a small matter such as omitting the date on his newspaper. People who demonstrate may not be arrested for assembly (though they sometimes are) but they can be arrested for not applying for permission, or for obstruction. If an obstruction is caused by persons supporting the Government, no action is taken.

Some newspaper reporters are so badly paid that they are open to corruption by such bodies as the police. Foreigners who speak up are liable to deportation, and local people, to intimidation. Lack of freedom is very subtle here, and is often little more than moral pressure, but in a small community that is very powerful, as it can ruin a person's whole career. One magistrate told me that some of his colleagues are afraid of losing their jobs,

---

[143] SCMP, 5 June 1972. The report 'Time to review HK Govt policy on radio and television' in Chang's Chinese Viewpoint column complained about the government-produced TV programme known as 'Viewpoint'. It was a 'Government-motivated, produced and researched' programme 'imposed on HK-TVB' by the 'direction of the Television Authority'. It was considered by the report as a propaganda programme and 'totally incompatible with a free society such as Hong Kong'. One of the episodes featured an interview with Governor Sir MacLehose on his Clean Hong Kong Campaign when he was inspecting North Point, see 'Viewpoint', Radio Television Hong Kong, broadcasted on 31 October 1972, https://app4.rthk.hk/special/rthkmemory/details/innovation/136

[144] The students' newspaper reported stories about the reasons behind the fact that none of the graduate applicants to the post of administrative officer of the Hong Kong government got employed; WKYP, 15 June 1976. Employment contracts of some of the lecturers involved in *Shatin News* were not extended; see Clement So, 'A Brief History of School of Journalism and Communication at CUHK', School of Journalism and Communication of Chinese University of Hong Kong, www.com.cuhk.edu.hk/zh-TW/about/school-history, originally posted on Ming Pao, 31 October 2015. Also recollection of senior journalist and editor Fung Tak-hung, 'Shatin News Incident', Sunday Mingpao, Facebook, 23 June 2013, https://zh-hk.facebook.com/SundayMingpao/posts/683174848375547/

[145] SCMP, 28 October 1979.   [146] Yu, 'Was Governor Maclehose a Great Architect?', 492.

and I have met Government servants who remained silent on injustice because they were afraid of losing job and pension.[147]

Vicky Barrett, chair of the Hong Kong Journalists Association, complained about being asked to delete from her speech content on 'conspiracies to suppress certain news stories' when she was invited to attend a luncheon organised by the Rotary Club. She also recalled how journalists had been threatened not to sail to the open sea near Hong Kong to cover the story of an arriving cargo ship carrying Vietnamese refugees. Journalists had been warned that they would be arrested for illegal entry into Hong Kong if they did not comply with the police request. As a result, no journalist dared cover the story.[148]

Silencing the ICCPR

In May 1976, the UK government ratified the International Covenant on Civil and Political Rights (ICCPR) and extended those rights to Hong Kong. The ICCPR requires state parties to protect citizens' freedom of expression, right to hold opinions and right to hold a peaceful assembly, amongst other rights considered to derive from 'the inherent dignity of the human person'.[149] The UK government was required to submit periodic reports regarding the ICCPR's implementation in Hong Kong, together with reports on other dependent territories, to the UN Human Rights Committee (HRC). The Hong Kong government did not publish any information on the ICCPR's extension to Hong Kong, and nor were there reports of such important news about citizens' rights and freedom published in the major English and Chinese newspapers.[150] Described by one scholar as merely paying lip service to the human rights situation in Hong Kong, the UK did not legislate local laws to give legal effect to the rights and freedoms protected under the ICCPR until more than twenty years later when the Bill of Rights Ordinance was passed in 1991, six years before Hong Kong was handed back to China, as we shall see in the next chapter.[151] Such deliberate inaction attracted ongoing criticism from the other state parties of the HRC. When the UK government was requested to submit its first periodic report to the HRC in 1978, the report contained just three sentences in a less than 100-word paragraph stating that 'the common law

---

[147] Elsie Tu, 'Speech delivered on Human Rights Day', 10 December 1972, *Elsie Tu Digitized Speeches*, Hong Kong Baptist University, https://libproject.hkbu.edu.hk/trsimage/elsie/speec h/es0021.pdf

[148] WKYP, 17 October 1979.

[149] ICCPR, Preamble. On freedom of expression and assembly, see ICCPR, articles 19 and 21.

[150] Max Wong, *Re-ordering Hong Kong: Decolonisation and Hong Kong Bill of Rights Ordinance* (London: Wildy, Simmonds & Hill, 2017), 40–1.

[151] *Ibid.*, 44.

knows of no restrictions on the right to hold opinions' and that it 'does not inhibit freedom of expression'.[152] The report did not mention the existence of the many political censorship laws against the freedom to publish and express opinions such as the CPCO, Education Ordinance and Regulations and Film Censorship Regulations.

In response to this superficial report, pressure groups and activists in Hong Kong wrote a joint report on human rights abuses in Hong Kong entitled 'Putting Justice and Human Rights in Focus' and submitted it to the HRC and to the British Parliament. The report's primary focus was recent instances of police brutality and the arbitrary arrest of petitioners for housing and labour rights. Many of the petitioners, including boat people who had petitioned the governor for proper housing and the employees of a suddenly closed TV station who petitioned the governor for compensation from their employer, were arrested and found guilty of unlawful assembly under the Public Order Ordinance.[153] Section 18 of the Public Order Ordinance prohibits any assembly of three or more people that is likely to cause any person to reasonably fear that the people so assembled will commit a breach of the peace.[154] The report argued that the Public Order Ordinance and the court's literal interpretation thereof granted unlimited power to the police and abrogated the freedoms of expression and peaceful assembly protected by the ICCPR.[155] The report attracted little attention from either the press or the public; hence, the Hong Kong government decided to make no comment on it so as not to 'give it the attention which it has so far failed to arouse', as written to the FCO by I. C. Orr, the Hong Kong government's assistant political advisor.[156]

In addition to its overt silence about this politically embarrassing report, the Hong Kong government also took its usual draconian measures against its writers. For example, the report's co-author Christine Vertucci, an American lawyer resident in Hong Kong for four years, who regularly engaged in activism on housing and other issues facing low-income citizens of Hong Kong, was ordered to leave Hong Kong by the Immigration Department, which gave no reason for the order but stated that 'the Director of Immigration ha[s] an absolute power to deny extensions of stay'.[157] Vertucci thought that the

[152] First Periodic Report on Hong Kong submitted by the UK to HRC, in *Yearbook of the Human Rights Committee 1979–1980*, Vol. 2 (New York: United Nations, 1989), 178; Wong, *Reordering Hong Kong*, 69–72.

[153] SCMP, 4 October 1978; SCMP, 8 January 1979, in which seventy-six boat people, including ten children, were arrested on their way to petition to the governor's residence for housing resettlement.

[154] Public Order Ordinance (Cap. 245), s. 18(1).

[155] 'Putting justice and human rights in focus: A report on Hong Kong to the human rights committee of the United Nations', August 1980, FCO 40/1188.

[156] Orr to P. J. Williamson (FCO), 25 November 1980, FCO 40/1188.

[157] SCMP, 28 and 31 January 1982.

government's action against her was 'a subtle form of repression and warning' to expatriates who were active in speaking out about social injustices, which echoes Elsie Elliot's observation above.[158]

Reforming Hong Kong 'for China'

Preparing Hong Kong for the eventual negotiations with China over its future, MacLehose initiated reforms that many in Hong Kong regarded as 'almost too good to be true'.[159] For more than 130 years, the people of Hong Kong had been living in a colonial society with minimal social welfare provision and medical care. Government schooling was hugely inadequate, with many children not even receiving a basic primary education. Many grassroots members of society lived in miserable slums and earned their livelihoods under the threat of alarmingly corrupt government bureaucrats and policemen. To rebuild Hong Kong as a better, freer society in comparison with the mainland, a series of unprecedented reforms were launched in housing, education, social welfare and medical care, leveraging the remarkable economic growth of the 1970s. Anti-corruption efforts then ensued following pressure from London over the corruption case of Police Superintendent Godber. MacLehose's government also attempted to erase the image of a suppressive, racist colony and to cultivate 'civic pride' in Hong Kong. The GIS tried to improve its public image as the major government news censor by removing its hand from the production of news bulletins for radio and TV. Both MacLehose and GIS head David Ford publicly discussed the importance of freedom of the press in Hong Kong at the same time that Special Branch was monitoring and suppressing the publications of students labelled as members of the New Left. Senior government officials for the first time participated in a 'Meet the Media' event in which they engaged in a spontaneous question-and-answer session in front of the camera without any filtering of questions by the GIS. Although research has recently revealed MacLehose's resistance to suggestions for better labour protection and a more representative legislature, as well as his half-heartedness during the anti-corruption campaign, his governorship was still much welcomed at the grassroots level, and continues to be fondly remembered as Hong Kong's 'golden years'.[160]

Nevertheless, behind the 'goldenness' lay the continuity of draconian laws, extensive police surveillance, covert control over political activists, and a close connection between the administration and senior judges of the court. The laws that had been used to censor and suppress the press and prosecute journalists,

---

[158] SCMP, 31 January 1982.   [159] Carroll, *A Concise History*, 161.
[160] Yep and Lui, 'Revisiting the Golden Era'; Yep, 'The Crusade against Corruption'; Lui, '"Flying MPs"'.

including the CPCO, Public Order Ordinance, Emergency Regulations Ordinance and Sedition Ordinance, remained on the statute books. TV and Radio Codes of Practice continued to impose legal responsibilities of political self-censorship on broadcasters. Films and theatrical plays still needed to be pre-censored on political grounds to avoid any provocation of Beijing. The Education Ordinance and Education Regulations continued to empower the director of education to prohibit teaching materials, restrict student activities, deregister teachers, dismiss principals, expel students or even close schools for political reasons, despite improving relations between China, Britain and the US making the exercise of such powers more difficult. At the same time, directives from Beijing to Hong Kong leftists to engage in peaceful united front work in Hong Kong also made open confrontation between the government and leftist journalists and the teachers and students of communist-controlled schools a much rarer phenomenon in the 1970s, rendering the need to use draconian laws less likely.

Despite the politically peaceful and economically prosperous environment, MacLehose did not take the potential threat of political undesirables lightly, and he continued to exercise covert control and surveillance over, and if necessary take legal action against, them, especially when they were not supported by local communists. Monitoring and bringing students under the New Left label and members of pressure groups to the courts are prime examples.

This chapter does not seek to undervalue Governor MacLehose's social welfare reforms or their significant impact on the people of Hong Kong, especially those born in and after the 1970s. Yet, it is a fact that aligning the rights and freedoms of the people of Hong Kong with international standards applied expressly to Hong Kong was not within MacLehose's modernisation blueprint despite domestic and international criticisms. Rather, keeping the silencing machine alive, albeit invisible, and its components (i.e. the law, police and court) functioning, enabled his government to take quick repressive action against any perceived threats to state security or his governance, yet without damaging the overall image of Hong Kong as a better and freer society with an 'open' government relative to that in China. Recalling his thoughts on how to govern Hong Kong in an oral memoir, MacLehose stated:

If [the Hong Kong government] provided things like security, housing, education, medical services, an environment in which people had a prospect of improving themselves, and to an extent obviously not available in China, that answered immediately any kind of 'hearts and minds' operation, whether it was by the Kuomintang or the Communists.[161]

---

[161] Transcript of interview with the Lord MacLehose of Beoch, interviewed by Steve Tsang on 13 and 16 April 1989, 12–14 and 29 March 1991, Mss. Ind. Ocn. S. 377, Commonwealth and African Studies Collection, Weston Library, Bodleian Libraries, University of Oxford, 91.

The subsequent first meeting between Margaret Thatcher and Deng Xiao-ping in September 1982 revealed that Britain still had hopes of retaining control of Hong Kong. So it was perhaps thought that retaining political censorship laws, appointing a former government administrator as chief justice, and maintaining wide and discretionary police powers and a legislature with no elements of election would benefit the continued authoritarian governance of this Crown Colony beyond 1997. As it turned out, Deng's attitude during his meeting with Thatcher in Beijing shattered such hopes.[162] The original planned Cabinet options that underlay MacLehose's governorship and aimed to maximise the Britain's bargaining power in preparation for negotiations with China, as discussed earlier in this chapter, suddenly became just one: an orderly withdrawal in 1997.[163] The silencing machine constructed by political censorship and the legal and judicial infrastructure of Hong Kong, which dated back to the late nineteenth century, began to be dismantled in the decade following Thatcher's dramatic fall on the steps of the Great Hall of the People in Beijing in September 1982. At the same time, the people of Hong Kong were for the first time in colonial history consulted as to the government's plan to introduce elections to the Legislative Council.

---

[162] For Thatcher's thoughts on possibly retaining British administration in Hong Kong beyond 1997 and an analysis of the meeting between Thatcher and Deng in 1982, see Mark Chi-kwan, 'To "Educate" Deng Xiaoping in Capitalism: Thatcher's Visit to China and the Future of Hong Kong in 1982', *Cold War History* 17.2 (2017): 161–80.

[163] In fact the Labour government (1976–9) also held the view that Britain would be able to retain Hong Kong beyond 1997 and conducted a series of studies on British negotiation strategies with China on Hong Kong's future; for details, see Chu Wai-li, 'We had no urge to do away an ex-colony: The changing views of the British government over Hong Kong's future, 1967–1979' (MPhil diss., Hong Kong Baptist University, 2017), chapter 5.

6   Liberating Hong Kong for China:
De-silencing the City

Human Rights Awakening

Following the UK's extension of the ICCPR to Hong Kong in 1976, the colonial government made no serious effort to incorporate its provisions into Hong Kong's statute book, and nor were the Hong Kong people officially notified of such international recognition of their rights to freedom of speech and assembly, amongst other rights.[1] There was very little public debate and few academic critiques of the government's failure to legislate to implement the ICCPR or protect human rights in Hong Kong. The UK's first periodic report on human rights in Hong Kong, submitted to the HRC in 1978, was not made available to the public, and the HRC's discussion and criticisms of the report were not publicised. The British government maintained the official view that most of the rights covered by the ICCPR were already protected by the existing laws of Hong Kong. Michael Hogan, a former chief justice of Hong Kong (1955–70) and a member of the delegation to the HRC, even argued in 1979 during the HRC's discussion of the first periodic report on human rights in Hong Kong that common law and equity offer 'an abundant number of remedies which safeguar[d] the rights of the citizen'.[2] Such an incomplete truth about the law of Hong Kong concealed an important fact: the traditional safeguards of rights under common law and equity had been considerably watered down, if not completely overridden, by the draconian legal regime of political censorship that had prevailed in Hong Kong since the nineteenth century and even been accentuated during the Cold War period pursuant to broad yet vague concerns over state security.

The government's low-key handling of the human rights situation in Hong Kong and Hong Kong's entitlements under the ICCPR underwent a 180-degree change in late 1984 after the signing of the Joint Declaration by the UK and PRC governments regarding the retrocession of Hong Kong to China upon the expiry of the New Territories lease in July 1997. It was stated in the Joint Declaration that rights and freedoms under the ICCPR, as they applied to

---

[1] Munn, A Special Standing in the World, 181–2; Wong, Re-ordering Hong Kong, 60–1.
[2] Munn, *A Special Standing in the World*, 181–2.

Hong Kong, would *remain* in force after 1997.[3] This was rather ironic, to say the least, given that most of those rights and freedoms were not in force as part of Hong Kong law at the time of the declaration's signing. Hence, immediately after the Joint Declaration's high-key manifestation of the ICCPR rights and freedoms to which the people of Hong Kong were supposedly entitled, public discussion and academic debate ensued concerning how to remedy the breaches in colonial law to ensure that a set of ICCPR-compliant laws would *remain* in force in Hong Kong after 1997. Compared with its relatively lukewarm discourse on the human rights situation in Hong Kong in the 1970s, the academic community began actively publishing articles and books on the situation and arguing for the importance of civil liberties in Hong Kong from the mid-1980s onwards.[4] Law academics and senior lawyers urged the colonial government to legislate for a separate bill of rights prior to 1997 to educate the public and enable human rights jurisprudence to be built up through trial cases so as to aid the smooth handover of Hong Kong's sovereignty to China.[5] There was also a marked increase in stories and commentaries on human rights and freedoms in Hong Kong in the major Chinese and English newspapers during the 1980s (see Tables 6.1 and 6.2 for a survey of news reports of two major newspapers on human rights and freedoms in Hong Kong in the 1970s and 1980s). Hong Kong society and the media alike seem to have been awakened to consciousness of the importance of human rights, freedom and the rule of law after having hitherto kept rather silent on these issues for more than a century. Around the same time, the people of Hong Kong were promised the gradual democratisation of governance through the introduction

[3] Article 13, Annex 1 of Joint Declaration of the Government of the United Kingdom of Great Britain and Northern Ireland and the Government of the People's Republic of China on the Question of Hong Kong, signed on 19 December 1984.

[4] For academic journal articles, see for example Albert H. Y. Chen, 'Civil Liberties in Hong Kong: Recent Controversies, Evolving Consciousness and Future Legal Protection', *Journal of Chinese Law* 2.1 (1988): 137–52; W. S. Clarke, 'Messrs Wong and Ng and the Universal Declaration of Human Rights', *Hong Kong Law Journal* 15 (1985): 137–49; Albert H. Y. Chen, 'A Disappointing Draft of Hong Kong's Bill of Rights (Editorial)', *Hong Kong Law Journal* 17.2 (1987): 133–6; Johannes Chan, 'The Control of Obscene and Indecent Articles Ordinance 1987', *Hong Kong Law Journal* 17.3 (1987): 288–306; Albert H. Y. Chen, 'Some Reflections on the Film Censorship Affair', *Hong Kong Law Journal* 17.3 (1987): 352–9; Nihal Jayawickrama, 'Human Rights in the Draft Basic Law – A Critique', *Hong Kong Law Journal* 18.3 (1988): 370–95; Raymond Wacks, 'Can the Common Law Survive the Basic Law', *Hong Kong Law Journal* 18.3 (1988): 435–44; Albert H. Y. Chen, 'Civil Liberties in Hong Kong: Freedoms of Expression and Association (Editorial)', *Hong Kong Law Journal* 19.1 (1989): 4–9. For book publications, see for example Albert Chen and Johannes Chan, eds., 人權與法治: 香港過渡期的挑戰 [Human rights and the rule of law: Challenges of Hong Kong during transitional period] (Hong Kong: Wide Angle Press, 1987); Raymond Wacks, ed., *Civil Liberties in Hong Kong* (Hong Kong: Oxford University Press, 1988); Raymond Wacks and Andrew Byrnes, eds., *Human Rights in Hong Kong* (Hong Kong: Oxford University Press, 1992).

[5] Munn, *A Special Standing in the World*, 182–3.

Table 6.1 *Comparison of the number of appearances of news reports on human rights and freedoms in SCMP, a major English-language newspaper, in the 1970s and 1980s*

Keywords used in searching[6]	Period	Number of appearances
Human rights	1970–9	46
	1980–9	774
Freedom of expression	1970–9	7
	1980–9	79
Freedom of speech	1970–9	11
	1980–9	221
Press freedom	1970–9	13
	1980–9	112
Civil liberties	1970–9	0
	1980–9	66
Civil rights	1970–9	4
	1980–9	97

Source: ProQuest Historical Newspapers: South China Morning Post, available at HKU Libraries.

of elections for the legislature, leading to the first Legislative Council election held in 1985.

Despite the rhetoric expressly emphasising human rights protection in the Joint Declaration and growing societal enthusiasm for such protection, London was much more interested in ensuring that ICCPR rights and freedoms were entrenched in the constitution of post-handover Hong Kong than in codifying them for colonial Hong Kong prior to the handover. Both Geoffrey Howe, the British secretary of state for foreign and commonwealth affairs, and Edward Youde, the governor of Hong Kong after succeeding MacLehose in 1982, agreed that no bill of rights for British Hong Kong should be enacted immediately. In discussing the issue, Youde advised the FCO – and Howe agreed – to 'play the matter long' for a number of reasons. First of all, passing a bill of rights at this stage 'would certainly not make the administration of Hong Kong any easier' and would 'create endless scope for disputes regarding the appropriate limitations on freedoms that are generally accepted in any democratic society'. Youde was right in pointing out how difficult, if not impossible, it would be to reconcile colonial laws that restricted freedom of speech and assembly in Hong Kong with the ICCPR's stipulations that restrictions on such freedoms are allowed only when necessary in a democratic society in the interests of national security, public safety or public order. Second, Howe,

---

[6] These keywords were used in conjunction with 'Hong Kong' to eliminate reports on foreign news.

Table 6.2 *Comparison of the number of appearances of news reports on human rights and freedoms in WKYP, a major Chinese-language newspaper, in the 1970s and 1980s*

Keywords used in searching	Period	Number of appearances
Human rights	1970–9	226
(人權)	1980–9	550
Freedom of speech / freedom of expression	1970–9	2
(言論自由)	1980–9	44
Press freedom	1970–9	18
(出版自由/新聞自由)	1980–9	124
Civil liberties	1970–9	4
(公民自由)	1980–9	25
Civil rights	1970–9	1
(公民權利)	1980–9	73

Source: The Old Hong Kong Newspapers Collection, available at the Multimedia Information System of Hong Kong Public Libraries (https://mmis.hkpl.gov.hk/web/g uest/old-hk-collection)

as one of the major negotiators with the PRC in the preparation of the Joint Declaration and drafting of the Basic Law, the mini-constitution of post-colonial Hong Kong, did not think that China would agree to 'apply the agreement with the UK, in explicit terms, as part of Chinese domestic law' at that stage. In fact, both Howe and Youde would rather 'attempt to influence the drafting of the Basic Law' to ensure that it would give legal force to the ICCPR in Hong Kong under Chinese rule.[7] Although the official stance of both the UK and PRC governments was that the drafting of the Basic Law was a matter for the latter, with the UK having no role in it, the reality is, as recent archival research shows, that both the UK and colonial Hong Kong governments were able to exert influence over it via behind-the-scenes diplomacy.[8] Third, making

[7] See detailed discussion between Hong Kong and London on why not to enact a Bill of Rights in telegram from Youde to the FCO, 24 September 1985; telegram in reply from J. N. Powell (FCO) to Youde, 26 September 1985; letter of comments from M. C. Wood, legal advisor of the FCO, to Powell, 7 October 1985; telegram from Geoffrey Howe (FCO) to Youde, 3 December 1985, FCO 40/1894. See also letter from R. J. F. Hoare of Hong Kong Colonial Secretariat to W. G. Ehrman of FCO, 23 August 1985, enclosing a memo on 'Fundamental Rights and Freedoms' from F. Burrows (Hong Kong Law Officer), 16 July 1985, FCO 40/1894. For the ICCPR's provisions on these freedoms and their restrictions, see arts. 19–22, ICCPR.

[8] For how behind-the-scenes British diplomacy influenced the drafting of the Basic Law, see Albert Chen and Michael Ng, 'The Making of the Constitutional Order of the Hong Kong SAR:

the ICCPR's rights and freedoms a part of the Basic Law would afford them 'a greater degree of entrenchment' because the Basic Law, as a constitutional document, could not be amended by the post-colonial Hong Kong government and was 'unlikely to be amended very often' by the PRC government. Youde advised that in any public debate about the need to enact a bill of rights for colonial Hong Kong, the government should take 'a relatively neutral stance' to avoid the refusal to pass such a bill before the handover being misinterpreted as an attempt to circumscribe the freedoms provided for under the ICCPR. 'Playing the matter long' via such a 'neutral stance' meant convincing the public that all necessary protections were contained within the common law and ICCPR, both of which are referred to in the Joint Declaration.[9]

The government's stance did not stop legal scholars, politicians and journalists from demanding passage of a bill of rights for Hong Kong in the final stage of the colonial era. Their demands were further propelled by the early drafts of the Basic Law falling short of legal scholars' recommendations to give full effect to the protections agreed by the UK government under the terms of the ICCPR.[10] Instead of giving legal effect to the full set of human rights thereunder by granting Hong Kong a separate bill of rights,[11] the colonial government adopted the piecemeal approach of liberalising the laws imposing political censorship on the media by revising them one by one. In a note forwarded to the FCO from the secretary for administrative services and information (SASI), it was pointed out that the intention of repealing the 'control' provisions in various Hong Kong ordinances was to 'ensure the continuation of a free press through and beyond the transition by liberalising the legal framework within which the press operates' during the run-up to 1997.[12]

Control of Publications Removed

Starting in the mid-1980s, the colonial government began to repeal, revise or depoliticise laws that imposed political censorship on the print media. The CPCO, described as giving the government 'far-reaching powers to gag press

---

The Role of Sino-British Diplomacy (1982–1990)', in *Constitutional Foundings of North East Asia*, ed. Kevin Tan and Michael Ng (Oxford: Hart, 2022).

[9] 'Fundamental Rights and Freedoms' from F. Burrows (Hong Kong Law Officer), 16 July 1985; telegram from Youde to the FCO, 24 September 1985, FCO 40/1894.

[10] See for examples A. Chen 'A Disappointing Draft', 133–6; Jayawickrama, 'Human Rights in the Draft Basic Law', 370–95; and 'The Basic Law and Human Rights', *Law Society of Hong Kong Gazette*, August 1988.

[11] See Munn, *A Special Standing in the World*, 183–4, for secret meetings between the attorney general and a group of legal academics and practitioners in 1987.

[12] Fax from SASI to the FCO, 12 May 1987, enclosing 'A Note on the Retention of the "False News" Provision in Hong Kong Laws', FCO 40/2338.

freedom', was revised and assigned the more politically neutral title of the Registration of Local Newspapers Ordinance in 1987.[13] Criticisms of the CPCO did not arise overnight. As early as 1970, it was being described as 'an anachronism' from 1951 that had been 'left stranded incongruously and unbecomingly in present-day Hong Kong'.[14] However, it was not until 1984 that the press started to widely denounce the CPCO and general press laws.

The public awakening of human rights consciousness coincided with fears about deteriorating freedoms in Hong Kong after the handover of sovereignty in 1997. The Hong Kong Journalists Association expressed concern over the possibility of the CPCO being used by Beijing to suppress press freedom after 1997.[15] In a submission to the attorney general, Legislative Council and British foreign secretary in November 1985, the association claimed that the CPCO was 'itself a bad law' and urged that it be repealed.[16] Legal experts echoed these media concerns. The Bar Association began to study the relationship between press freedom and the future Basic Law and to review those laws that might be used to suppress press freedom, including the CPCO and Objectionable Publications Ordinance (OPO).[17] In December 1986, the Hong Kong government announced a major overhaul of the CPCO.[18]

In this 'legal cleansing' exercise, most of the suppressive provisions in the CPCO were repealed, including the power to prosecute the publishing of content considered to be of a subversive nature or prejudicial to the security of the colony; to suspend the publication of newspapers pending the determination of trial proceedings; to prohibit the importation of publications considered harmful to public order, safety, health or morals; and to authorise the police to enter press premises to search and seize anything in relation to suspected crimes under the CPCO. The revised CPCO became a politically neutral procedural law governing the administrative procedures for maintaining a register of newspapers and news agencies in Hong Kong. The colonial government attempted to retain one controversial power under the CPCO by moving it to the Public Order Ordinance: the power to prosecute the publication of false news likely to cause alarm to the public or disturb public order. The 'false news' provision also placed the burden of proving innocence on the defendant. The provision's retention faced 'unprecedented opposition' both inside and outside the Legislative Council before it was incorporated into the Public Order Ordinance.[19]

As it turned out, the relocated 'false news' provision survived for less than two years. The colonial government moved to repeal it in December 1988, a month after the UK government was 'grilled' by the HRC in Geneva for delaying to remedy existing ICCPR-infringing laws and pass new local laws

[13] SCMP, 19 December 1986.   [14] SCMP, 26 April 1971.   [15] SCMP, 7 June 1985.
[16] SCMP, 13 November 1985.   [17] SCMP, 09 August 1985.   [18] SCMP, 19 December 1986.
[19] Henry Litton, 'The Public Order (Amendment) Ordinance: Alarming the Public (Editorial)', *Hong Kong Law Journal* 17.2 (1987): 136–8.

(such as a bill of rights) to give effect to the rights and freedoms guaranteed by the ICCPR.[20] In justifying the Hong Kong government's embarrassing 'mental somersault' in repealing the 'false news' provision, whose retention it had fiercely fought for just two years' previously, the SASI explained that the repeal was 'a logical final step in the process of liberalizing control over publications, started by the Government two years ago'.[21]

Another piece of legislation aimed at punishing the distribution of objectionable publications was also revised and de-politicised. The Objectionable Publications Ordinance (OPO) had been enacted in 1975 to reduce teenagers' exposure to publications deemed undesirable on obscenity or political rebelliousness grounds. Objectionable publications under the OPO included articles likely to be read by juveniles that were of an indecent, obscene or revolting nature or portrayed the commission of crimes in such a way as to bring into contempt the forces and institutions entrusted with the enforcement of law and order.[22] It was replaced in 1987 by the Control of Obscene and Indecent Articles Ordinance. Such conventional references to seditious behaviours as to 'bring into contempt the forces and institutions entrusted with the enforcement of law and order' and 'revolting' were removed from the definition of content subject to regulation under the new ordinance. It thus became a politically neutral law intended primarily to control or ban obscene and indecent magazines targeting a juvenile readership.[23]

Film Censorship Loosened

With growing awareness of human rights, rising concerns over human rights protection under Chinese rule after 1997, and loosened control over the media and press, it was sometimes difficult for the colonial government to 'manage' the pace of liberalisation according to its schedule. The liberalisation of film censorship regulations that had been in place since 1953 was to a considerable extent forced by public demand and investigative journalism. Despite repeated complaints by filmmakers, the film censorship system continued to impose political censorship on film content prior to the 1980s. As mentioned in Chapter 4, in addition to censoring films on the grounds of sex, violence, and stimulating racial and religious hostilities, censors were authorised to ban or censor films considered likely to 'provoke hatred or contempt of the government', 'damage good relations with other territories' or 'encourage public disorder'.[24] Films from

[20] SCMP, 18 December 1988.
[21] Official Report of Proceedings of Hong Kong Legislative Council, 14 December 1988 and 11 January 1989.
[22] Objectionable Publications Ordinance 1975, s. 3.
[23] Control of Obscene and Indecent Articles Ordinance 1987.
[24] Television and Films Division, *Film Censorship Standards: A Note of Guidance*, Secretariat for Home Affairs (Hong Kong: Hong Kong Government, 1973).

mainland China that were considered to contain communist propaganda, films from Taiwan that were regarded as having the potential to provoke Beijing and films critical of the Hong Kong government were either banned or cut under the censorship regime.[25]

Until its revelation in an article by journalist Frank Ching in the *Asian Wall Street Journal* in March 1987, the Hong Kong public was unaware that the exercise of such censorship power in fact lacked a proper legal basis.[26] Films had for the past thirty-four years been censored on the basis of political and moral principles stated in administrative guidelines (known as *Film Censorship Standards: A Note of Guidance*), not on the basis of statutes.[27] Ching's article also cited a leaked Executive Council memorandum revealing that the government had been advised by its legal advisors as early as 1972 about the illegality of film censorship powers, and yet had taken no remedial action 'for fear of embarrassment and of arousing public attention on the sensitive issue of censorship of films on political grounds'. Described by the press as 'one of the greatest scandals in Hong Kong history' and 'the biggest leak to hit the government in decades', the incident stirred up heated debate and led to criticisms that the government had been covering up its illegal censorship practices for three decades.[28] In response, the government rushed to draft a new film censorship ordinance for public consultation with the aim of replacing the 'illegal' censorship guidelines.

There was not only widespread media coverage and heated debate in Legislative Council meetings, but also intense discussion between the governor, his political advisors and FCO officials. The major issue was how to reconcile the government's power of political censorship with article 19 of the ICCPR, which protects freedom of expression. Journalists, law lecturers and liberal legislative councillors, particularly those newly elected in the first-ever Legislative Council election held in 1985, advocated for the removal of political censorship powers from the new film censorship ordinance owing to the powers' contradiction with the ICCPR. Governor David Wilson, who succeeded Youde after the latter passed away in his sleep during a 1986 visit to Beijing, wanted to retain the power to ban films for political reasons. He sought advice from the FCO, which agreed to a proposal to retain such power because Hong Kong needed 'to maintain good relations with China'.[29] Allowing the showing of films that risked jeopardising such relations would, in the FCO's view, 'complicate the delicate dialogue' with the Chinese over other Hong Kong issues in 1987–8[30], a period in

---

[25] Lai-to Herman Yau, 'The progression of political censorship: Hong Kong cinema from colonial rule to Chinese-style socialist hegemony' (PhD diss., Lingnan University, 2015).

[26] *Asian Wall Street Journal*, 17 March 1987.

[27] Television and Films Division, *Film Censorship Standards*.

[28] A. Chen, 'Some Reflections', 352-3.

[29] Geoffrey Howe, Foreign Secretary to Hong Kong, 29 April 1987, FCO 40/2338.

[30] FCO to Hong Kong, 13 April 1987, FCO 40/2338.

which the process of drafting a basic law for post-colonial Hong Kong was well underway. The UK government was engaged in private discussions with Chinese officials 'behind the scenes' to gain influence despite its official stance that the law was the sole responsibility of China in consultation with the people of Hong Kong.[31] Amongst the more sensitive 'Hong Kong issues' at hand was how to gain Beijing's acquiescence in the inclusion of some element of direct elections for the post-colonial Legislative Council in the Basic Law and endorsement of a 1988 British White Paper introducing direct elections for the colonial Legislative Council in 1991. Cooperative UK–China relations and careful manoeuvring were needed if the Chinese government was to accept Britain's suggestions. As Governor Wilson recalled in his oral memoir, the British were very careful to ensure that those suggestions were not made public, which would have embarrassed China and made it harder to achieve what the British wanted because they 'had no direct locus' in drafting the Basic Law.[32] Notwithstanding Britain's public rhetoric that the drafting of the Basic Law was a Chinese affair, much of its input was included in the drafts released in April 1988 and February 1989. Hence, the British team, including Prime Minister Thatcher, was satisfied that the law that was 'emerging [was] a very satisfactory one, both from [the British] point of view and for Hong Kong'.[33]

Amidst such secretive British–Chinese diplomacy in drafting a constitution for post-colonial Hong Kong, the FCO placed considerable importance on retaining the governor's power to ban films that might jeopardise the cooperative environment for high-level diplomats' discussions about the future of post-1997

[31] Letter enclosing a paper entitled 'Hong Kong' for prime minister's meeting with governor on 22 February 1989 from R. N. Peirce, private secretary of the FCO, to Powell, 17 February 1989, PREM 19/2727. In fact, as early as a few months after the Basic Law drafting exercise commenced in mid-1985, British foreign secretary Howe reminded his colleagues that when they responded to press enquiries regarding the British role in the drafting process, it was important to convey a coherent message that 'the drafting of the Basic Law is a matter for the Chinese government'. Howe thought 'it would be most unwise to imply that the UK government (or the Hong Kong government) might have any role (even a secondary role) in the drafting process'; see Howe's reminder in Howe to Hong Kong, telno. 1501 entitled 'Representative Government and the Basic Law', 8 October 1985, FCO 40/1869. For how behind-the-scene Sino-British diplomacy influenced the drafting of Basic Law in the late 1980s, see A. Chen and Ng, 'The Making of the Constitutional Order'.

[32] Interview with Lord Wilson, 51–2, 19 September 2003, GBR/0014/DOHP, British Diplomatic Oral History Programme, Churchill Archives Centre, referred to Wang-lai Gao, 'Sino-British negotiations on democratic reforms in Hong Kong' (PhD diss., Waseda University, 2009), 129; see such careful maneuvering in A. Chen and Ng, 'The Making of the Constitutional Order'.

[33] Prior to June 1989, Howe and his team felt satisfied that their inputs were taken on board in the first and second drafts of the Basic Law released in April 1988 and February 1989, respectively. The inclusion of British inputs in relation to direct elections of the post-colonial legislature were particularly commended by Margaret Thatcher. Thatcher agreed with Howe that 'the outcome is highly satisfactory' and 'attaches particular importance to having secured Chinese agreement to provide for direct elections in the Basic Law'; see Powell to A. C. Galsworthy, Private Secretary of the FCO, 5 October 1987, PREM 19/2727; Howe to the Prime Minister, 6 January 1988, PREM 19/2727, as cited in Chen and Ng, 'The Making of the Constitutional Order'.

Hong Kong. The FCO's legal advisors advised that amongst the three existing principles of political censorship (i.e. provoking hatred or contempt for the government, encouraging public disorder and damaging good relations with other territories), the first two were already included under sedition offences in the Crimes Ordinance, and hence the government's power would not be diminished by their absence in the new film censorship ordinance. Further, the third principle, in the view of the FCO's legal advisors, fell under the exception in article 19 of the ICCPR allowing freedom of expression to be restricted on national security grounds: 'it would seem strange if one territory could not ban activities within its borders which might be seen as damaging to good relations with another territory' given that the 'comity of nations underlies international law'.[34] With the backing of the FCO's legal advice, the Hong Kong government pushed through passage of the Film Censorship Ordinance, which retained the 'damage good relations' clause despite widespread criticisms from the media and legal scholars that the clause breached article 19 of the ICCPR.[35]

Although the Hong Kong government did not expressly admit that the clause was tailor-made to preserve good relations with China, declassified documents show that it was used for that purpose in most cases. In April 1987, the government provided the FCO with a list of films that had been banned between 1973 and 1986 on the grounds that they were 'likely to damage good relations'. Of the seventeen films so banned, half had been produced in Taiwan. Some of these Taiwanese films were banned because they showed lifestyles of corrupt CCP members and criticised the Chinese government for its policies and the lack of human rights.[36] Although the Film Censorship Ordinance authorises the government censor to view films and make censorship decisions, declassified correspondence between Hong Kong and London reveals that the actual deliberations on whether to ban a film based on the 'damage good relations' clause very often took place between the governor of Hong Kong and FCO officials in London. Input from the governor's political advisor and British Embassy in Beijing also played an important role in decision-making. Having reached a decision with the FCO and received ministerial approval thereof, the governor would inform his political advisor to tell the commissioner for television and entertainment licensing (who appointed film censors under the Film Censorship Ordinance) to

---

[34] Memo entitled 'Hong Kong: Film Censorship' from Paul Fifoot, FCO's Legal Advisor, to C. E. Leeks of the FCO, 8 April 1987, FCO 40/2337; Governor Wilson to the FCO, 28 April 1987; the FCO's legal advisors' opinion stated in Geoffrey Howe to Hong Kong, 29 April 1987, 12 May 1987, FCO 40/2338.

[35] For the Hong Kong government's reliance on the FCO's legal advice, see Official Record of Proceedings of the Hong Kong Legislative Council, 9 March 1988, 895–6, and 18 May 1988. For criticism from legal scholars and the press, see J. Chan, 'Freedom of Expression', 215–21. Also SCMP, 18 April 1987, 3 May 1987 and 3 July 1987; SCMP, 3 July 1987, as cited in A. Chen, 'Some Reflections', 356.

[36] Letter from J. Michie, SASI, to C. E. Leeks, FCO, 28 April 1987, FCO 40/2338.

implement the decision.[37] Consideration over whether to ban a given film was influenced by how the Hong Kong and British governments interpreted signals from China on its attitude towards the film. For instance, with respect to a Taiwan-produced film, it was noted that a member of the NCNA had made it clear to the deputy political advisor of Hong Kong that it would be 'greatly disturbed' by the showing of the film.[38] Similarly, in warning the Hong Kong government and FCO against the showing of a French comedy that featured a hypothetical communist invasion of France and life in Paris under communist rule, the British Embassy in Beijing expressed concern over the film's mocking of the PLA. It was also concerned that the film's showing would coincide with China's national day and the run-up to the Sino-British Joint Liaison Group's discussions of Hong Kong's transition to 1997.[39]

The same China-sensitive approach was also applied to the liberalisation of the political censorship of theatrical performances from the mid-1980s. As mentioned in Chapter 4, the scripts of all plays and words of all songs had to be sent to government authorities (including but not limited to the Secretariat for Home Affairs, Television and Entertainment Licensing Authority and Police Special Branch) for censorship before a public performance permit could be granted under the Places of Public Entertainment Ordinance.[40] As a result, politically undesirable titles were filtered out from the stage from the 1950s to the 1970s. In 1984, the pre-censorship of play scripts was dropped, and yet the government kept the power to do so in law and reserved the right to request the submission of scripts when it deemed necessary. In that year, a theatrical troupe staging a play whose title featured the name Deng Xiao-ping was asked to submit the script for pre-censorship.[41]

A Careful Touch in Making the Judiciary Independent

Whilst Hong Kong society heatedly debated the Film Censorship Ordinance and Regulations, the colonial government managed to make a very significant structural change to the judicial system, albeit in a low-key but still impactful way. In 1986, Peter Robinson, a former deputy secretary of the Lord Chancellor's Department in the UK, was commissioned by the chief justice

---

[37] Governor Wilson to the FCO, 30 January 1989, FCO 40/2823; for appointment of film censors, see Film Censorship Ordinance 1988, ss. 3 and 5.

[38] Governor Wilson to the FCO, 23 April 1987, FCO 40/2338. The film concerned was *The Coldest Winter in Peking* that told the story of an underground movement in China after the Cultural Revolution.

[39] British Embassy in Beijing to the FCO, 9 September 1989, FCO 40/2823. The film was titled *Les Chinois a Paris*.

[40] J. Chan, 'Freedom of Expression', 208–9; Cheung Chui-yu, '香港政府', chapter 2.

[41] The play was titled *Opium War – Four Letters to Deng Xiao-ping*; see Cheung Chui-yu, '香港政府', 93–4.

of Hong Kong, Denys Roberts, to study and propose reforms to the administration and structure of the judiciary of colonial Hong Kong. In addition to
suggesting measures to improve the courts' efficiency in hearing cases and
streamlining administration of the judiciary, Robinson's study considered 'how
to give the Judiciary the best possible start in the SAR which will have its high
degree of autonomy but be under the sovereignty of China'.[42] In a letter to Sir
Derek Oulton, the then permanent secretary of the Lord Chancellor's
Department, summarising his recommendations, Robinson expressed his 'concern for the need for preparation for judicial independence in the Special
Administrative Region of HK after 1997', quoting his conversation with the
late Governor Youde in support of such a need. He further pointed out that
a number of matters in the colonial judicial structure 'tend[ed] against judicial
independence [in Hong Kong]'.[43] These matters included judges being subject
to the same civil service regulations as those applicable to civil servants
working for the executive branch, judges' salaries being linked to the civil
service pay scale and determined by committees governing civil service salaries and conditions of service, and the magistrates who tried over 90 per cent of
criminal cases in Hong Kong not enjoying tenure of employment, as their
higher court colleagues did. Such a system, as the SCMP reported, had 'led to
accusations that magistrates are not truly independent, because they have the
psychological pressure of knowing their contracts are periodically up for
renewal'.[44] Although Robinson had been commissioned to report to Chief
Justice Roberts, who had headed up the government's legal service for many
years before becoming chief secretary and chief justice, Robinson was frank in
advising that another impediment to judicial independence in Hong Kong was
that 'the legal civil service was a fully acknowledged – and jealously guarded –
field of recruitment for the bench'.[45] Although the FCO's legal advisors were
not particularly pleased with Robinson's argument against judicial promotion
and appointment from the civil service, they agreed that a demonstrable separation of the judiciary from the civil service was important in the run-up to 1997.
Governor Wilson also reported to London that the difficulty in recruiting local
legal professionals to the bench was due in part to the local Bar's view that the
judiciary did not enjoy 'a sufficiently independent status'.[46] Moreover, because

---

[42] Letter from Peter Robertson to Derek Oulton, permanent secretary of Lord Chancellor's
Department, 7 February 1987, FCO 40/2174/1.
[43] *Ibid.*
[44] SCMP, 12 January 1988. Of the more than 21,000 criminal cases dealt with in Hong Kong from
January to October 1986, magistracies disposed of 19,904 cases, as described in 'Study of the
Hong Kong Judiciary 1986 by Peter D. Robinson, C.B. submitted to the Honourable Sir Denys
Roberts, KBE, Chief Justice of Hong Kong, December 1986,' Appendix, 'Some Statistics
Collected for the Study,' 119, December 1986, FCO 40/2174/1.
[45] Letter from Peter Robertson to Derek Oulton.
[46] Wilson to the FCO, 22 April 1987, FCO 40/2174/1.

of its structural link to the civil service, the judiciary's salary package was not very attractive to talented lawyers, who could earn much more in the private sector.

To prepare for Hong Kong's retrocession to China, the colonial government initiated a restructuring of the 'relation' between the judiciary and the executive with the aim of 'distancing the judiciary from the civil service' to produce 'a favorable effect on public confidence of any measures which enhance the independence of the judiciary'.[47] Given the relative consensus between the British and Chinese governments on the need for pre-1997 policies that would survive the handover of sovereignty, Hong Kong and London agreed to sound out Beijing on the plan for judicial reform.[48] However, Geoffrey Howe reminded the Hong Kong government, which was asked to prepare an explanatory note on the reform plan for the Chinese government, that 'it is presentationally important' to describe the plan 'to the Chinese in terms of the practical need for localization', not as a measure for 'distancing the judiciary from the civil service' or 'enhanc[ing] the independence of the judiciary'. Howe's warning stemmed from 'Deng Xiao-ping's recently expressed reservations about strict separation of powers on the US model'.[49]

The British Embassy in Beijing echoed Howe's approach, asking the Hong Kong government to avoid any reference 'to the need for separation of the judiciary from the executive' or 'strengthening the "independence" of the judiciary', as such reference 'might provoke an unhelpful reaction from the Chinese' and spark 'constitutional debate'. It was important to 'minimize the risk of the Chinese seeing a sinister British constitutional plot in these proposals'.[50]

Taking into account the recommendations of Robinson's report and advice from the FCO and British Embassy in Beijing, the Hong Kong government took actions to make the judiciary free for the first time in Hong Kong's history from the structural control of the executive by establishing a separate pay scale for judges and an independent committee to determine judges' salaries and terms of employment, increasing the judiciary's representation on the Judicial Services Commission that determined the appointment and promotion of judges, freeing members of the judiciary from the regulation of civil service rules and drawing up separate judicial service regulations for governance of the judiciary and judges, and, last but not least, awarding security of tenure to magistrates. In line with Robinson's recommendations, the independence and special role of judicial officers was clearly indicated by an official classification

---

[47] Wilson to the FCO, 11 May 1987, FCO 40/2174/1.
[48] Wilson to the FCO, 22 April 1987; Howe to Hong Kong, 24 April 1987, FCO 40/2174/1.
[49] Howe to Hong Kong, 11 May 1987, FCO 40/2174/1.
[50] Richard Evans, British Ambassador to the PRC, to the FCO, 19 May 1987 and 20 May 1987, FCO 40/2174/1.

that distinguished them as 'one homogeneous group from all other public servants'.[51] In May 1987, after gaining the approval of ministers in London, a note explaining the reform was presented to Beijing.[52] The note was 'carefully worded' to stress the importance of the reform in terms of 'improving the local/expatriate balance rather than in terms of increasing the independence of the judiciary'. From London's perspective, the reform was 'fully defensible in simple localization terms', and its packaging would avoid 'as far as possible a discussion with the Chinese focused on the constitutional/Basic Law implication of what [was being] proposed'. Revealing that the aim was actually to enhance judicial independence would likely cause Beijing to 'feel obliged to scrutinize any such proposals very closely' owing to its 'reservations about the theory of a separation of powers'.[53] The explanatory note was amended numerous times to ensure that the slightest reference to the reform's constitutional implications was removed. For example, the following paragraph, which appeared in an earlier draft, was deleted from the final note presented to Beijing upon the advice of the British Embassy in Beijing:

It is considered that the above measures will not only create a climate within the judiciary which is more conducive to local lawyers but will also help meet the need to *give clearer public expression to the important principle that there should be no interference with the judiciary by the executive*.[54] [Emphasis added.]

The end result was that the twenty-five-paragraph explanatory note sent to Beijing on 29 May 1987 was presented as an examination of 'the terms of employment of members of the judiciary with a view to attracting more local candidates'.[55] Although Beijing's reaction remains unknown, as the relevant letters of exchange between the Hong Kong government, British Embassy in Beijing, and head of Chancery and senior Chinese officials have been redacted, it appears that the reform faced little opposition, and the public was informed of the government's plan to 'divorce the judiciary from the Government and make it independent in appearance as well as in form' in December 1987.[56] Just two months earlier, Queen Elizabeth II had approved the appointment of fifty-eight-year-old high court judge Yang Ti-liang as the

[51] 'Study of the Hong Kong Judiciary 1986 by Peter D. Robinson, CB, submitted to the Honourable Sir Denys Roberts, KBE, Chief Justice of Hong Kong, December 1986,' chapter 9 'Recommendations and Implementation', 103, FCO 40/2174/1.

[52] Hong Kong was informed of ministers' agreement to present the paper to the Chinese side; see Howe to Hong Kong, 26 May 1987, FCO 40/2174/1. The paper was delivered to the Chinese side on 29 May 1987; see Wilson to the FCO, 17 June 1987, FCO 40/2174/1.

[53] Confidential note of the FCO from Christopher Hum to McLaren and Renton, 21 May 1987, FCO 40/2174/1.

[54] Wilson to the FCO enclosing a draft note on the judiciary to Beijing, 18 May 1987, FCO 40/2174/1.

[55] Final draft of the note to Beijing in Wilson to the FCO, 22 May 1987, FCO 40/2174/1.

[56] SCMP, 10 December 1987; SCMP, 12 January 1987.

first Chinese chief justice in colonial Hong Kong history to succeed the retiring Denys Roberts. Unlike Roberts, who had occupied such top government positions as attorney general and chief secretary before heading up the judiciary in 1979, Yang had never been involved in the executive branch and had begun his judicial service as a magistrate in 1956. He was then promoted to justice of appeal in 1980 after having served as a district court and high court judge.[57] This historic appointment, together with the structural reforms of the judiciary, represented the complete independence of the judiciary from the executive under the English rule of law, independence that did not exist in Hong Kong until the final decade of colonial rule and constituted a significant decolonisation step in preparing Hong Kong for its reversion to China.

The very few declassified records on Hong Kong from the 1980s make it difficult to ascertain completely the British and Hong Kong governments' motives for liberalising the law and legal system and loosening restrictions on the media and freedom of expression in the last decade of the colonial era.[58] Nevertheless, a secret paper prepared for a meeting held by the UK Cabinet's Defence and Oversea Policy Committee in June 1984 on how to democratise Hong Kong before 1997 sheds light on the UK's perspective on liberalising Hong Kong from the mid-1980s:

A balance would have to be drawn between the need for adequate control to be exercised from London during the period until 1997, particularly in emergencies, and the need to avoid over-elaborate external control arrangements which could be used by the Chinese after the transfer of power to diminish autonomy within the proposed Hong Kong Special Administrative Region.[59]

In addition to striking the aforesaid precarious balance in keeping Hong Kong under Britain's colonial control and liberating it from China's post-colonial control, the UK government was also mindful of the need not to provoke Beijing's resentment of its liberalisation programme for two reasons. First, there was general consensus between London and Beijing on the need for convergence in dealing with Hong Kong in the transition to 1997, that is, the need to ensure that the measures and laws put in place before 1997 would converge with what was to be stipulated in the Basic Law and survive the change of sovereignty in July 1997. Second, through

---

[57] SCMP, 14 October 1987.

[58] Hong Kong, unfortunately, does not have archives law. It was up to the government's decision as to how and when to release past records for public access.

[59] 'Hong Kong: Constitutional Development Before 1997', in paper of minutes of meeting of Cabinet's Defence and Oversea Policy Committee (Sub-committee on Hong Kong), 28 June 1984, CAB 148/241. The meeting discussed the publication of the Green Paper on introducing the first-ever election to Hong Kong Legislative Council and the role and appointment of the Hong Kong governor before 1997.

behind-the-scenes diplomacy, the FCO tried to influence the drafting of the Basic Law, and the willingness of the Chinese side to take its input on board was highly dependent on a relative atmosphere of trust between London and Beijing over the question of Hong Kong. Prior to June 1989, both the FCO and Percy Cradock, a major advisor to Thatcher during the Sino-British negotiations over Hong Kong, were happy that all of the provisions in the Joint Declaration were reflected in the second draft Basic Law and, further, that 'the Chinese ... [had] been responsive to [the British side's] persuasions'.[60] The general atmosphere of trust began to evaporate, however, after the violent crackdown on the student demonstrations at Tiananmen Square in Beijing on 4 June 1989, a crackdown that shocked the world.

The Tiananmen Trigger

Several weeks before the crackdown, professional bodies with a combined membership of 25,000, including lawyers, architects and medical doctors, met with members of Parliament's Foreign Affairs Committee during their visit to Hong Kong to urge the enactment of a Bill of Rights, but the Hong Kong government continued to insist that no human rights legislation could be enacted until after the Basic Law's promulgation. Its stance took a 180-degree turn, however, after television footage of the crackdown in Beijing appalled the world, including the people of Hong Kong. Geoffrey Howe told the House of Commons in early July that events in Beijing had 'badly shaken' confidence in Hong Kong and announced that a Bill of Rights would be introduced as soon as possible.[61] A draft Bill of Rights was then published in March 1990 for consultation. Despite the open opposition of the Chinese government, the bill passed in June 1991, becoming the first statute in Hong Kong legal history to expressly protect individual freedoms, including the freedom of expression.[62] It was also the first 'entrenched' or legally superior ordinance in Hong Kong, repealing any ordinances that contradicted

---

[60] Such 'convergence' consensus was made public; see Hong Kong's attorney general Jeremy Mathews' justified his refusal in enacting a pre-1997 Bill of Rights by remarking that that 'local legislation would have to converge with the Basic Law', in SCMP, 5 October 1988. Peirce to Powell, 17 February 1989, PREM 19/2727; confidential memo from Percy Cradock to Thatcher, 21 February 1989, PREM 19/2727. See A. Chen and Ng, 'The Making of the Constitutional Order' for consensus of convergence before June 1989 and the behind-the-scene diplomacy in drafting the Basic Law.

[61] SCMP, 6 July 1989.

[62] See Chinese opposition to the Bill of Rights Ordinance in Nihal Jayawickrama, 'The Bill of Rights', in *Human Rights in Hong Kong*, ed. Raymond Wacks (Oxford: Oxford University Press, 1992): 73–6; Munn, *A Special Standing*, 195.

it.[63] Article 16 of the Bill of Rights Ordinance is a word-for-word reproduction of the freedom of expression stipulation in article 19 of the ICCPR:

(1) Everyone shall have the right to hold opinions without interference. (2) Everyone shall have the right to freedom of expression; this right shall include freedom to seek, receive and impart information and ideas of all kinds, regardless of frontiers, either orally, in writing or in print, in the form of art, or through any other media of his choice.[64]

Nihal Jayawickrama, a long-time advocate for a Bill of Rights for Hong Kong and a senior law lecturer, expressed the hope that 'when the countdown to the transition [to 1997] ends, the six million people being handed over to a highly authoritarian orthodox Communist regime will be a small but strong and vibrant human-rights-conscious community'.[65]

Soon after that hope was expressed, Margaret Thatcher's own hope of prolonging her time in office vanished. With insufficient support from fellow members of the Conservative Party, Thatcher resigned, with John Major assuming leadership of the party and being appointed prime minister on 28 November 1990. Major's prime ministership marked a change in UK policy vis-à-vis China, with the British government adopting a tougher line with regard to Hong Kong's future. In the summer of 1992, two 'old China hands' who had played a major role in advising Thatcher's government on China affairs in relation to Hong Kong retired. Governor Wilson left office, and his mentor Percy Cradock stepped down as chairman of the Joint Intelligence Committee and foreign affairs advisor to the prime minister at almost the same time.[66] Chris Patten, a former chairman of the Conservative Party who had recently lost his seat in the House of Commons despite the party's victory in the 1992 general election, was appointed the last governor of British Hong Kong. Patten's appointment departed from the previous practice of appointing career diplomats to the post. His approach in dealing with Beijing also differed from that of his China-expert predecessors. The controversies surrounding Patten's political reforms to accelerate the democratisation of the Hong Kong legislature are well-documented in previous works. Beijing accused the proposed reforms of contravening the Joint Declaration, as well as the consensus on convergence between Britain and China. I am not going to rehash the controversies, as their impact on colonial and post-colonial Hong Kong have been thoroughly studied.[67] What is of interest here is an equally impactful

---

[63] For the rather complicated legal scheme (with the assistance of an amended Letters Patent) that made the Bill of Rights Ordinance legally 'superior' than other laws, see Johannes Chan, 'Hong Kong's Bill of Rights: Its Reception of and Contribution to International and Comparative Jurisprudence', *International and Comparative Law Quarterly* 47.2 (1998): 307.

[64] Hong Kong Bill of Rights Ordinance, art. 16.   [65] Jayawickrama, 'The Bill of Rights', 76.

[66] SCMP, 19 April 1992 and 2 July 1992.

[67] For an overview of these controversies and impact, see Carroll, *A Concise History*, 198–238; Tsang, *A Modern History*, 254–67; and Zheng Chi-yan, '戰後香港政治發展' [Policy

liberalisation exercise that was carried out speedily in the last few years of the colonial era and took place behind the highly dramatised arguments between Governor Patten and Chinese officials over Hong Kong's constitutional reforms.

From 1991 to late 1995, nearly forty ordinances were amended to make them consistent with the Bill of Rights Ordinance.[68] As a result, additional restrictions were placed on police powers to stop, search and arrest, and various offences that required those accused to prove their innocence were removed or modified. The licensing of public assemblies and processions under the Public Order Ordinance was replaced with a notification system.[69] In June 1995, the government tendered a legislative proposal to deal with the Emergency Regulations Ordinance, the historical origin of the colonial newspaper pre-vetting and censorship system that had begun in the 1920s. A government official was quoted as saying that the emergency laws were 'anachronistic and outdated' and that some of the regulations therein could no longer be applied.[70] Although the proposal repealed past regulations made under the Emergency Regulations Ordinance, it did not repeal the ordinance itself.[71] Hence, the power to make regulations in future should the government perceive 'an occasion of emergency or public danger' without the need to obtain prior approval from the legislature was retained. Patten's government oversaw a number of other changes that did indeed unlock the colonial chains on free speech and a free press, however; changes that have been largely neglected in previous studies.

Classrooms Freed

In contrast to the pre-1980s laws and policies discouraging and, if necessary, banning political discussion in schools, in 1984 the Hong Kong government introduced civic education to the school curriculum soon after the signing of the Joint Declaration and release of a White Paper on developing representative government in Hong Kong. To prepare for the first-ever indirect election of Legislative Councillors in 1985, the White Paper emphasised the need to promote civic education in schools to ensure that the people of Hong Kong were 'educated more effectively and comprehensively in political and

development in post-war Hong Kong], in 香港史新編/*Hong Kong History: New Perspectives*, ed. Wang Gung-wu (Hong Kong: Joint Publishing, 2016), 1:155–9.

[68] According to the statement issued by the Hong Kong Attorney General's Chambers, thirty-six ordinances had been amended since 1991 to bring them in line with the Bill of Rights Ordinance; see Attorney General's Chambers, 'Statement on the Bill of Rights Ordinance,' in *Hong Kong's Bill of Rights: Two Years Before 1997*, eds. George Edwards and Johannes Chan (Hong Kong: Faculty of Law of the University of Hong Kong, 1995), Appendix C.

[69] Munn, *A Special Standing*, 187.

[70] SCMP, 24 June 1995. M. Ng, Zhang and Wong, 'Who But the Governor?', 446.

[71] SCMP, 24 June 1995; Emergency Regulations (Repeal) Order (L.N. 254 of 1995).

constitutional matters'. The Education Department issued guidelines on civic education in schools in 1985 to help schools to formulate syllabuses to, inter alia, emphasise the value of free and informed discussion, educate students on the meaning of citizenship and enhance their political awareness so as to 'develop in young people the sort of knowledge, attitudes and skills necessary for them to become rational, politically sensitive and responsible citizens who can contribute constructively to the process of political and social change'.[72] To facilitate the development of civic education, legal obstacles that might inhibit free speech and the free flow of political ideas in schools were also removed within a few years' time.[73]

Whilst Hong Kong society was deliberating on the consultation draft of the Bill of Rights Ordinance, revolutionary changes were made to the Education Ordinance in July 1990, with the governor's powers to impose political censorship on teaching materials and school activities, which had been in place for most of the colonial period, being largely scrapped. Abolished was the governor's power to make regulations 'prohibiting political, subversive or tendentious propaganda in schools and among teachers and pupils'.[74] According to the director of education, that power had been necessary from the 1950s to 1970s 'when our education system was in danger of disruption by contending political forces emanating from outside Hong Kong' but now appeared 'out of date, defective or inappropriate'.[75] Many of the director of education's political censorship powers under the Education Regulations were also abolished. The regulations were amended such that schools were no longer required to teach according to a syllabus approved by the director of education, and he or she could no longer request schools to submit instruction materials for prior approval, prohibit 'the presence of any specified document in school premises' or ban 'the use of any specified documents by schools'.[76] The director's previous fearful power to expel students if they participated 'in processions, propaganda or political activities or in any dispute between employer and his employees, or in any disorderly assembly' was also abolished,[77] as was a provision prohibiting activities of a 'political or partly political nature and prejudicial to the public interest'[78] and a prohibition against the presence of salutes, songs, dances, slogans, uniforms, flags and documents of a political nature.[79]

---

[72] Curriculum Development Committee, Education Department of Hong Kong Government, *Guidelines on Civic Education in Schools*, August 1985, 4, 10.
[73] For a discussion on the relationship between amending the Education Ordinance and the promotion of civic education, see Official Report of Proceedings of Hong Kong Legislative Council, 21 March 1990 and 4 July 1990.
[74] Education (Amendment) Ordinance 1990, s. 10.
[75] Per secretary for education and manpower in Official Report of Proceedings of Hong Kong Legislative Council, 21 March 1990.
[76] Education (Amendment) Regulations, 1990 (L.N. 268/1990), reg. 8.   [77] *Ibid.*, reg. 10.
[78] *Ibid.*, reg. 11.   [79] *Ibid.*

A follow-up amendment in early 1993 further removed the director of education's power to refuse the registration of a school for political reasons such as affiliation with an organisation of a political nature.[80] Given the government's view that the governor's 'special powers to refuse or cancel the registration of teachers' for similar reasons were no longer necessary, they were also dropped in the same amendment.[81] The only power the government retained was the power to give directions to schools on 'the dissemination of information or expression of opinion of a political nature' to ensure that 'that information or opinion is unbiased'.[82] Political censorship and the control of ideas, information, speech and materials in schools had formed a crucial legal and formal component of Hong Kong's education system since passage of the Education Ordinance in 1913. Such a regime of censorship and control had continued to expand in scope and strengthen through the Education Ordinances of 1952 and 1971, the numerous education regulations made thereunder, and the cross-departmental surveillance of teachers and students implemented by Special Branch and the Education Department's Special Bureau. Just five years before Hong Kong's return to China, its classrooms were finally set free from controls that had been in place for nearly a century.

Television and Radio Untied

Another unprecedented legal relaxation, which took place in 1993, freed television stations from government action and the threat of political censorship, which had been in place since the Television Ordinance was passed in 1964. With the arrival of colour television broadcasting in Hong Kong in the early 1970s and the growing economic power of the average household, television had by the mid-1970s superseded radio as the most influential electronic medium for the people of Hong Kong.[83] As discussed in the previous chapter, the period also saw the loosening of strict control over the content of electronic media programmes such as news programmes. Yet, under the Television Ordinance the government still retained the power to pre-censor TV programmes if it was of the opinion that such programmes might affect 'the peace and good order of Hong Kong', although one TV veteran recalled that such power had not been exercised since the mid-1970s.[84] The government was

---

[80] Education (Amendment) Ordinance 1993, s 7.
[81] Per secretary for education and manpower in Official Record of Proceedings of the Hong Kong Legislative Council, 21 April 1993; Education (Amendment) Ordinance 1993, s. 22.
[82] Education (Amendment) Ordinance 1990, s. 10. Legislative councillor Christine Loh proposed in 1996 to remove this remaining power to block 'biased' information in school but failed to get her private member's bill passed in 1997; SCMP, 29 October 1996 and 15 May 1997.
[83] Shi, '香港的大眾文化', 671–9.
[84] Television Ordinance (Cap. 52) 1989, s. 33. Recollection of Selina Chow, then director of Asia Television Limited, in Official Record of Proceedings of Hong Kong Legislative Council, 31 March 1993.

also empowered to prohibit the broadcasting of any programme it believed to threaten 'the peace and good order of Hong Kong'. The broadcasting of a prohibited programme was a criminal offence that was liable to six months' imprisonment.[85] The governor could also make rules to regulate the standard of programmes that contained political material.[86] One such programme standard prohibited the broadcasting of programmes that were 'undesirable in the public interest', although the precise meaning of that standard was not elaborated in any detail.[87] The governor could also revoke a television licence 'if it appear-[ed] to him that the security of Hong Kong so require[d]'.[88] Television regulations required broadcasters to broadcast news content only 'from sources or services approved by' the government.[89] In January 1993, the Hong Kong government proposed the abolition of all of these political censorship powers by amending the Television Ordinance, as they were now considered 'unnecessary' and 'perhaps [overly] wide'. Described by a newspaper as a bill that was 'set for a quick reading', the amended Television Ordinance was passed in less than three months and scrapped all of the aforementioned powers.[90] The new ordinance left the government only with the highly limited power to apply to the high court for an order prohibiting the broadcasting of programmes likely to incite racial hatred, result in a breakdown of law and order, or gravely damage public health or morals.[91]

Shortly thereafter, the Telecommunication Ordinance was also revised to hand over the power to prohibit content of the aforementioned nature to the high court. As with the revised Television Ordinance, it abolished the governor's power to prohibit broadcasting on 'peace and order' grounds. The Radio Code of Practice on Programme Standards was also revised in 1995 such that programmes that provoked hatred of the government, damaged good relations with other territories, or were undesirable in the public interest were no longer considered by law to contain 'objectionable' content.[92] One final move to remove the strictures on radio broadcasting took place as late as October 1996. As mentioned in Chapter 4, commercial radio stations in Hong Kong had since 1959 been subject to stringent content censorship conditions in their licences, which, unlike the law, remained inaccessible by the public. Such licence conditions empowered the government, if it considered it to be in the public interest, to prohibit the broadcasting of any content. They continued to be included in the renewed licences of commercial radio stations for nearly four decades, until the

---

[85] Television Ordinance (Cap. 52) 1989, s. 35.   [86] *Ibid.*, s. 27.

[87] Broadcasting Authority, *Television Code of Practice on Programme Standards,* 1 March 1993, para. 4(a)(iii). This paragraph was deleted in the revised *Code of Practice on Programme Standards*, 1 April 1995.

[88] Television Ordinance (Cap. 52) 1989, s. 14(3)(c).

[89] Television (Standards of Programmes) Regulations (Cap. 52) 1989, reg. 5(c).

[90] SCMP, 23 March 1993.   [91] Television (Amendment) Ordinance 1993, s. 33.

[92] Broadcasting Authority, *Radio Code of Practice on Programme Standards,* 1 April 1995.

government determined in 1996 that they were 'excessive', had 'impact on press freedom or the freedom of expression' and should be repealed.[93] The last colonial government, with only a few months left in power, thus requested that the Legislative Council 'advance the scrutiny' of its proposed amendment of the Telecommunication Ordinance, as it was one of the bills that the administration considered important to pass before 1 July 1997.[94] The executive power to set a licence condition allowing the government to require a radio broadcaster to refrain from broadcasting content specified by the government was duly abolished by the revised Telecommunication Ordinance passed by the Legislative Council on 23 October 1996, just nine months prior to the end of the British lease. As a result, the government's wide censorship powers were removed from the licence conditions of the two commercial radio broadcasters operating in Hong Kong, Commercial Radio and Metro Broadcast, right before the handover.[95]

The last five years of the colonial era saw the hurried legislative cleansing of long-standing draconian restrictions on freedom of the press. As of May 1996, fifty-three provisions in twenty-seven ordinances had been reviewed under what the government called a 'press freedom review exercise'. Thirty-one provisions were either amended or repealed for potentially threatening freedom of expression. The result was to repeal what the government called 'old and excessive regulations' to deal with emergencies and to remove powers allowing for the pre-censorship of TV and radio broadcasts. The review exercise also resulted in the abolition of the power of the commissioner for television and entertainment licensing to issue permits or impose conditions on permits for public performances and entertainment based on their content. It also removed police powers to close places of public entertainment on grounds other than public order or safety, restricted police powers to regulate public meetings and processions, restricted the powers of law enforcement agencies to enter premises to search for and seize journalistic materials, and removed the criminal offence of maliciously publishing defamatory libels, amongst the other modifications.[96]

---

[93] Official Record of Proceedings of Hong Kong Legislative Council, 22 May 1996, 67–8. Note that not all licences of commercial broadcasters were available in the Hong Kong Public Records Office. I possessed only a copy of licences for Commercial Radio granted in 1959 and 1979, respectively. Both of the licences contained such a condition: 'The Director [of Information Services in 1959 or the Commissioner for Television and Entertainment Licensing in 1979] may in his direction require the licensee to refrain from broadcasting any specified matter except on such conditions, if any, as that officer may see fit to prescribe if the Director considers it is in the best interest of the public so to do, and the licensee shall comply with every such requirement.' The Official Record of Proceedings of Hong Kong Legislative Council, 23 October 1996, confirmed the existence of the same condition in the licences of Commercial Radio and Metro Broadcast.

[94] Report of the Bills Committee on Telecommunication (Amendment) Bill 1996, para. 4.

[95] Official Record of Proceedings of the Hong Kong Legislative Council, 23 October 1996, 52–4.

[96] As at July 1996, thirty-one amendments were made to fourteen pieces of legislation, including the Television Ordinance (ss. 14, 27, 29, 33, 35, 36, 39, regs. 4, 6); Telecommunication Ordinance (s. 13M); Broadcasting Authority Ordinance (s. 18); Places of Public Entertainment

Building a Colonial Legacy by Erasing Marks of Colonialism

As we have seen throughout this book, unfettered freedom of expression was nearly undreamt of in Hong Kong during most of the colonial era. Editorial independence was subject to the government's political concerns, both local and global. Newspaper publishers and editors were regularly sued for criminal libel for criticising senior British officials, and were also prosecuted for criticising Britain's allies such as Japan and France for military aggression against China. By law, all Chinese-language newspaper articles had to be pre-censored, not only during emergencies but even in peacetime. Failure to comply with the pre-censorship regulations led to heavy fines and the imprisonment of publishers and editors. Both KMT- and CCP-controlled newspaper presses were shut down for political reasons. During the height of the Cold War, journalists, school principals, teachers and students were detained and deported without trial. School textbooks, syllabuses and activities were subject to pre-censorship, and students who engaged in activities or discussions of a political nature could be expelled. Schools were shut down for maintenance of colonial 'peace and order'. Extensive surveillance of students, teachers, school principals, and pressure group activists was conducted by Special Branch, assisted by inspectors from the Special Bureau of the Education Department and the government's funding agency for universities. GIS 'fed' news bulletins and scripts to radio and television stations for broadcasting. Even when these stations were allowed to produce their own news reports in the 1970s, they could obtain information only from 'approved' news sources according to the law. RTHK's senior management pre-censored even non-news entertainment programmes and gramophone recordings to ensure that minimal political elements were contained in radio programmes. Licence conditions and so-called programme standards for radio and television stations imposed restrictions on programme content on political grounds such as

Ordinance and Regulations (s. 8(2), reg. 174(1)); Registration of Local Newspapers Ordinance (three regulations); Emergency Regulations Ordinance (subsidiary legislation); Summary Offences Ordinance (s. 8(d), s. 4(29)); Public Order Ordinance (ss. 6, 9, 13, 14, 17, 17D); Complex Commercial Crimes Ordinance (s. 19); Criminal Procedure Ordinance (s. 123); Judicial Proceedings (Regulations of Reports) Ordinance (s. 3(1)(a)); Defamation Ordinance (s. 6); Juvenile Offenders Ordinance (s. 3D(4)); and Police Force Ordinance (s. 50(7)). For details of the government's plan for such legislative changes, see statement by the secretary for home affairs made to the meeting of the Legislative Council's Information Policy Panel on 25 July 1995; Home Affairs Branch to the Legislative Council's Information Policy Panel, 'Review of Legislation Having an Impact on Press Freedom,' April, July 1996, available at the Database of Legislative Council (www.legco.gov.hk/general/english/library/search_records_col lection.html). The controversial power to ban films that were considered likely to damage good relations with other territories in s. 10(2)(c) of the Film Censorship Ordinance was also removed in 1994; Official Record of Proceedings of Hong Kong Legislative Council, 7 December 1994, 1347–9.

provoking hatred of the government, damaging good relations with other territories or being undesirable in the public interest.

Well-rehearsed common-law cases and remedies that safeguarded freedom of the press and freedom of expression were not applicable to Hong Kong in practice because they were simply watered-down or overruled by repressive colonial legislation until the late 1960s and early 1970s, when the future of Hong Kong after 1997 first appeared on London's policy agenda. Despite the open opposition of the press and Chinese elites to restrictions on the press and freedom of expression since the early twentieth century, it is clear that what happened in mainland China, in global geopolitics, and in China's relations with Britain, the US and their allies mattered much more to the British and colonial governments than did the people of Hong Kong in determining the freedoms they enjoyed.

Governor MacLehose's liberated Hong Kong to some extent in the 1970s was part of London's blueprint to cultivate civic pride in the people of Hong Kong as citizens of British Hong Kong to maximise Britain's bargaining position in its negotiations with China over the potential continuation of British administration beyond 1997. Although his governorship featured a relaxation of government intervention in the media and free speech, he actually changed few, if any, colonial laws and regulations enabling the government to censor the media and suppress free speech whenever it saw the necessity of doing so.

The governorships of Wilson and Patten, in contrast, liberated Hong Kong to prepare for the discontinuance of British colonial rule from July 1997. Thanks to the efforts of negotiators on both sides, the Joint Declaration signed in 1984 stated that the law and judicial system in force in Hong Kong prior to 1 July 1997 would be *maintained* thereafter, which means that the British side had more than a decade (1984–97) to rectify the draconian colonial laws and 'imperfections' in the judicial system that it did not wish to be 'maintained' after Hong Kong's retrocession to China. Wilson's government swiftly repealed the most repressive of the laws and regulations used to suppress the print media and film studios, lifted the restrictions on discussions of politics in schools and introduced civic education to the school curriculum to raise young people's awareness of political affairs. Whilst MacLehose made very few changes to the colonial legal and judicial systems and appointed a former colonial secretary as chief justice, Wilson's government skilfully ensured that the judiciary, for the first time in the history of Hong Kong, satisfied the traditional English doctrine of judicial independence by separating the judiciary from the executive's manpower and administrative system and extending tenure of employment to all judges, including magistrates. And he was able to do so without attracting much opposition from Beijing. Yet, bearing the guiding principle of 'convergence' in mind, Wilson and Cradock's team in London was pulled back from liberating Hong Kong to the extent that people in Hong Kong and the international community were demanding in the mid- to late-1980s.

Had the Tiananmen crackdown not occurred, it is doubtful whether the Bill of Rights Ordinance would have been passed, given the lukewarm attitude of both the Hong Kong and British governments towards a human rights law for Hong Kong prior to the incident. Another unexpected trigger was Thatcher's loss of office to Major, which brought about a change not only in Hong Kong's governorship but also in the China advisory team at Downing Street, which had formerly comprised Chinese-speaking sinologists. Accordingly, 'convergence' was no longer the golden principle in Britain–China relations with regard to the legal and policy changes in colonial Hong Kong in the run-up to 1997. If the Youde and Wilson eras featured primarily behind-the-scenes diplomatic consultation with China on important policy and legal changes in Hong Kong, Patten's governorship, in sharp contrast, featured a series of highly publicised wars of words and friction with Beijing over constitutional reforms in Hong Kong. Behind the angry exchanges over Hong Kong's pace of democratisation was the hurried erasure of draconian legal provisions against freedom of expression. This legal liberation exercise ran until the week before Hong Kong was decolonised on 1 July 1997 despite an understanding that some of the last-minute changes in the law might not be given effect after the handover.[97]

At the farewell ceremony for colonial Hong Kong, Chris Patten stressed that Britain's main contribution to Hong Kong was the scaffolding that had enabled the people of Hong Kong to ascend, scaffolding that included the rule of law, the values of a free society and the rich fabric of civil society.[98] Those who grew up in Hong Kong in the 1980s and 1990s without hearing much from their elders about the colonial past probably do appreciate such 'scaffolding' without realising that the liberal legal and institutional infrastructure constituting it was actually constructed only during the final decade of British rule. Those who were born and grew up in the 1950s or 1960s, however, may perhaps view the legal liberation efforts of Patten and Wilson more as 'de-scaffolding', that is, as

---

[97] The Hong Kong SAR's chief executive designate Tung Chee-hwa did not accept certain laws passed in colonial Hong Kong to take effect in Chinese Hong Kong, SCMP, 25 June 1997. Legal changes stalled as a result include Crimes (Amendment) (No. 2) Ordinance 1997 passed in the Legislative Council on 24 June 1997, which added the requirement of inciting violence in establishing an offence of seditious behaviour; see Hua-ling Fu, 'Past and Future Offences of Sedition in Hong Kong', in *National Security and Fundamental Freedoms: Hong Kong's Article 23 Under Scrutiny*, ed. Hualing Fu, Carole Petersen and Simon Young (Hong Kong: Hong Kong University Press, 2005), 230–1 . Loosening of restrictions for protests and rallies without notification under the Public Order Ordinance was reversed after the handover. The repealed provision which prohibits connection of local societies with foreign political groups under the Societies Ordinance was restored in post-colonial Hong Kong. For some of these reversed laws, see SCMP, 20, 21 January 1997.

[98] Quoted from Patten's speech given on 30 June 1997. For its full text, see SCMP, 1 July 1997.

the dismantling of the iron-like legal scaffold that caged their freedoms until very late in the day.

Would the unprecedented liberation that Hong Kong experienced in the years prior to the handover have occurred if British administration had continued beyond 1997? Albeit rather ahistorical, this question, which I posed at the beginning of the book, is a thought-provoking one. It is possible that the documents that would provide an answer will not be declassified during my lifetime. Nevertheless, an inference can be drawn from the archival materials I have read as to British strategies for handling China's potential demand for the return of Hong Kong: MacLehose's efforts to liberalise the media and confer individual liberties were in large part a strategy to maintain a 'civic gap' between Hong Kong and mainland China. Such a gap accompanied by economic prosperity was thought to be the best defence against any Chinese claim to Hong Kong. At the same time, MacLehose sought to retain colonial legal powers to suppress the media and individual liberties should colonial 'peace and order' require just in case British administration continued beyond 1997. Accordingly, the legal overhaul undertaken under the Wilson and Patten governorships that abolished most of the executive powers to tamper with the media and freedom of expression is probably best seen as part of Britain's game plan to prepare for Hong Kong's non-negotiable return to China, an overhaul that was accelerated and accentuated by events in Beijing (the Tiananmen incident) and London (change of prime ministership). As I have said, however, only time and the availability of additional declassified documents will tell whether that view is correct.

Conclusion and Epilogue

Back in 2013 when I was preparing a proposal seeking research funding to support this archival study, I had an interesting conversation with a colleague who had migrated from England to teach law in Hong Kong quite some time ago. After reading my proposal, he 'advised' me (as a newly joined faculty member) not to conduct research that sought to condemn the English rule of law. To condemn it, he said, was easy, but in doing so I would leave out the fact that maintaining peace and order sometimes warrants a departure from the rule of law.

As a historian, I was trained to read against the grain and to unfold different ways of seeing a narrative. My colleague's advice, and the defence of the English rule of law in colonial Hong Kong embedded within his narrative, reassured me that it would be a worthwhile academic pursuit to investigate the use of law to ease colonial anxiety about 'peace and order' in the contexts of Hong Kong's 155-year colonial history, the history of modern China and the history of Britain.

This book offers neither a condemnation nor a celebration of the English rule of law in Hong Kong. It is also not to be read as a general denial of common law's contributions to Hong Kong. The book focuses on how free speech was weighted against the state's political and economic interests within an undemocratic polity despite the theoretical oversight of a democratic parliament in London. In the thousands of pages of declassified documents that I have read, I have not found a single debate amongst senior officials in London and Hong Kong on the imposition of censorship laws and policies or initiation of press prosecutions that was premised upon the rule of law. Even when the FCO's lawyers advised that certain censorship regulations were procedurally ultra vires and lacked legality, they remained in force. Accordingly, there is considerable doubt as to whether the English rule of law is an informative framework for analysing the colonial system of political censorship that operated through the law, given that historically it was not a significant factor, if a factor at all, considered worthy of consideration amongst policymakers in the metropole and colonies. Rather than ascertaining conceptually whether the rule of law existed in colonial Hong Kong, this book investigates empirically the thought and work processes of colonial officials that underpinned the design and operation of the regime of information control and epistemic intervention that prevailed under the colonial legal system.

It draws on archival sources to situate political censorship in colonial Hong Kong within the contexts of local politics and ever-shifting global geopolitics rather than viewing it through the lens of the highly contested and elusive concepts of the English rule of law.[1] The foregoing chapters have amply demonstrated the hitherto unappreciated fact that the laws of colonial Hong Kong responded not only to local factors but also, and perhaps to an even greater extent, to the global geopolitics surrounding relations amongst Britain, various Chinese regimes and the rest of the world during the nineteenth and twentieth centuries. The following concluding note highlights what has been omitted in previous studies of colonial Hong Kong and imperial history and points to useful directions for future research that this book does not afford the space to cover.

Uncommon Common-Law System

The English common-law system practised in colonial Hong Kong was very much uncommon in comparison with the system practised in England and Wales at the same time. The freedom of expression enshrined in English case law never fully applied, if it applied at all, to Hong Kong simply because the law was superseded by numerous pieces of legislation imposing political censorship. The press was suppressed; editors and publishers were prosecuted and imprisoned; journalists, teachers and school principals were deported and detained without trial; and daily newspaper reports appeared with crosses, dots and boxes to replace politically censored words struck out by government censors in the pre-vetting process of newspaper proofs, all in accordance with the law. Further, the law was not equally applied. Some censorship regulations explicitly applied only to Chinese-language publications. Even if a regulation was supposedly applicable to all newspapers, in practice the government's control over the English-language media was much less stringent. Independence of the judiciary was also a textbook doctrine rather than a reality in colonial Hong Kong. Magistrates, who dealt with the majority of political censorship prosecutions, were not governed by the judiciary but reported to the colonial secretary until 1939, when they came under the leadership of the chief justice of Hong Kong. However, the chief justice was very often selected from amongst senior officials of the executive branch. The

---

[1] See Brian Tamanaha, *On the Rule of Law: History, Politics, Theory* (Cambridge: Cambridge University Press, 2004) and McLaren, 'Chasing the Chimera', 21–36, on the discussion and implication of the undefined nature of the concept of the rule of law.

deep structural connection between the executive and the courts continued until less than a decade before Hong Kong's retrocession to China. Worse still, the law of political censorship was so broadly and vaguely drafted that the colonial government enjoyed the sole power to judge whether it was in the public interest to impose political censorship, a power that was difficult to challenge by law even under the most impartial judge. This brief summary illustrates the dangers of taking at face value the conventional textbook narrative that colonial Hong Kong historically practised the English common-law system and English rule of law. Without explaining the systematic differences between that system/rule's operation in metropole and colony, readers will inevitably be misled. The considerable divergence in the law and legal ideas between the central imperial and peripheral colonial is hence an understudied yet highly significant area of research in the field of law and colonialism.

Common Language in Colonial Laws: 'Peace and Order', 'Public Order' and 'Public Interest'

Despite its stark contrast with the legal system practised in England, the common-law system of colonial Hong Kong had many features in common with the systems of other British colonies, particularly those of such non-settler colonies as Malaya, Singapore and India. In addition to such widely studied features as racism, inequality and corporeal violence, another less known common feature was the widespread embedment of state security provisions in colonial legislation. It is common to find such legal phrases as 'peace and order', 'public order' and 'the public interest' in many of the statutes of colonial Hong Kong, which lacked a standalone state security law, to justify restrictions on individual liberties. These vaguely defined phrases afforded the governor of Hong Kong wide and unfettered discretion to restrict freedom of expression whenever he perceived a state security threat. The three state security keywords appeared in colonial laws and regulations empowering the government to politically control and censor publications, films, radio and television programmes, and teaching materials; restrict public assembly; and detain and deport political dissents. As we have seen, once such laws/regulations were available, they were used not only to deal with emergency situations but on a daily basis to mute opposing voices and crack down on political dissents. Even if they were not used frequently, their mere existence on the statute books, together with the powerful surveillance machine operated by Police Special Branch and other government departments, exerted deterrent effects on journalists, media operators, teachers, students and ordinary citizens. As discussed, the colonial Hong Kong government used the tactics of prosecuting a few newspapers and schools, deporting a few leading activists and directing Special Branch officers to pass on tacit messages to a few media workers to deter their peers from speaking out and/or attempting to cross political red lines. Declassified documents show that censorship prosecutions were deliberately selective and highly strategic and that decisions to prosecute on political grounds were collective decisions made by Hong Kong and London. Previous studies claiming that colonial Hong Kong enjoyed freedom of expression and a free press because censorship laws were only sparingly used overlook the self-censorship that resulted from the mere existence of relevant statutes. The sophisticated censorship regime that comprised (but was not limited to) various laws and regulations for maintaining 'peace and order', the governor, the colonial secretary, the political advisor, senior officials in the Home Affairs Department (formerly the Secretariat for Chinese Affairs), GIS, RTHK, Police Special Branch, the Attorney General's Office, and officials in the FCO and British Embassy in Beijing remained operative (with or without the need for prosecution) during most of the colonial era. Comparative studies of the *continuous* state security concerns shared amongst former colonies promise to link British imperial history with the history of global geopolitics during the twentieth century.

Common Friend and Foe: China

China was probably the greatest friend and foe for all Hong Kong governors. Whilst keen to keep a foot in the door of a huge potential market for British traders, the colony's governors had for a century been wrestling with what they perceived as potential state security risks flowing across the border as a result of the rapid and unexpected political changes occurring both within China and in its relationship with the wider world. Hence, most of the political censorship laws and measures curtailing freedom of expression were designed to nip 'the China problem' in the bud, although what that problem was shifted over time. Accordingly, the press was prosecuted for publishing pro-Qing China and anti-European government stories in the nineteenth century, whilst anti-Qing China and pro-Nationalist revolutionary commentaries were suppressed at the turn of the twentieth century, and pro-Nationalist China but anti-Japanese news reports in the 1930s. The loss of China to the CCP, outbreak of the Korean War and launch of the subsequent Cold War placed Hong Kong at the heart of the US–UK special relationship and the two countries' efforts to prevent Hong Kong from being used as a base to spread communist propaganda in Asia. Communist newspapers and their journalists and communist schools and their teachers, principals and students were closely watched and censured when deemed necessary. Amidst escalating Cold War tensions, many Hong Kong governors justified restrictions on free speech under the glorified notions of the Anglo-American 'free world'. However, the 'free world' did not necessarily promise the colonised the freedoms enjoyed by other denizens of that world. For many post-war governors, as long as Hong Kong was afforded greater freedom, a more stable political environment and brighter economic prospects than communist China, they had accomplished their anti-communist propaganda job sufficiently to foster the loyalty of the colonial population. Blatant breaches of agreed international human rights standards did not overly concern officials in Hong Kong and London. A desire to hedge China-related risks underpinned most of the political censorship measures, and eventual relaxation thereof, in colonial Hong Kong history. Hong Kong's freedoms were amongst the variables in Britain's geopolitical arbitrage vis-à-vis China, and sometimes even the US. Small but strategically located colonies such as British Hong Kong, Singapore, Cyprus and Gibraltar offer a rich but under-explored history as part of the grand strategy of Britain in the long twentieth century. Behind the well-rehearsed commercial stories, the colonial history of Hong Kong actually has much to tell us concerning its role in international relations, military intelligence, the world's China strategy and China's view of the world powers, stories that are yet to be fully told.

Uncommon Colonial Ending

The negotiated retrocession of a colony to its former sovereign was a new experiment for the British Empire in decline. The way in which that experiment was carried out from the 1970s to the 1990s defined and confined the freedoms of the people of Hong Kong. After the painful end to the 1967 riots in Hong Kong, which coincided with the devaluation of the British pound and subsequent official announcement of military retreat from the East of Suez, a certain consensus view developed in London. First, if China chose to take Hong Kong back prior to 1997, there was nothing Britain could do about it. Second, unilaterally declaring Hong Kong independent or fully democratising it would only invite China to march across the border and take Hong Kong back even earlier, rendering the usual options of independence and democratisation for former British colonies unworkable for Hong Kong.[2] Third, there might be a chance for British administration of Hong Kong to continue beyond 1997, failing which an orderly withdrawal had to be implemented. Fourth, gauging that chance could only be done through negotiation with the Chinese government, and the Mao regime was not a reasonable negotiator. Last but by no

---

[2] There was a brief moment immediately after the British victory in the Falklands War and during a deadlock in discussions with Beijing in 1982 when Margaret Thatcher thought of making Hong Kong independent, a thought that she was quickly talked out of by her advisors on China affairs, including Cradock and Howe; see 'Record of a Discussion at No. 10 Downing Street at 1615 Hours on Monday, 7 March, 1983', PREM 19/1054, cited in Man Hok-yin, 'A re-examination of the governors autonomy: Three selected case studies during the Sino-British talks over Hong Kong's future, from 1982–1985' (MPhil diss., Lingnan University Hong Kong, 2018).

means least, London believed that prior to Mao's death, living standards and civic pride in Hong Kong had to be raised to an exemplary level, and well above those in communist China, to give Britain more bargaining chips during its eventual negotiation with a post-Mao regime concerning the future of Hong Kong. As part of this blueprint for boosting the confidence of the Hong Kong people in British rule prior to its demise, Hong Kong in the 1970s experienced what earlier works have called 'colonial benevolence' – extensive improvements in social welfare and the unprecedented loosening of media control and restrictions on freedom of expression – facilitated by unexpectedly peaceful relations with Beijing and a remarkable period of economic growth. The careful yet speedy lifting of media censorship laws and strengthening of an independent judiciary took place only once an orderly retreat from Hong Kong had become the only option for Britain in 1984. During the 1980s, Hong Kong underwent a metamorphosis, transforming from a place where the 'administration [was] the best judge of what the people can be trusted to hear and see' to one of the freest cities in the world.[3] That metamorphosis was the result not so much of how hard the people of Hong Kong fought for freedoms or how hard the international community pressed for human rights in Hong Kong as of what China's relationship with Britain and the rest of the world required.

Colonial Legacy and Legality

Despite the determined liberalisation of individual freedoms in Hong Kong in the 1980s and 1990s, a small number of draconian laws against freedom of expression were left in place upon Hong Kong's return to China. Additional declassified documents are needed for future researchers to ascertain the rationale for leaving these laws on the statute books. The 2019–21 period has seen the recycling of some of these colonial leftovers. For example, the Emergency Regulation Ordinance once used to arrest leftists was used to prohibit face-covering during the massive anti-extradition bill protests of 2019, and the sedition law formerly used to prosecute the left-wing press was used in 2020 to charge media workers and politicians over what they had published. Similarly, the Public Order Ordinance, which was widely used in the 1970s to prosecute the New Left for unlawful assemblies, was invoked in 2021 to jail pro-democracy legislative councillors for unauthorised assembly. RTHK, once responsible for censoring broadcasting content in the colonial era, was recently accused of censoring politically sensitive programmes, and the

---

[3] A description of the freedom of expression of colonial Hong Kong used in Yash Ghai, 'Freedom of Expression', in *Human Rights in Hong Kong*, ed. Raymond Wacks (Oxford: Oxford University Press, 1992), 378.

Education Department has been accused of deregistering teachers on political grounds. The people of Hong Kong's freedom of expression, which was once subject to London's state security considerations in the name of 'public order' and 'the public interest', is now subject to Beijing's national security considerations under the newly passed National Security Law. The once hotly debated, and eventually repealed, 'offence of spreading fake news' is currently being considered by the post-colonial government. In this age of increasing division or even disengagement amongst world powers, it remains to be seen how evolving international relations, geo-economic rivalries and the geopolitical power equation will influence the scope of freedoms enjoyed in Hong Kong. But one thing is certain: the protesters who recently waved the colonial flag in demonstrations against the post-colonial Hong Kong government and who hold a fanciful nostalgic imagination of the freedoms enjoyed under the colonial legal regime are no doubt surprised by the alacrity with which the current government has moved to embrace that supposedly liberal regime. They may wish to ask themselves whether that constitutes a step forward or backward for the people of Hong Kong.

Glossary of Chinese Newspapers[1]

Afternoon News	今午報
Chi Po	時報
Chung Hwa Yat Po	中華日報
Chung Kwok Yat Po[2]	中國日報
Chung Ngoi San Po[3]	中外新報
Hong Kong Evening News	香港夜報
Hwa Shiang Pao[4]	華商報
Kung Sheung Daily News[5]	工商日報
Kung Sheung Evening News	工商晚報
Kung Yik Po	公益報
Kwok Man Yat Po[6]	國民日報
Min Bao[7]	民報

[1] Information on these papers was obtained from a variety of sources including Chow Kai-wing, 香港報刊與大眾傳播 [Newspapers, periodicals and mass media in Hong Kong] (Hong Kong: Cosmos, 2017); Kan Lai-bing and Grace Chu, *Newspapers of Hong Kong: 1841–1979* (Hong Kong: University Library System of the Chinese University of Hong Kong, 1981); Li Kwok-sing, 香港報業百年滄桑 [One hundred years' history of Hong Kong newspapers] (Hong Kong: Ming Pao, 2000); Lee Siu-nam, '香港的中西報業', 563–604; and *Hong Kong Annual Reports* of various years published by the Hong Kong government. The English transliterated or translated titles of newspapers follow the titles used in historical sources and documents.

[2] Published from 1900 to 1913, *Chung Kwok Yat Po* was founded by revolutionary leader Chen Shao-bai and supported by Sun Yat-sen.

[3] Published from c. 1869 to 1919, *Chung Ngoi San Po* was one of earliest Chinese newspapers in colonial Hong Kong.

[4] *Hwa Shiang Pao* (published from 1941 to 1949), *Ta Kung Pao* (Hong Kong edition published since 1938) and *Wen Wei Po* (Hong Kong edition published since 1948) were regarded as 'orthodox' communist newspapers by the colonial Hong Kong government. *Tin Fung Daily*, *Afternoon News* and *Hong Kong Evening News* were regarded as 'fringe' left-wing papers that enjoyed a much smaller circulation.

[5] Published from 1925 to 1984, *Kung Sheung Daily News* was a major Chinese newspaper owned and operated by the Hotung family since 1929. It was run by Robert Ho until 1984. It also published *Kung Sheung Evening News*.

[6] *Kwok Man Yat Po* was established by the KMT in Hong Kong in 1939 as its propaganda channel. It ceased operation in 1947.

[7] *Min Bao* was published by Tongmenghui (同盟會), a secret anti-Qing society founded by a group of revolutionary leaders including Sun Yat-sen and Song Jiao-ren.

Ming Pao	明報
Nam Chung Po	南中報
Nam Keung Yat Po	南強日報
New Life Evening Post	新生晚報
People's Daily	人民日報
Shat Po	實報
Shun Po	晨報
Siu Yat Po[8]	小日報
Ta Kung Pao	大公報
Tin Fung Daily	田豐日報
Tsun Wan Yat Po[9]	循環日報
Wa Tsz Yat Po[10]	華字日報
Wah Kiu Man Po	華僑晚報
Wah Kiu Yat Po[11]	華僑日報
Wai San Yat Po[12]	維新日報
Wen Wei Po	文匯報
Yin Cheong	現象報

[8] A short-lived left-wing newspaper published from 1929 until 1930 when it was suppressed by the Hong Kong government.

[9] *Tsun Wan Yat Po* is one of the earliest Chinese newspapers in Hong Kong. It was founded by the famous intellectual and reformist Wang Tao in 1874. It ceased operation in 1946.

[10] Published from 1872 until 1941, *Wa Tsz Yat Po* was initially affiliated to *China Mail*, a leading English newspaper in Hong Kong. It remained a leading Chinese newspaper until its closure due to the Japanese occupation of Hong Kong.

[11] *Wah Kiu Yat Po* was founded in 1925 and remained one of the most popular Chinese newspapers in Hong Kong until the 1990s. It was sold to SCMP in 1992 and ceased operation in 1995. It also published a number of affiliated papers including *Chung Hwa Yat Po*, *Nam Keung Yat Po*, *Nam Chung Po* and evening paper *Wah Kiu Man Po*.

[12] *Wai San Yat Po* was published from 1879 until 1908. It was founded by advocates of constitutional reforms of the Qing government.

Bibliography

Archival Sources

The National Archives of the UK

Cabinet Office: Defence and Oversea Policy Committee: Minutes and papers: CAB 148
Colonial Office Records: CO 129, CO 141, CO 371, CO 537, CO 962, CO 968, CO 1027, CO 1030, CO 1035
Foreign and Commonwealth Office Records: FCO 21, FCO 40, FCO 141
Foreign Office Records: FO 371
Prime Minister's Office Records: PREM 19

Hong Kong Public Records Office

Hong Kong Manuscript Series: HKMS 189
Hong Kong Record Series: HKRS 41, HKRS 70, HKRS 163, HKRS 313, HKRS 376, HKRS 508, HKRS 545, HKRS 890, HKRS 934, HKRS 935, HKRS 952, HKRS 1225, HKRS 1448, HKRS 2139

University of Oxford

Transcript of interview with Lord MacLehose of Beoch, interviewed by Steve Tsang on 13 and 16 April 1989, 12–14 and 29 March 1991, Mss. Ind. Ocn. S. 377, Commonwealth and African Studies Collection, Weston Library, Bodleian Libraries, University of Oxford

Special Collections and the Law Library of the University of Hong Kong Libraries

Annual Departmental Report by the Director of Information Services
Film Censorship Standards: A Note of Guidance
Historical Laws of Hong Kong Online (https://oelawhk.lib.hku.hk/exhibits/show/oelawhk/home)
Hong Kong Annual Report

Hong Kong Government Gazette
香港年鑑 (Hong Kong Year Book)
Hong Kong Government Reports Online (https://sunzi.lib.hku.hk/hkgro/index.jsp)
Hong Kong Hansard
Laws of Hong Kong
Ng Bar Ling Collection
Radio Code of Practice on Programme Standards
Television Code of Practice on Programme Standards
Yearbook of the Human Rights Committee

Newspapers and Journals

Asian Wall Street Journal
China Mail
Daily Worker
Far Eastern Economic Review
Hong Kong Daily Press
Hong Kong Star
Hong Kong Telegraph
Hong Kong Times
Kung Sheung Daily News
Kung Sheung Evening News
Min Bao
Ming Pao
Nam Keung Yat Po
New Life Evening Post
New Statesman
New York Herald Tribune
People's Daily
South China Morning Post
Ta Kung Pao
The Standard
The Times
Wa Tsz Yat Po
Wah Kiu Man Po
Wah Kiu Yat Po
Wen Wei Po

Secondary Works

Asian Human Rights Commission. *Hong Kong, Human Rights Issues Prior to 1997*. Hong Kong: Asian Human Rights Commission, 1992.
Attorney General's Chambers [HK]. 'Statement on the Bill of Rights Ordinance'. In *Hong Kong's Bill of Rights: Two Years Before 1997*, edited by George Edwards and Johannes Chan, 171–81. Hong Kong: Faculty of Law of the University of Hong Kong, 1995.

Ban, Kah-choon. *Absent History : The Untold Story of Special Branch Operations in Singapore, 1915–1942*. Singapore: Raffles, 2001.

Benton, Lauren. *Law and Colonial Cultures: Legal Regimes in World History, 1400–1900*. Cambridge: Cambridge University Press, 2002.

Buckley, Roger. *Hong Kong: The Road to 1997*. Cambridge: Cambridge University Press, 1997.

Carroll, John M. *A Concise History of Hong Kong*. Lanham, MD: Rowman and Littlefield, 2007.

  Edge of Empires: Chinese Elites and British Colonials in Hong Kong. Hong Kong: Hong Kong University Press, 2007.

Census & Statistics Department, Hong Kong. *Hong Kong Statistics 1947–67*. Hong Kong: Hong Kong Government, 1969.

Chan, Johannes. 'Freedom of Expression: Censorship and Obscenity'. In *Civil Liberties in Hong Kong*, edited by Raymond Wacks, 208–42. Hong Kong: Oxford University Press, 1988.

  'Hong Kong's Bill of Rights: Its Reception of and Contribution to International and Comparative Jurisprudence'. *International and Comparative Law Quarterly* 47.2 (1998): 306–36.

  'The Control of Obscene and Indecent Articles Ordinance 1987'. *Hong Kong Law Journal* 17.3 (1987): 288–306.

Chan, Ming K. 'Hong Kong in Sino-British Conflict: Mass Mobilization and the Crisis of Legitimacy'. In *Precarious Balance: Hong Kong between China and Britain, 1842-1992*, edited by Ming K. Chan and John D. Young, 27–57. Hong Kong: Hong Kong University Press, 1994.

  'The Legacy of the British Administration of Hong Kong: A View from Hong Kong'. *China Quarterly* 151 (1997): 567–82.

Chanock, Martin. *Law, Custom and Social Order: The Colonial Experience in Malawi and Zambia*. Cambridge: Cambridge University Press, 1985.

Cheesman, Nick. *Opposing the Rule of Law: How Myanmar's Courts Make Law and Order*. Cambridge: Cambridge University Press, 2015.

Chen, Albert H. Y. 'A Disappointing Draft of Hong Kong's Bill of Rights (Editorial)'. *Hong Kong Law Journal* 17.2 (1987): 133–6.

  'Civil Liberties in Hong Kong: Freedoms of Expression and Association (Editorial)'. *Hong Kong Law Journal* 19.1 (1989): 4–9.

  'Civil Liberties in Hong Kong: Recent Controversies, Evolving Consciousness and Future Legal Protection'. *Journal of Chinese Law* 2.1 (1988): 137–52.

  'Some Reflections on the Film Censorship Affair'. *Hong Kong Law Journal* 17.3 (1987): 352–9.

Chen, Albert and Johannes Chan, eds. 人權與法治: 香港過渡期的挑戰 [Human rights and the rule of law: Challenges of Hong Kong during transitional period]. Hong Kong: Wide Angle Press, 1987.

Chen, Albert, Christopher Munn and Michael Ng. '殖民地時代香港的法制與司法' [The legal system and administration of justice in colonial Hong Kong]. In 香港史新編, 上冊/*Hong Kong History: New Perspectives, Vol. 1*, edited by Wang Gung-wu 王賡武, 445–82. Hong Kong: Joint Publishing 三聯, 2017.

Chen, Albert and Michael Ng. 'The Making of the Constitutional Order of the Hong Kong SAR: The Role of Sino-British Diplomacy (1982–1990)'. In

Constitutional Foundings of North East Asia, edited by Kevin Tan and Michael Ng, 41–71. Oxford: Hart, 2022.

Chen, Percy. *China Called Me: My Life inside the Chinese Revolution*. Boston: Little Brown, 1979.

Chen Yun 陳雲. 一起廣播的日子: 香港電台八十年 [Broadcasting together: The 80th anniversary of RTHK]. Hong Kong: Ming Pao, 2009.

Cheng Kai-ming 程介明. '教育的回顧 (下)' [Looking back at education, II]. In 香港史新編, 下冊/*Hong Kong History: New Perspectives, Vol. 2*, edited by Wang Gung-wu 王賡武, 533–61. Hong Kong: Joint Publishing 三聯, 2017.

Cheung, Anne. *Self-Censorship and the Struggle for Press Freedom in Hong Kong*. The Hague: Kluwer, 2003.

Cheung Chui-yu 張翠瑜. '香港政府治理戲劇的策略, 1945–1997' [Hong Kong government's strategies in governing theatres]. MPhil diss., Chinese University of Hong Kong, 2013.

Cheung, Gary Ka-wai 張家偉. 六七暴動:香港戰後歷史的分水嶺/*Hong Kong's Watershed: The 1967 Riots*. Hong Kong: Hong Kong University Press, 2012.

Ching Cheong 程翔. 香港六七暴動始末 : 解讀吳荻舟 [1967 riots in Hong Kong: Reading from Wu Di-zhou] (Hong Kong: Oxford University Press, 2018).

Chow Kai-wing 周佳榮. 香港報刊與大眾傳播 [Newspapers, periodicals and mass media in Hong Kong]. Hong Kong: Cosmos, 2017.

Chu, Wai-li. 'We had no urge to do away an ex-colony: The changing views of the British government over Hong Kong's future, 1967–1979'. MPhil diss., Hong Kong Baptist University, 2017.

Clarke, W. S. 'Messrs Wong and Ng and the Universal Declaration of Human Rights'. *Hong Kong Law Journal* 15 (1985): 137–49.

Clayton, David. 'The Consumption of Radio Broadcast Technologies in Hong Kong, c. 1930–1960'. *Economic History Review* 57.4 (2004): 691–726.

Comber, Leon. *Malaya's Secret Police 1945–60 : The Role of the Special Branch in the Malayan Emergency*. Singapore: Institute of Southeast Asian Studies, 2008.

Dicey, A. V. *An Introduction to the Study of the Law of the Constitution*, 10th ed. London: Macmillan, 1959.

Dikötter, Frank. *Mao's Great Famine: The History of China's Most Devastating Catastrophe, 1958–62*. London: Bloomsbury, 2010.

Du, Ying. 'Censorship, Regulations, and the Cinematic Cold War in Hong Kong (1947–1971)'. *China Review* 17.1 (2017): 117–51.

Edwards, George and Johannes Chan, eds. *Hong Kong's Bill of Rights: Two Years Before 1997*. Hong Kong: Faculty of Law of the University of Hong Kong, 1995.

Endacott, G. B. *A History of Hong Kong*. London: Oxford University Press, 1958.

Evans, Julie. 'Colonialism and the Rule of Law: The Case of South Australia'. In *Crime and Empire 1840–1940*, edited by Barry Godfrey and Graeme Dunstall, 57–75. Portland, OR: Willan Publishing, 2005.

Final Report of the Committee of Inquiry into the Precious Blood Golden Jubilee Secondary School. Hong Kong: Hong Kong Government, 1978.

Fitzpatrick, Peter. 'Custom as Imperialism'. In *Law, Society and National Identity in Africa*, edited by Jamil Abun-Nasr, Ulrich Spellenbergt and Ulrike Wanitzek, 15–30. Hamburg: Buske, 1990.

Foster, Hamar, Benjamin L. Berger and A. R. Buck, eds. *The Grand Experiment: Law and Legal Culture in British Settler Societies*. Vancouver: University of British Columbia Press, 2009.

Fu, Hua-ling. 'Past and Future Offences of Sedition in Hong Kong'. In *National Security and Fundamental Freedoms: Hong Kong's Article 23 Under Scrutiny*, edited by Hua-ling Fu, Carole Petersen and Simon Young, 217–49. Hong Kong: Hong Kong University Press, 2005.

Fu, Hua-ling and Richard Cullen. 'Political Policing in Hong Kong'. *Hong Kong Law Journal*, 33.1 (2003): 199–230.

Fu, Poshek. 'Entertainment and Propaganda: Hong Kong Cinema and Asia's Cold War'. In *The Cold War and Asian Cinemas*, edited by Poshek Fu and Man-Fung Yip, 238–62. London: Routledge, 2019.

'More Than Just Entertaining: Cinematic Containment and Asia's Cold War in Hong Kong, 1949–1959'. *Modern Chinese Literature and Culture* 30.2 (2018): 1–55.

Gao, Wang-lai. 'Sino-British negotiations on democratic reforms in Hong Kong'. PhD diss., Waseda University, 2009.

Ghai, Yash. 'Freedom of Expression'. In *Human Rights in Hong Kong*, edited by Raymond Wacks, 369–409. Oxford: Oxford University Press, 1992.

Grantham, Alexander. *Via Ports: From Hong Kong to Hong Kong*. Hong Kong: Hong Kong University Press, 1965.

Hampton, Mark. *Visions of the Press in Britain, 1850–1950*. Illinois: University of Illinois Press, 2004.

Hewitt, Martin. 'The Press and the Law'. In *Journalism and the Periodical Press in Nineteenth Century Britain*, edited by Joanne Shattock, 147–64. Cambridge: Cambridge University Press, 2017.

Huang Yong 黃永, Feng Zhi-feng 馮志豐 and Huang Pei-feng 黃培烽. 十八樓C座為民喉舌卅年 [18/F Flat C, thirty years of broadcasting for the people]. Hong Kong: Liangguang wenhua, 2008.

Ip, Eric. *Law and Justice in Hong Kong*. Hong Kong: Sweet & Maxwell, 2014.

Jayawickrama, Nihal. 'The Bill of Rights'. In *Human Rights in Hong Kong*, edited by Raymond Wacks, 37–85. Oxford: Oxford University Press, 1992.

'Human Rights in the Draft Basic Law: A Critique'. *Hong Kong Law Journal* 18.3 (1988): 370–95.

Jin Ruoru 金堯如. 中共香港政策秘聞實錄：金堯如五十年香江憶往 [Secrets of CCP's Hong Kong policies: Jin Ruoru's fifty years of recollection]. Hong Kong: Tianyuan 1998.

Jones, Carol and Jon Vagg. *Criminal Justice in Hong Kong*. London: Routledge-Cavendish, 2007.

Kan, Lai-bing and Grace Chu. *Newspapers of Hong Kong: 1841–1979*. Hong Kong: University Library System of the Chinese University of Hong Kong, 1981.

Kian Kwan-sang, 中共在香港, 下卷 [The CCP in Hong Kong, Vol. 2]. Hong Kong: Cosmos, 2012.

Kibata, Yoichi. 'British Imperialism in Asia and Anglo-Japanese Relations, 1930s–1950s'. In *The International Order of Asia in the 1930s and 1950s*, ed. Shigeru Akita and Nicholas J. White, 49–60. Farnham, England: Ashgate, 2010.

Klein, Richard. 'The Empire Strikes Back: Britain's Use of the Law to Suppress Political Dissent in Hong Kong'. *Boston University International Law Journal* 15.1 (1997): 18.

Kolsky, Elizabeth. *Colonial Justice in British India*. New York: Cambridge University Press, 2010.

Kuiken, Kees. 'Hong Kong and Macau,' in *Censorship: A World Encyclopaedia* (Vol. 2), edited by Derek Jones, 1096–102. New York: Routledge, 2001.

Lee, Francis. *Talk Radio, the Mainstream Press, and Public Opinion in Hong Kong*. Hong Kong: Hong Kong University Press, 2014.

Lee Shuk-man 李淑敏. 冷戰光影: 地緣政治下的香港電影審查史 [Screens of the Cold War: History of film censorship in Hong Kong under geopolitics]. Taipei: Jifengdaiwenhua, 2018.

Lent, John A., ed. *Newspapers in Asia: Contemporary Trends and Problems*. Hong Kong: Heinemann Asia, 1982.

Lee Siu-nam 李少南. '香港的中西報業' [Chinese and English press in Hong Kong]. In 香港史新編, 下冊/*Hong Kong History: New Perspectives, Vol. 2*, edited by Wang Gung-wu 王賡武, 563–604. Hong Kong: Joint Publishing 三聯, 1997.

Li Kwok-sing 李谷城. 香港報業百年滄桑 [One hundred years' history of Hong Kong newspapers]. Hong Kong: Ming Pao, 2000.

Litton, Henry. 'The Public Order (Amendment) Ordinance: Alarming the Public (Editorial)'. *Hong Kong Law Journal* 17.2 (1987): 136–8.

Lowe John and Eileen Yuk-Ha Tsang, 'Securing Hong Kong's Identity in the Colonial Past: Strategic Essentialism and the Umbrella Movement', *Critical Asian Studies* 50.4 (2018): 556–71.

Lu, Xun. 'The American Cold War in Hong Kong, 1949–1960: Intelligence and Propaganda'. In *Hong Kong in the Cold War*, edited by Priscilla Roberts and John Carroll, 117–40. Hong Kong: Hong Kong University Press, 2016.

Lu, Yan. *Crossed Paths: Labor Activism and Colonial Governance in Hong Kong, 1938–1958*. (New York: Cornell University Press, 2019).

Lui, Tai-lok. '"Flying MPs" and Political Change in a Colonial Setting: Political Reform under MacLehose's Governorship of Hong Kong'. In *Civil Unrest and Governance in Hong Kong: Law and Order from Historical and Cultural Perspectives*, edited by Michael Ng and John D. Wong, 76–96. London: Routledge, 2017.

Man, Hok-yin. 'A re-examination of the governors autonomy: Three selected case studies during the Sino-British talks over Hong Kong's future, from 1982–1985'. MPhil diss., Lingnan University Hong Kong, 2018.

Mark, Chi-kwan. 'Development without Decolonisation? Hong Kong's Future and Relations with Britain and China, 1967–1972'. *Journal of the Royal Asiatic Society* 24.2 (2014): 315–35.

   The Everyday Cold War: Britain and China, 1950–1972. London: Bloomsbury, 2017.

   'Everyday Propaganda: The Leftist Press and Sino-British Relations in Hong Kong, 1952–67'. In *Europe and China in the Cold War: Exchanges Beyond the Bloc Logic and the Sino-Soviet Split, New Perspectives on the Cold War*, edited by Janick Marina Schaufelbuehl, Marco Wyss and Valeria Zanier, 151–71. Leiden: Brill, 2019.

   Hong Kong and the Cold War: Anglo-American Relations 1949–1957. Oxford: Oxford University Press, 2004.

'To "Educate" Deng Xiaoping in Capitalism: Thatcher's Visit to China and the Future of Hong Kong in 1982'. *Cold War History* 17.2 (2017): 161–80.

Mason, Anthony. 'The Role of the Common Law in Hong Kong'. In *The Common Law Lectures Series 2005*, edited by Jessica Young and Rebecca Lee, 1–26. Hong Kong: Faculty of Law, Hong Kong University, 2005.

McLaren, John. 'Afterword: Looking from the Past into the Future'. In *The Grand Experiment: Law and Legal Culture in British Settler Societies*, edited by Hamar Foster, Benjamin L. Berger, and A. R. Buck, 268–76. Vancouver: University of British Columbia Press, 2008.

'Chasing the Chimera: The Rule of Law in the British Empire and the Comparative Turn in Legal History'. *Law in Context* 33 (1) (2015): 21–36.

Merry, Sally E. 'Law and Colonialism'. *Law and Society Review* 25.4 (1991): 889–922.

Miners, Norman. 'The Use and Abuse of Emergency Power'. *Hong Kong Law Journal* 26.1 (1996): 47–57.

Mok, Florence. 'Chinese communist influence in Chinese left-wing press in Cold War Hong Kong, c. 1949–1970' (unpublished manuscript).

Morris, Paul and Anthony Sweeting. 'Education and Politics: The Case of Hong Kong from an Historical Perspective'. *Oxford Review of Education* 17.3 (1991): 249–67.

Munn, Christopher. *Anglo-China: Chinese People and British Rule in Hong Kong, 1840–1880*. Hong Kong: Hong Kong University Press, 2009.

'Our Best Trump Card: A Brief History of Deportation in Hong Kong, 1857–1955'. In *Civil Unrest and Governance in Hong Kong: Law and Order from Historical and Cultural Perspectives*, edited by Michael Ng and John Wong, 26–45. London: Routledge, 2017.

A Special Standing in the World: The Faculty of Law at the University of Hong Kong, 1969–2019. Hong Kong: Hong Kong University Press, 2019.

Murray, David. *Colonial Justice: Justice, Morality, and Crime in the Niagara District, 1791–1849*. Toronto: University of Toronto Press, 2002.

Ng, Kenny K. K. 'Inhibition vs. Exhibition: Political Censorship of Chinese and Foreign Cinemas in Postwar Hong Kong'. *Journal of Chinese Cinemas* 2.1 (2008): 23–35.

Ng, Michael. 'Rule of Law in Hong Kong History Demythologised: Student Umbrella Movement of 1919'. *Hong Kong Law Journal* 46.3 (2016): 829–47.

'When Silence Speaks: Press Censorship and Rule of Law in British Hong Kong (1850s–1940s)'. *Law and Literature* 29.3 (2017): 425–56.

Ng, Michael and John Wong, eds. *Civil Unrest and Governance in Hong Kong: Law and Order from Historical and Cultural Perspectives*. London: Routledge, 2017.

Ng, Michael, Shengyue Zhang and Max Wong. 'Who But the Governor in Executive Council Is the Judge?: Historical Use of the Emergency Regulations Ordinance'. *Hong Kong Law Journal* 50.2 (2020): 425–61.

Norton-Kyshe, James William. *The History of the Laws and Courts of Hong Kong from the Earliest Period to 1898*. Hong Kong: Vetch and Lee, c. 1971; originally published by London: T. Fisher Unwin, 1898.

Roberts, Denys. *Another Disaster: Hong Kong Sketches*. London: Radcliffe Press, 2006.

RTHK. *RTHK-50 Years: Broadcasting in Hong Kong from 1928–1978*. Hong Kong: Government Printer, 1978.

RTHK. 從一九二八年說起: 香港廣播七十五年專輯 [Since 1928: Broadcasting for seventy-five years in Hong Kong]. Hong Kong: RTHK, 2004.

Shi Wen-hong 史文鴻. '香港的大眾文化與消費生活' [Popular culture and consumption in Hong Kong]. In 香港史新編, 下冊/*Hong Kong History: New Perspectives, Vol. 2*, edited by Wang Gung-wu 王賡武, 665–90. Hong Kong: Joint Publishing 三聯, 2017.

Simpson, Brian. *Human Rights and the End of Empire: Britain and the Genesis of the European Convention*. Oxford: Oxford University Press, 2001.

Sinn, Elizabeth. *Power and Charity: The Early History of the Tung Wah Hospital, Hong Kong*. Hong Kong: Oxford University Press, 1989.

Sun Yang 孫揚. 國民政府對香港問題的處置 [Nationalist government's policies towards the Hong Kong question]. Hong Kong: Joint Publishing 三聯, 2017.

Sweeting, Anthony. *Education in Hong Kong, 1941–2001: Visions and Revisions*. Hong Kong: Hong Kong University Press, 2004.

Tamanaha, Brian. *On the Rule of Law: History, Politics, Theory*. Cambridge: Cambridge University Press, 2004.

Tan, Carol. *British Rule in China: Law and Justice in Weihaiwei 1898–1930*. London: Wildy, Simmonds & Hill, 2008.

Tang, James T. H. *Britain's Encounter with Revolutionary China, 1949–54*. London: Macmillan, 1992.

'From Empire Defence to Imperial Retreat: Britain's Postwar China Policy and the Decolonization of Hong Kong'. *Modern Asian Studies* 28.2 (1994): 317–37.

Television and Films Division. *Film Censorship Standards: A Note of Guidance*, Secretariat for Home Affairs. Hong Kong: Hong Kong Government, 1973.

Tsai Jung-fang 蔡榮芳. 香港人之香港史 *1841–1945/The Hong Kong People's History of Hong Kong 1841–1945*. Hong Kong: Oxford University Press, 2001.

Tsang, Steve. 'Commitment to the Rule of Law and Judicial Independence'. In *Judicial Independence and the Rule of Law in Hong Kong*, edited by Steve Tsang, 1–18. Hong Kong: Hong Kong University Press, 2001.

A Modern History of Hong Kong 1841–1997. London: I. B. Tauris, 2004.

Tse, Kin-Lop. 'The denationalization and depoliticization of education in Hong Kong, 1945–92'. PhD diss., University of Wisconsin, Madison, 1998.

Tu, Elsie. *Colonial Hong Kong in the Eyes of Elsie Tu*. Hong Kong: Hong Kong University Press, 2003.

TVB. *TVB* 開心三十年 [TVB 30th anniversary] (Hong Kong: TVB, 1997).

Undergrad of Hong Kong University Students Union 金禧事件特刊 [The Precious Blood Golden Jubilee Secondary School incident]. Hong Kong: Undergrad, 1978.

Wacks, Raymond. 'Can the Common Law Survive the Basic Law'. *Hong Kong Law Journal* 18.3 (1988): 435–44.

, ed. *Civil Liberties in Hong Kong*. Hong Kong: Oxford University Press, 1988.

Wacks, Raymond and Andrew Byrnes, eds. *Human Rights in Hong Kong*. Hong Kong: Oxford University Press, 1992.

Wang, Xiao-jue. 'Radio Culture in Cold War Hong Kong'. *Interventions*, 20.8 (2018): 1153–70.

Welsh, Frank. *A History of Hong Kong*. London: HarperCollins, 1993.

Wesley-Smith, Peter. 'Anti-Chinese Legislation in Hong Kong'. In *Precarious Balance: Hong Kong between China and Britain, 1842–1992*, ed. Ming K. Chan and John D. Young, 91–106. Hong Kong: Hong Kong University Press, 1994.

Wiener, Martin. *An Empire on Trial: Race, Murder, and Justice under British Rule, 1870–1935*. Cambridge: Cambridge University Press, 2009.

Wong, Max. *Re-ordering Hong Kong: Decolonisation and Hong Kong Bill of Rights Ordinance*. London: Wildy, Simmonds & Hill, 2017.

Yang Guo-xiong 楊國雄. 香港戰前報業 [Hong Kong pre-war newspaper industry]. Hong Kong: Joint Publishing 三聯, 2013.

Yau, Lai-to Herman. 'The progression of political censorship: Hong Kong cinema from colonial rule to Chinese-style socialist hegemony'. PhD diss., Lingnan University Hong Kong, 2015.

Ye Lin 葉霖.在中國的影子下: 美國對香港的外交政策 *1945–1972* [In China's shadow: US foreign policy towards Hong Kong 1945–1972]. Hong Kong: Chung Hwa, 2018.

Yep, Ray. 'The Crusade against Corruption in Hong Kong in the 1970s: Governor MacLehose as a Zealous Reformer or Reluctant Hero?' *China Information* 27.2 (2013): 197–221.

'"Cultural Revolution in Hong Kong": Emergency Powers, Administration of Justice and the Turbulent Year of 1967'. *Modern Asian Studies* 46.4 (2012): 1007–32.

'The 1967 Riots in Hong Kong: The Domestic and Diplomatic Fronts of the Governor'. In *May Days in Hong Kong: Riot and Emergency in 1967*, edited by Robert Bickers and Ray Yep, 21–36. Hong Kong: Hong Kong University Press, 2009.

Yep, Ray and Robert Bickers. 'Studying the 1967 Riots: An Overdue Project'. In *May Days in Hong Kong: Riot and Emergency in 1967*, edited by Robert Bickers and Ray Yep, 1–18. Hong Kong: Hong Kong University Press, 2009.

Yep, Ray and Tai-lok Lui. 'Revisiting the Golden Era of MacLehose and the Dynamics of Social Reforms'. *China Information* 24.3 (2010): 249–72.

Yu, Andrew C. K. 'Was Governor Maclehose a Great Architect of Modern Hong Kong?' *Asian Affairs* 51.3 (2020): 485–509.

Zhang Zhen-dong 張振東 and Li Chun-wu 李春武. 香港廣播電視發展史 [The history of broadcasting in Hong Kong]. Beijing: Zhongguo guangbo dianshi chubanshe, 1997.

Zheng Chi-yan 鄭赤琰. '戰後香港政治發展' [Policy development in post-war Hong Kong]. In 香港史新編, 上冊/*Hong Kong History: New Perspectives, Vol. 1*, edited by Wang Gung-wu 王賡武, 145–69. Hong Kong: Joint Publishing 三聯, 2017.

Zhou Yi 周奕.香港左派鬥爭史 [History of struggles of leftists in Hong Kong]. Hong Kong: Li wen, 2002.

Index